TO DESTROY YOU
IS NO LOSS

TO DESTROY YOU IS NO LOSS

The Odyssey of a Cambodian Family

JOAN D. CRIDDLE
and TEEDA BUTT MAM

THE ATLANTIC MONTHLY PRESS, New York

959.604
Tee

Copyright © 1987 by Joan D. Criddle

FIRST EDITION

Library of Congress Cataloging-in-Publication Data

Teeda Butt Mam.
   To destroy you is no loss.

   Autobiography of Teeda Butt Mam as told to Joan
Criddle.
      1. Teeda Butt Mam.   2. Cambodia—History—1975-
3. Refugees, Political—Cambodia—Biography.   I. Criddle,
Joan.   II. Title.
DS554.83.T44A3   1987   959.6'04   87-1396
ISBN 0-87113-116-1

Published simultaneously in Canada
Printed and bound in the United States of America

First Printing, June 1987

Design by Laura Hough

To Dick,
my friend, lover,
and eternal companion

—Joan D. Criddle

Acknowledgments

I wish to express a special thanks

to my husband, Richard, for suggesting that I write this book, for his professional critique through every step, and for his unfailing support and encouragement;

to my literary agent, George Ziegler, for his counsel throughout each phase of bringing this book to print;

to Teeda and her family for a willingness to recount painful experiences in order to make their ordeal public;

to my family and many friends for reading portions of the manuscript, and for their continued interest and concern.

Joan D. Criddle

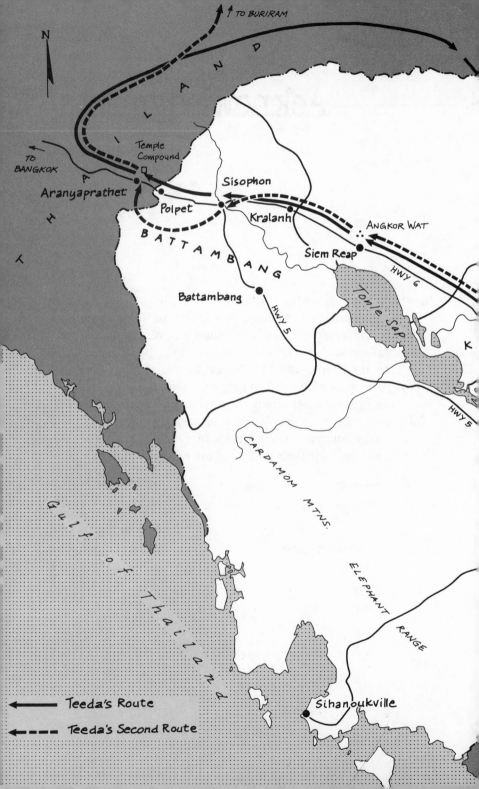

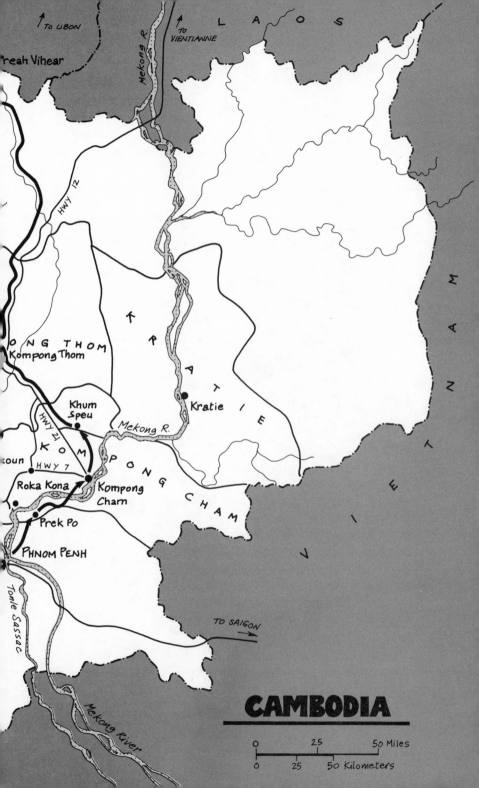

CAMBODIA

0   25   50 Miles

0   25   50 Kilometers

To keep you is no benefit:
To destroy you is no loss.
—Khmer Rouge slogan

TO DESTROY YOU
IS NO LOSS

Chapter One

I woke with a start. Something was different—wrong. Faint morning light filtered through the shuttered window. I was in my own bed; the knot of fear I had lived with for so long was still there. So what was different? Then it came to me. It was silence—an eerie silence. Something awesome had happened, for Phnom Penh was never quiet, especially with the noise of war our constant companion for over four months. This morning, not only had the cannons and rockets ceased, but even ordinary street sounds were missing—blaring horns, the cries of vendors. There were no barking dogs, no crowing roosters. It was as though someone had thrown a switch. Silence.

For the past five years, one-third of my life, war had engulfed Cambodia in constant internal strife and spillover of fighting from Vietnam. Communist guerrilla bands had harassed outlying villages for as long as I could remember.

Each year more and more children had crowded the city's schools as villagers flocked to Phnom Penh to escape the escalating war. My mother had complained bitterly about food shortages in the markets and soaring prices, and Papa looked increasingly worried. He and my brothers-in-law, Keang and Leng, sometimes remained at work day and night. Still, the naked ugliness of war hadn't penetrated my child's world until sustained rocket bombardments jolted the city itself and the streets teemed with ragged refugees from the embattled countryside. Not until the Khmer Rouge again launched their annual Tet offensive against our government forces near Phnom Penh had my schoolgirl's life lost its tranquillity. School was reduced to half days, then dismissed entirely after a devastating rocket blast wrecked a private school and killed many students. Saboteurs and rioting youths had razed power stations and ripped out water mains.

Mum told my older sisters, "I think Teeda hates being cut off from her classes and friends more than she minds the dreadful rockets."

It was true. I hated the isolation from schoolmates. I was the youngest, and a tomboy, in a family of four girls, and always needed reminding that I was now a young lady who must learn to sit quietly, talk less, keep my opinions to myself. Fortunately, Papa indulged me, encouraging my independent bent and curiosity. He had often tried to explain the war to me, managing to make it appear less frightening. However, on this morning, the seventeenth of April, 1975, the silence unnerved me.

I slipped from my mosquito-net-draped bed, careful not to wake my older sister Soorsdey. Even at this early hour, the day was sticky hot. I put on a loose-fitting blouse, and wrapping and tucking a floral-print *sampot* at the waist, I tiptoed across the polished teak floor and into the hall. A tattoo of gunfire sounded faintly in the distance.

We lived on a narrow side street in a quiet neighborhood of southern Phnom Penh, not far from the intersection of Monereth Boulevard and Mao Tse-tung Road. Our modern, box-shaped house was one of those cement, two story, Western-style homes that were popular in the city. A deep, elevated balcony wrapped around the second story, where we lived. Stairs led up from the encircling balcony to a rooftop patio and down to three ground-floor apartments. Tenants rented two of the apartments.

The third was Keang and Mearadey's. Mum's nephew, Samol, had lived with them since he'd fled his war-torn village.

On the second story were our living room, dining room, kitchen, three bathrooms, and four bedrooms. One bedroom was for Soorsdey and me, another was for my ailing grandmother. Leng and Rasmei and their small son and daughter shared a large bedroom suite. My parents slept in the master bedroom.

Several months before, we had constructed a makeshift bomb shelter in front of Keang and Mearadey's apartment, using our overhanging front balcony for the shelter's roof.

It was amazing how quickly we had adjusted to wartime Phnom Penh. In January of 1975, when the first sustained bombardments of Chinese-supplied rockets pounded the city, we had cowered silently in our dark shelter most of the time. But within days, we had learned to distinguish various rocket sounds, and only when explosions were near did we bother to use the muggy retreat.

If you were caught on the street during the awesome whistle of an incoming rocket, there was time only to fall face down, put your arms over your head, and pray that the explosion would not be too close. Then you'd jump up and run for cover. People darted from doorway to doorway listening for the distinctive, high-pitched whine of the next incoming rocket, then, between shrapnel-filled blasts, they ran for home or the safety of a real shelter.

During attacks, rockets had poured into one or more sectors of the city, often for hours. When a barrage had centered on southern Phnom Penh, we'd huddled in our shelter and made a game of sitting quietly until everyone's eyes grew accustomed to the dark. Calmly and deliberately, the adults had ignored the frightening explosions. Because they had remained calm, so had I. When rockets burst in another part of town, I'd pitied those unfortunate families but rejoiced for my own. I knew we were safe from attack as long as I could hear reassuring, distant explosions.

Recent barrages had been aimed first at one, then another, residential area, rather than at factories, harbors, government buildings, or other strategic targets. Psychologically wearing down the populace was more important to the enemy than physically destroying structures.

During the final weeks of the war we had continued to work and even play much as usual, but our leisure-time activities held added elements of risk. Gasoline-filled bottle bombs had been tossed so often into crowds at restaurants, sporting events, movies, and dances that many parents, my own included, refused to let their children participate in any group outings.

Upon entering the dimly lit living room, I found not only my worried parents, but also my sisters, Rasmei and Mearadey, and their husbands, Leng and Keang, and my twenty-year-old cousin, Samol. All of them kept vigil near the stubbornly silent radio; Radio Phnom Penh had gone dead almost twenty-four hours before. Bleary-eyed, my family nervously awaited the resumption of broadcasting, hoping for some announcement.

"Morning, Teeda" was all anyone said as I slipped onto the couch between my parents. My father's troubled face kept me mute.

We listened. Worried, the adults paced. What did the sudden stillness mean? Was the war really over? What should we do now? Was the curfew lifted? Who was in charge?

Noise in the street drew me to the window. I peered through the shutters and saw frightened government soldiers retreating toward Monereth Boulevard, shedding weapons and uniforms as they fled. A white flag of surrender draped the government tank stalled in the intersection.

By eight-thirty, there was still no sound from the radio.

My father's sister, her husband, and two other neighbors

came to consult with Papa. Cautiously, I joined them in the front yard. Our four families had previously decided to act together when the time came. Was this the moment?

A loud volley of shots and artillery fire erupted from the heart of the city. My little nieces and my nephew screamed in terror. I prepared to dash to our bomb shelter, but Papa reassuringly put his arm around my shoulder. He said the great burst of gunfire no doubt announced war's end.

Apparently, others in the neighborhood agreed, for some civilians cheered. To our surprise, even government soldiers joined the salute to the Communist victors by repeatedly firing their guns into the air. The disabled government tank in the intersection raised its muzzle into the morning sky and boomed a salvo to the new regime. The din reverberated through the city, crescendoed, sputtered, died.

Papa and our neighbors agreed that it was premature to settle on a course of action, so each family went home.

Just before nine-thirty, our radio crackled to life with earsplitting military music. Soorsdey lunged to turn down the volume. We clustered expectantly around the set, but half an hour went by before the music finally was interrupted. In unison, we leaned toward the radio as the voice of Cambodia's beloved Buddhist patriarch, Samdech Sangh Huot That, assured us all was well: the war was over, there would be peace. The Communist armies had defeated the Republic's forces. Today, no one was to go to work—we were to stay inside and remain calm. Then a weary-voiced General Mey Si Chan, from Lon Nol's defeated army, ordered all government forces to lay down their weapons. Peace negotiations were in progress; further announcements would follow. Military music resumed.

Remain calm. For weeks we had been poised to fight or to flee. Now, along with anxiety, we felt some relief. Peace at any price seemed preferable to the nightmare of the past few months.

Defeat of the Republic would mean major adjustments in our family. Papa was sure he would lose his government post, and did not expect the Communist regime to use his services. But surely, he told us, an educated man could always find work, and our family savings would tide us over these uneasy times.

Fifteen years earlier, under Prince Sihanouk, Papa had been elected as a deputy minister in the National Assembly. He served for eight years. For the past seven he had worked in Phnom Penh's Land Registry Office; two years under the prince and five in the same position after his friend President Lon Nol effected the bloodless coup that established the Khmer Republic.

I was giddy with relief that my father was not important enough to be one of the "Traitorous Seven"—those top government officials on the widely publicized list of "traitors" to be executed. In a government riddled with intrigue and corruption, Papa had maintained his integrity. Choun Butt had served his country well, worked hard, and husbanded his financial resources wisely.

Keang also expected to be jobless. He had been with the Ministry of Information in the Khmer Republic. My other brother-in-law, Leng, was manager of the international airport and thought he might be able to retain his position. But the men expressed no deep concern about work. Keang, once a lawyer and teacher of philosophy, could turn to one of these professions, and Leng's talents would always be in demand in a country where a good education was rare. My fears were lulled by the men's studied efforts to treat defeat casually. We still had our large home, financial resources, our good health. Most precious of all, we had each other. The war was over and we were alive.

"War or peace, people expect to be fed," my practical mother muttered. Soon she and my two married sisters were busy cooking rice for a belated breakfast. We were without fresh fruits and vegetables from the open-air market, since produce had been woefully scarce for months. But Mum had stock-piled bags of rice and other staples. Our meals were monotonous, but we were better off than many, and occasionally Mum bought vegetables on the black market.

Mearadey, twenty-four, and Rasmei, two years younger, were Mum's regular helpers. The three of them normally ran our household with the aid of one or two servants and occasional help from Father's mother, Grandmother Butt.

Soorsdey and I seldom helped. We were absorbed in studies and being teenagers, but this morning we willingly set the table, then entertained our nephew and nieces in the living room so the women could cook in peace.

The men sat on the balcony overlooking the street and debated what options were likely under the Khmer Rouge. They discounted wild stories of reprisals. At worst, Papa might be jailed for a while. This alarmed me, but they speculated that, more likely, he would simply be allowed to quietly seek private employment, provided he kept a low profile during the transition period.

Compared to some—who lived in lavish villas with spacious walled gardens and uniformed guards—ours was not a wealthy or ostentatious family. We were, however, comfortably situated. My parents had built our house when they moved to the city just before I was born. Mum had recently purchased a second house next door, where one of my father's sisters and her family had taken refuge when their village was overrun. In addition to our two houses, we owned three cars and leased a large one for Papa's official use. My father's income provided for the household needs of all fifteen people in our extended family, which included my parents, their four daughters, two sons-in-law, four grandchildren, my father's mother, my mother's nephew, and a servant. As was common in many upper-class households, the earnings of my brothers-in-law were spent as they and their wives wished, on extra things, such as cars or travel abroad, or saved toward purchasing homes of their own. We were well off, and the men expected to find life under the Khmer Rouge not much different. Our family would at least be physically safe, and if the new regime was not to our liking, we could always live in France or America like so many of our friends.

Good smells were coming from the kitchen. Mum had hoarded a small tin of canned ham, some of which she had added to the soup in honor of the promised peace.

By ten, breakfast was ready. The four young children and our serving girl were already in the kitchen eating by the time the men finally left the veranda and joined the rest of us in the dining room. With the kitchen door closed on the children's chatter, we reminisced about the dangers of recent months. Now that the repeated bombardments and the war's ordeal were over, we felt a compelling need to talk about our near misses. Like the time Keang had been eating lunch in the shade of a tree near his office and a rocket exploded directly overhead. When he regained his senses, he discovered only a few cuts and bruises. The tree's thick foliage had saved him, yet across the street mutilated people twisted and screamed in agony or lay lifeless.

We teased Mum and Papa about the time a rocket attack sent the family racing to the bomb shelter, only to find that Mum was not with us. She had been taking a shower, oblivious to the attack. Sick with fear over her fate, we were unable to reach her while rockets whistled directly overhead, sending thousands of white-hot shards flying in every direction as they exploded. When the short-lived attack ended, my mother turned off the water and serenely emerged from the shower surprised to find a frantic husband at her door. We could at last joke about it.

The end of war would mean that my nieces and nephew could play outside in safety again without fear of snipers, and we older ones could return to school as soon as the damaged classrooms were rebuilt.

Soorsdey, Samol, and I had continued our studies at home, but it was not a satisfactory arrangement. Mearadey had insisted that seven-year-old Tevi do basic arithmetic problems and practice reading each day. With few books and no classmates, it had been hard to hold the little girl's interest.

During the war, we occasionally had watched distant bombardments from our rooftop patio. In fear and fascination, we had traced the path of exploding rockets through the night sky as government-launched missiles arced out from the capital and Khmer Rouge rockets stabbed at the city's heart. The rockets reminded me of the fireworks, for which Phnom Penh was famous in quieter times. In the almost forgotten days of peace, I had loved seeing the night sky explode into a rainbow of color as fireworks shot out over the Mekong River.

Other nights we'd gathered on the covered rooftop to watch sadly as our beloved city burned. This morning, as we sat at breakfast, Phnom Penh was still burning.

We heard cheering in the distance and ran to the third-story patio, where we could see the street. Khmer Rouge soldiers approached from the city's outskirts—the dreaded Communist guerrillas. They looked timid and friendly, like shy country cousins.

I stared in disbelief. Could the enemy have been nothing more imposing than this ragtag group? They were no older than Soorsdey and I!

Covered with jungle grime, wearing black, ill-fitting pajama uniforms with colorful headbands or peaked Mao caps, they seemed ill at ease—gawking peasants who had never seen a city. How naïve they seemed. Yet I was struck by the wary, exhausted look even their spirit and youth could not hide.

Some soldiers walked. Others, with great delight, careened out of control on appropriated motorbikes, carts, pedicabs. After crashing into a building or a car, they simply walked away, laughing. Clearly, they had never steered such vehicles

11

before. Some soldiers were scarcely taller than the cumbersome Russian AK-47 rifles or the captured American M-16s they carried. Still, they looked hard—gaunt and hard—these thirteen- and fourteen-year-old veterans. Recruited when the Khmer Rouge overran their villages and pressed them into service, they had fought in the jungles since they were old enough to aim a weapon.

Residents cautiously cheered them on. Some neighbors waved white flags and draped sheets from balconies and windows, or tied white handkerchiefs to handlebars and car antennas. White, the color of surrender, was now the color of welcome. One daring boy tentatively joined the Khmer Rouge marching past. Then others ventured forth. Before long, there was singing of folk songs and dancing in the street. I wanted to join in the fun, but one look at Papa's face told me no.

My father said that to the majority it made little difference at this point which side won or lost. Many originally had fled the countryside, sickened by Khmer Rouge atrocities there, but after years of being uprooted, they just wanted to go home. They were tired of war. All that mattered to the beaten populace today was peace.

Catching the mood of the city and our neighbors, my young nieces and nephew started to cheer. Papa silenced them.

I gazed in fascination at the advancing conquerors, who had slogged through the lowlands to reach the capital. I could barely tell where their feet ended and their muddy, homemade sandals began. They all had short, close-cropped hair. I elbowed Soorsdey and, in a whisper, shared a startling realization: some of the soldiers were girls.

As we turned from the rooftop railing and the cheering throng, Mum marshaled her daughters, grandchildren, and serving girl into the house below. It was after eleven; the beds were unmade and breakfast dishes cluttered the table. She and the rest of us needed the security of routine this morning.

Rasmei, Mearadey, and Mum again began preparing soup and rice. For good or ill, this was a momentous day—Mum wanted our meals to reflect it.

Soorsdey and I hurried to our room to discuss the events so far. Perhaps the greatly feared enemy was only a paper tiger. We were relieved that the dire predictions of slaughter seemed unfounded. We had seen the soldiers. Those young boys were far from frightening. And the girls—well, the dirty, unkempt girls were . . . pathetic.

The mirror reflected our animated faces as we brushed each other's long, shiny-black hair and chatted. My father claimed I had a ready smile, dancing eyes, and vivacious manner. I hoped it was true, for those were traits I admired in my sisters. My quick wit, good humor, and practicality were inherited from Mum, I was told, and the family consensus was that my intelligence came from Papa. No one had to point out where I got my jug-handle ears. Anyone who knew Choun Butt knew I was his daughter. "Da, they give your countenance an almost pixie quality," Mum would say.

Soorsdey was quieter and more studious than I was. As a brand-new eighteen-year-old, she had a more mature outlook on life. I admired her, though she wasn't as much fun since she'd become a "young lady."

After dressing, I played with my dogs. In a class at the private English school I attended, I'd read about a dog named Blacky, and I'd chosen what I considered to be exotic English names for them: Blacky and Brownie. When I saw Rasmei feeding the chickens, I joined her. Seven months before, she, Mearadey, and Papa had imported five hundred chicks from Singapore and turned our garage into a chicken coop. It would have been a worthwhile business venture, but with bombs bursting overhead, few eggs were laid by the nervous hens.

Returning to the house with a basket of eggs, I could hear the men talking on the roof patio. I wanted an excuse to join

13

them, so I volunteered to carry the tea tray my mother was preparing. Papa, Keang, Samol, Leng, and some of our neighbors, including Uncle Suoheang from next door, were settled in deck chairs discussing in detail the likely consequences of the takeover and wishing they had more information about the new government. Radio bulletins had added little new information.

Nodding toward the festive sounds in the streets, a neighbor expressed pleasant surprise that the victors seemed to be so lenient. He'd feared a bloodbath; instead, there was dancing. My father had reservations. He did not expect the harsh reprisals some had predicted, but he did anticipate curfews and controls, and imprisonment or exile ordered for top officials. Few Cambodian leaders had accepted the American offer to flee when the American embassy personnel were evacuated. Acting President Saukham Khoy, one of the "Super Traitors" marked for death by the Khmer Rouge, did leave, and President Lon Nol, who had earlier suffered a stroke, was already in Hawaii. Most government officials, however, remained at their posts.

Papa, Leng, and Keang, like their colleagues, had felt no pressing need to dislocate our family, to abandon possessions and homeland. They decided to adjust to the new order of government, or, if necessary, to leave the country later. My father's longtime friend, Prime Minister Long Boreth, had chosen to remain, to help organize an orderly surrender, prompting Papa to say, "If Long Boreth doesn't fear a change in government, why should we?"

Throughout history, we Cambodians have constantly adapted to successive regimes, the way bamboo shifts with each new current of air. To bend in a strong wind and right oneself after the fury of the storm has passed is a form of strength the Asian mind understands well. In his time, my father had already lived under six diverse political systems: French colonial rule, a teenaged figurehead king, the Japanese occupation forces, an independent kingdom, a partial democracy with a king–turned–

prince–politician, and finally a republic. Even today, he said he felt sure we could accommodate yet another government. The men on the veranda nodded agreement.

In the mid-1960s, Papa had been part of a goodwill delegation to China. He prized a photo from that trip that pictured him with the Chinese premier, Chou En-lai. Although he did not favor communism, he felt we could live comfortably under a system similar to what he had seen in China. The Khmer Rouge, with their strong Chinese backing, seemed to offer such a government.

Noise in the street below drew my attention. Sensing a different tone in the merrymaking, I hurried to the rooftop railing. The men followed.

Additional foot soldiers had arrived in the neighborhood, and still more approached in jeeps, army trucks, and an odd assortment of commandeered vehicles. People scurried to get out of their way. These grim-looking soldiers no longer joined in celebrations. Their mood in no way resembled that of their fellow Khmer Rouge who had wandered through the neighborhood only a few hours earlier. This new contingent shunned camaraderie. The crowd grew concerned and the carnival air dissipated. Brandishing weapons, soldiers stopped hungry civilians from looting neighborhood shops, even as they covered themselves with gaudy trinkets and pocketed handfuls of ballpoint pens.

From our sequestered balcony, we watched an army truck career into the narrow, winding street. A brash Khmer Rouge driver braked sharply and forced the truck into reverse. The vehicle lurched to a halt a few feet from a neighbor's house. Five dusty soldiers hopped from the back, and, kicking open the elaborately carved teak door, they began loading household possessions into the truck, heaving some things into the street. The owners looked on in shocked silence. A few minutes later, the driver, draped in a woman's pink coat, banged the tailgate

15

closed and roared away, jamming gears as he went, his comrades shouting as they raced to catch him.

We were dumbfounded. What had been the point of that raid? Why that particular neighbor? Could others in the neighborhood expect the same?

More foot soldiers turned the corner and entered the street a block away. From our vantage point, we saw soldiers enter other streets as well. These pajama-clad youths looked grim. Shots rang out, and the crowds were ordered off the streets. Soldiers killed a stray dog to show they meant business.

Our sobered guests quietly returned to their own homes by way of the back garden. Just then, eight mud-stained Khmer Rouge entered our front yard. My father ordered me to stay put. Hastily, he descended the outside staircase to intercept them. The soldiers wanted to bathe and to eat.

"Ean Bun, girls, bring these young countrymen something to eat, something to drink." Tensely, my mother and sisters rushed to provide refreshments.

Fearfully, I held my breath when I realized what my father had in mind.

He presumed these villagers had never seen indoor plumbing, so instead of inviting them into the house to shower, he pointed out the garden hose. Six of the soldiers stripped to the waist and took turns bathing. The concept of water running through a hose on demand appealed to them. Turning the faucet on and off was a novelty. I breathed a sigh of relief. Had they suspected that there were facilities for showering inside, they would have been insulted.

Two soldiers watched the other six in stony silence. Mum and my sisters nervously tried to encourage them to avail themselves of the shower, but they repeatedly grunted refusal. Then it became apparent to us; they were *neary*—female soldiers.

I watched until the last of the males boisterously filed out the front gate, followed by their two stoic companions.

16

We returned to our vigil at the radio, but the news bulletins just repeated earlier ones. Finally, we heard a new item. Men in the Ministry of Information were directed to go to the radio station, to operate equipment and help with news releases.

Keang hesitated to leave his wife and two little daughters. He questioned the motives of the Khmer Rouge for issuing the order. A few hours after this announcement, he became doubly suspicious when Radio Phnom Penh stated that *all* ministers, generals, and other government officials were to report at once to the Ministry of Information to help organize the country.

He and my father decided to wait. They had expected the transfer of power to be fairly smooth, but it seemed unlikely that former leaders would be consulted, let alone included in the new government at the start.

A truck with loudspeakers moved slowly through the neighborhood announcing an order more in keeping with what my father had expected—all doors must be propped open. Windows could be shuttered against the intense afternoon heat, but no homes were to be locked. Anyone possessing arms must bring them out immediately. Something called Angka Loeu—Organization High—wanted all weapons. The exact meaning of "Angka Loeu" was unclear, but none of us doubted the necessity of obeying.

Three teenaged soldiers approached our front gate to collect weapons. I was in Mearadey's ground-floor apartment with my two little dogs when the armed youngsters marched boldly into the yard. As required, the door to the apartment was wide open, but a mosquito net covered the entrance. Brownie and Blacky barked as they bounded through this flimsy curtain. The soldiers opened fire. Aghast, I shrank against the wall. Leng dashed down the outside stairs pleading with the soldiers to stop—his children were in danger. Quickly, Papa and Keang proffered our guns, handles first. The soldiers swaggered from the yard.

17

Miraculously, the children were only shaken and both dogs unharmed, but Mearadey's riddled doorframe was graphic proof of our vulnerability. Papa ordered everyone to remain indoors and out of sight from then on. I was too frightened to protest.

From the privacy of our balcony, we noticed a trickle of residents from other districts trudging down the streets. By early afternoon, the trickle had become a flood. Rumor had it that everyone must prepare to leave the city. At once! The Angka "requested" it. Soldiers claimed whatever pleased them by pointing weapons at the owner and suggesting he loan the object to Angka Loeu. In our neighborhood, no soldiers came to enforce an order to leave, so my father and brothers-in-law chose to disregard the mass evacuation as a false rumor. Without real conviction, we invented explanations for the movement of so many people burdened with large bundles. Perhaps they were merely villagers anxious to return home, perhaps they had done something to incur the wrath of the Khmer Rouge and had been kicked out. They were evicted squatters, slum dwellers, perhaps. As more and more frightened people crowded the streets, it became apparent that the order to leave was no rumor, but did it mean everyone?

Herded along by the Khmer Rouge, frightened residents streamed toward the four main thoroughfares leading to the city outskirts. The din on Monereth Boulevard and Mao Tse-tung Road could be heard even in our tightly shuttered home. Those moving too slowly, turning aside to rest, or even stopping to adjust their loads were threatened by gun-wielding soldiers. With occasional shots fired overhead, the masses were kept moving.

Shaken by what had happened during the past few hours, our family sat down to dinner shortly after two. While we were eating, a neighbor rushed in to report that the entire city was to be emptied of residents for three or four days while the Khmer

Rouge "cleaned up Phnom Penh." We analyzed possible meanings of "clean up." It could mean clearing the city of snipers and reputed CIA-led resistance. Perhaps it meant removal of all the filth and rubble three million residents and tons of rockets had inflicted on the city. A passerby, running to warn friends and relatives, yelled that everyone must leave quickly because the Americans were preparing a massive bombing of Phnom Penh. No one was sure if this or any other explanation was correct, but all those fleeing the city seemed anxious to comply at once.

Papa, as chief provider and undisputed head of our extended family, felt differently. He did not believe that anyone—not even this mysterious Organization on High—could possibly empty an *entire* city of three million people. The idea was absurd. Where would they all go? How could they all be fed, sanitation provided? What reason could the Khmer Rouge have for wholesale evacuation? They might well be planning to remove all the recent refugee-squatters from the parks, alleys, and temporary camps around the city, he argued, even those from slums and heavily damaged areas. But not *everyone.* It made no sense. The Butt family, he decided, would remain quietly behind our shutters until the confusion passed.

Family members were accustomed to agreeing with my father. He made final decisions in our home not only by reason of his patriarchal position, but also because he was a wise man who held our interests and needs above his own. He was a kind, gentle husband and father, much loved and respected.

Several times during the long afternoon, soldiers with portable loudspeakers drove through our neighborhood, issuing conflicting orders. One said people must leave immediately. The next that everyone should prepare to leave tomorrow. Papa chose to wait and see, and hope. At 4:00 P.M. the first official announcement of victory was broadcast, followed immediately by a formal order to evacuate.

The order was distressing. Even more alarming to my

father and brothers-in-law was the victory statement itself: "This is the United National Front of Kampuchea. We are in the Ministry of Information. We have conquered by arms and not by negotiation. Long live the extraordinary revolution of Kampuchea."

By arms and not by negotiation. That arrogant statement left little hope for compromise with the former government or moderation in stated Communist goals. Our bubble of optimism burst. Darkness falls swiftly near the equator: there is little twilight at Cambodian latitudes. Political darkness fell just as fast.

Solemnly, we ate an evening meal of leftovers prepared in the gathering darkness. No lights were turned on or candles lit this first night under the new regime. Soorsdey, the children, and I went to bed early. It had been a long, draining day. Still, I could not sleep. I lay listening fearfully to the continuing bedlam in the streets while my mind sifted the day's happenings.

Mum's youngest brother, a forest ranger, lived near Thailand, just one kilometer from the border. He had urged us a few weeks before to leave Phnom Penh and stay with his family in the quiet frontier village. However, Leng needed to be at the airport daily; Keang had his work with the Ministry of Information. Papa felt he should keep his office open and stay abreast of final decisions even as the government collapsed. Wives and children refused to go without husbands and fathers. Besides, all we owned, all that was familiar, was in Phnom Penh. So the kind offer had been turned down and, though we did not know it yet, the borders were being sealed.

Under cover of darkness, many of our neighbors buried treasured items in their gardens, secured valuables inside walls, pried up floorboards to create secret vaults. Jewelry was sewn in skirt hems and jacket linings; radios, cameras, silver bowls, candlesticks, and silverware were concealed in bags of rice and beans. Not my family; my practical mother had packed our things weeks before.

20

From my bedroom, I heard Mum make her usual nightly round of the house. Even in the dark, she moved with assurance, pausing at each door. My frail grandmother slept deeply, as did the serving girl who shared her room.

In contrast to the unusual quiet in which I woke, I drifted to sleep amid noises my shuttered windows could not keep out: the insistent cries of hungry children, the distant moans of weary families trying to settle on the hard pavement, the angry shouts of black-uniformed youths.

Chapter Two

Khmer Rouge soldiers were on the streets when I awakened before dawn. Four- to six-man patrols moved through the avenues and alleys of Phnom Penh evicting everyone from homes, shops, and shelters. No delays were permitted. No requests allowed. Troublemakers were killed on the spot. Often, animals were slaughtered to intimidate owners.

Already, on this second day of evacuation, orphanages and monasteries, hotels and hospitals, stood empty. Within hours of the takeover, people staying in these places had been driven from the city at gunpoint. Doctors and staff were killed if they resisted expulsion. Hospital patients too weak to walk were shot in their beds. Others, carrying still-attached plasma bottles, hobbled from the wards. Hospital beds, filled with the sick and dying, were pushed through the streets by relatives and friends.

For nearly four hundred miles, the border between Cambodia and Thailand curves through mountains, jungles, and across rivers. The Khmer Rouge methodically evacuated all villages within five miles of the border, creating a no-man's-land that extended from the southern fishing villages on the Gulf of Thailand to the ancient Khmer temple of Preah Vihear in the north and beyond.

Borders with Laos and Vietnam were likewise secured, and all roads into the country closed, jungle paths booby-trapped and mined. The Cardamon Mountains and the Elephant Range to the southwest completed the cordon. A lethal web was being cast over Cambodia. Angka Loeu, the spider at the center, was even then issuing the orders that would entrap each citizen in servitude and fear. For millions of my fellow countrymen, this web would become a shroud.

North, south, east, and west, the four official exits from Phnom Penh filled with people. Friendship Highway, built with U.S. aid during the Vietnamese War, had once transported military supplies eastward from the port city of Kompong Som through Cambodia to Vietnam. Now it carried the human flotsam of civil war.

With first light, a thorough emptying began street by street, block by block, house by house, from the center of the city outward. The rich, the poor, the sick and lame, filed past our door. Mum packed additional supplies. Papa urged us to remain quietly inside as long as possible. Mearadey and Rasmei pressed him to leave. If the neighborhood was emptied, we could more readily be singled out. Better to move now and be part of the faceless mass, they reasoned.

Papa was reluctant to leave the shelter of our yard. "If we leave our home, we will never return." There, he had said it.

Pushing through the multitudes outside, Uncle Ban and three of his grown children arrived, breathless, at our front gate and joined our worried neighborhood council. He had left four of his daughters and his wife—my father's other sister—frantically packing in their apartment a few blocks away. Even at this early-morning hour, he dripped with sweat from exertion and apprehension.

Uncle Ban and his son, Si Ton, echoed our fears; reality did not match what we were being told by the Khmer Rouge. If Phnom Penh was being emptied for fear of retaliation by pockets of resistance, there was no need to evacuate those in hospitals and orphanages, certainly not by dumping them into the streets at gunpoint. Besides, snipers and resisters could easily melt into the crowds.

If American B-52s were going to bomb the Communist-held city, why did the Khmer Rouge confiscate cars, making rapid exit next to impossible? Not everyone's auto was being appropriated—everything seemed random and unorganized—yet most people on the streets were without transportation, and those with vehicles were allowed to use them merely to carry possessions while they pushed. Cars could not be started within the city. If the Khmer Rouge feared bombing, why not keep people in their homes? A home offered some protection against bombs, the streets none. We had already survived attacks by using homemade shelters. It seemed implausible that the Americans would attack. What would bombing accomplish? The Khmer Rouge could not be destroyed by destroying Phnom Penh.

Finally, Father agreed that it was best to leave our home before we were forced out at gunpoint. We would try to cross the city in a northerly direction and stop outside Phnom Penh as soon as allowed. If worse came to worst, we could go on to Khum Speu in Kompong Cham Province and stay with relatives. Samol's parents and two of Mum's brothers and other kin lived in Khum Speu.

Armed at last with a course of action, Uncle Suoheang from next door, our neighbors, and Uncle Ban's family went to pack. The group would reassemble at our home prepared for the journey.

Easing into the throng, Uncle Ban, his daughter, and two sons set out for their apartment. They never reached it. Soldiers blocked the way. On the other side of the intersection, civilians were being shunted toward the southern exit. Those on our side were forced east. Soldiers would not let my frantic uncle cross the barrier. Finally, with tears of despair, he and my cousins worked their way back to our home. They had no alternative now except to go with us. Uncle Ban's wife and four daughters were lost in the tide of humanity ebbing away to the south.

We tried to comfort our distraught relatives. In anguish, I helped Mum gather additional rice and food for Uncle Ban and my cousins. Articles of clothing and bedding were jammed into suitcases and we scurried to load Rasmei's and Papa's small cars. The cars would secure a place for us in the crowds, carry needed supplies, and allow Grandmother Butt and the four children to ride. We would leave the other two autos behind.

Already packed were gold, American dollars, jewelry, and other small objects of value, plus our best clothing. We did not expect to need expensive garments, but knew they would offer irresistible temptation to soldiers rummaging through our house. I pocketed a delicate, gold Buddha necklace given to me as a child. I prized it more for its sentimental importance than its monetary value, and I did not want some soldier claiming it.

With three million people on the road, we realized that few could be accommodated in hotels or homes, so we took sleeping mats, pots, pans, dishes, and water, as well as a month's supply of rice, beans, pickled eggs, and more—for nineteen people. We also took sheets of plastic to use as canopies in case we didn't return before the rains came.

Tevi, my oldest niece, packed a little satchel of favorite things—objects she wanted to keep safe or play with while we were gone. No one paid attention then to the wrinkled family photos and other childish treasures she chose.

Mearadey and Rasmei took a few toys for Moni, Rota, and Chenda Poong, then hurried once more through the house scooping up items they thought might be useful. On impulse, Rasmei grabbed bottles from the almost-empty medicine cabinet. Mum took two antique silver bowls from the locked cupboard, cherished wedding presents she decided not to leave.

At the last minute, a lounge chair, which could be folded into a cot, was wedged into the trunk of Rasmei's Suzuki. Then Soorsdey's and Si Ton's motorbikes were hastily tied behind.

The chickens! We'd forgotten all about the five hundred chickens. Without constant care, they would die in the heat. We decided to give the chickens and eggs to neighbors and any passing refugees who wanted them. Better to feed friend than foe. Rasmei and Mearadey grabbed fifty of the largest laying hens, stuffed them into bamboo baskets and piled the baskets on the luggage in the backseat of each car, then invited neighbors to help themselves.

I pushed Brownie and Blacky into the backyard, leaving them with a tub of water and a large mound of food, and prayed they'd be safe until I returned.

Into the fray we descended. The nightmare began. Once we joined the masses moving slowly through the congested lane, all choice of direction was taken from us. We just shuffled along and pushed our cars whenever we were able to move forward. A solid bank of buildings and high cement walls lined the winding streets, creating narrow canyons filled to overflowing with the thousands. Occasionally, an army truck, horn blaring, roared down upon us. We, who thought we couldn't pack together any tighter, frantically pushed against buildings and people to make room for the advancing vehicle. Soldiers kicked, insulted, clubbed. People screamed. Loose dogs, ducks, geese, chickens, and pigs added their fearful cries to the din.

The still air in these city canyons was over 100 degrees, and I was nauseated by the stench of unwashed bodies wedged against me. The streets had become toilet facilities as well as home for thousands. Through this hell we struggled to keep the cars near each other and the group together. It was like being squeezed through a steamy sewer.

Intersections and crossroads presented a serious hazard. There, the merging rivers of people caused dreadful currents.

Papa ordered us to hold on to the car tightly as we approached each side street. All about us people were separated from their families. Mothers and fathers, who fought to regain a child, were forced to move on or were clubbed for disobeying orders. One family in our neighborhood group vanished.

By sundown, we were on Mao Tse-tung Road, only a quarter mile from home, straining to reach Monivong Boulevard, the city's main southeast artery. The column nearly came to a halt when aged wood apartments and tinder-dry storefronts alongside streets erupted into flame. I eased myself to the side of the car, away from the heat. Burning shops blocked roads to the left. Flames filled alleys, and buildings tumbled around us. With more refugees pressing in from behind, and nowhere to go in front, there was hysteria. People clawed their way toward safety and the weak were trampled all around us.

After dark, soldiers finally stopped shouting at us to keep moving, but no one could stop for the night until he found a place safe from the crowds and fires. As we neared the huge Bokor Cinema, Papa announced that he hoped to reach his cousin's villa, which was not far from there. She had fled the capital earlier, when a bomb damaged her home. Although the house was in ruins, Papa thought it would at least offer a place where we could spend the night.

As we passed Bokor Cinema, I glanced through its open doors. There, in the ornate lobby, lay the bloated bodies of soldiers who'd been killed in the final assault on the city. Before Papa could direct my eyes elsewhere, I saw the maggot-covered faces, the exposed cheekbones where worms had eaten away stinking flesh. I nearly fainted.

A new fear swept through the exhausted crowd: a gas station at the intersection ahead was in the path of advancing fires. If the flames got much closer, the tanks might explode.

Although our relative's house was only a block away, we could not possibly reach it before morning at the rate we were progressing. Another place to sleep had to be found and soon. We had been battling the crowds for over twelve hours.

We spotted a dark, dead-end alley to the right. It was a risk to enter a passageway with no exit at the other end, but to remain where we were offered little hope of escaping fires or fear-maddened crowds. Grabbing our valuables, a small amount of food, and our baskets of chickens, we locked the cars and hurried down the alley. Our neighbors and relatives followed.

Near the end of the cul-de-sac I spied a friend's house. We piled into the deserted yard and tried to settle the weary children, but it proved impossible. In the dark, we had inadvertently set up camp near a stagnant fishpond, and even mosquito nets could not keep the thousands of bloodthirsty insects away. While my mother and sisters and I repacked and comforted sobbing children, the men scouted for another place. They led us to an old cement mansion not yet claimed by too many others. An orange glow from myriad fires beyond Bokor Cinema provided enough light to see. Everyone was exhausted and needed food. On the marble floor, the men soon had a small pile of broken furniture blazing. We boiled pots of rice and bedded down the children.

Checking our belongings, Rasmei discovered that many of our chickens were dead. The rest would soon follow. If we were to salvage anything to add to our food supply, we had to kill, pluck, clean, cook, and preserve those fifty birds before going to sleep. Our neighbors had almost as many to process. It was early morning before the task was completed, but our heavily salted meat would not spoil before it could be consumed.

At last we could rest, but sleep did not come readily. The roar of fires raging across the boulevard drowned out all efforts to talk without shouting. We lay huddled in benumbed silence, willing sleep to claim us. Cowering in the darkest corner, I turned my face to the wall that seemed to dance in fire-cast shadows.

Too weary to go elsewhere, we could only hope that the

tanks at the service station would not explode; that fire would not cross Mao Tse-tung Road; that the cement mansion would protect us if it did.

We were saved for another day of hell by a shift in wind direction. Danger from the fires was gone by morning. We were routed from the mansion at dawn only to find our two autos in the litter of the burned-out street. Rasmei's Suzuki was badly damaged by fire and vandals—four tires slashed and windshield smashed. It had to be abandoned. Most of the food we'd left in the cars had been stolen, spilled, or burned. Yet, we felt blessed. We were still together and unhurt; we still had some belongings and one car for Grandmother and the children to ride in.

Hastily transferring the salvageable belongings to the second car, we began inching forward again with the press of people. Si Ton, Samol, Leng, and Keang forged ahead to our relative's bomb-gutted mansion. Scrambling over a broken garden wall, they went in search of food and other useful items, but returned almost instantly. Fierce fighting had apparently taken place there, and the stench of bloated bodies in the roofless, shell-pocked rooms made it impossible to remain long enough to scavenge. I was glad I hadn't gone with them, and thankful that Papa's cousin was not there to see the carnage that had taken place in her once sedate parlor.

My father attempted to divert my attention whenever we passed a fly-shrouded body, but turning away did not block my other senses. I plugged my nose against the assault of rotting flesh and breathed through my mouth, but the stench of death also had a taste. Nor could I be deaf to the anguished cries of an exhausted mother, lying on a curb, laboring to bring new life into this world turned upside down. Relatives tried to screen the woman from view with their long skirts, but we all could hear her screams of pain.

During those first days of the evacuation, people unable to keep up were clubbed. However, once the Khmer Rouge had the entire population moving like a herd of dumb oxen, it took only shouts and occasional prodding to keep us in line.

In peacetime, Phnom Penh, with its stylish shops, sidewalk cafés, cream-colored mansions, walled villas, tropical foliage, and tree-lined boulevards, had always seemed elegant, but the alleys hid cardboard and corrugated-tin hovels where the poor eked out a miserable existence. Until our march from the city, however, I'd had little knowledge of this other world. Now I rubbed shoulders with not only those who'd recently fled the advancing Khmer Rouge, but also with peasants who had abandoned their villages earlier for the promise of wealth in the city. These poor people had been reduced to selling vegetables on the street, pedaling the three-wheeled pedicabs, or driven to begging, prostitution, theft. Many had been unwell and underfed even before being forced to make this grueling march back into the countryside. By the third day, many impoverished peasants began to die.

Stifling heat, lack of food, and bad water also took their toll of the old, the infirm, and the young. Dysentery and dehydration were felling many. Water supplies had been shut off to encourage residents to leave the city, so those not carrying their own water were soon reduced to drinking from ponds and ditches. Though my family used bottled water, little Tevi soon became deathly ill. Mearadey tried to ease her pain, but we were not allowed to stop long enough to care for her properly.

Inching along Monivong Boulevard, we finally reached Keang's old law school. It had taken us four horrendous days to travel less than two miles. We took shelter in classrooms where Keang had sat for exams. Charred remains of desks littered the tiled floors where refugees cooked rice. The corners of rooms were used as toilets.

My English school, next door, was a stinking shambles. Windows were smashed, the lovely grounds trampled, trees destroyed. Textbooks had provided fuel and light for squatters.

That I could understand, but I could not understand the Khmer Rouge's wanton burning of books. Stacks of books had been simply tossed out library windows and set afire. Even the law library was destroyed.

Most books in Phnom Penh's many libraries were in French. Ever since our independence from colonial rule twenty-two years before, Cambodians had felt resentful of continued French influence. But French was undeniably our second language, the language of the educated. It was the language that made contact with the outside world possible. But it wasn't just hatred for the French that prompted the Khmer Rouge to burn books; it seemed to be hatred for any learning. Books written in Cambodian were also tossed to the ravenous flames, and book-stores, newsstands, and stationery shops torched. Rare, price-less volumes in special collections had been eliminated without a second's thought. Even illiterate peasants, filing past the burning books, were devastated by the senseless destruction.

Money was also burning. At first people grabbed fistfuls of bills from the burning piles in front of banks. The soldiers laughed. Money wouldn't be needed in the new Cambodia, they said. This was a new era, a starting over, year zero—*Tchap Pdum Pee Saun*. Angka Loeu would take care of us from now on. They told refugees to throw their useless riels into the flames. A few gullible people believed the soldiers and unbur-dened themselves of bulky moneybags, but most, ourselves in-cluded, refused to believe that our hard-earned riels were totally worthless, even though it had recently required a shopping bag of bills to purchase a bag of rice.*

---

*Between 1970 and the takeover in 1975, inflation drove the value of the riel down from 35 per dollar to 3000 per dollar. What this major devaluation meant to the everyday economy is best illustrated in considering the change in prices of basic comodities. Rice increased from 4 riels per kilogram to 1800 riels per kilogram, and the cost of a traditional soup meal rose from 3 riels to 1500 riels.

As food shortages increased, rice became the measure of value. A car or costly watch was the price demanded for a fifty-pound bag. More often, no proffered wealth could pry rice from a lucky owner.

Famished refugees chewed leaves and even tree bark to dull hunger pangs. Stripping the once majestic teak, jacaranda, and Nandi flame trees, they boiled leaves and bark in polluted water to make tea. Years before, Prince Sihanouk had spent large sums on spacious parks and grandiose public buildings, with the goal of making Phnom Penh rival Saigon as "the Paris of the Orient," but it was the gracious tree-lined boulevards that provided so much of the city's charm. As we shuffled toward the bridge that spanned the Bassac River, rows of denuded trees stood as battered sentinels of our broken nation.

Fierce fighting had taken place the week before at Monivong Bridge. Mutilated soldiers lay where they had fallen, rotting in the intense tropical heat. A buzzing, black cloud of flies lifted from bloated bodies as we approached, then settled once more when we passed. Looking down into the Bassac River, I saw books and magazines by the hundreds floating in lazy eddies; the river was awash with soggy French literature.

Ten miles east of Phnom Penh, we took refuge under an unclaimed tree in a cucumber patch near Highway 1, even as thousands of our countrymen trudged past. Ten miles. It had taken us just over a week to reach this spot where we could camp long enough to tend to Tevi's needs. The child was little more than skin and bones. Death seemed imminent.

Shortly after our arrival in the cucumber patch, a Communist officer noticed Tevi's illness. In an inexplicable humane gesture, he used his influence to secure the streptomycin that saved Tevi.

Our car, parked between the highway and the tree, offered us some privacy from the crowds. We tied a plastic tarp between the tree and the car for a shade canopy, and later the tarp was useful in collecting rainwater. Mosquito nets, suitcases, and rolled sleeping mats were stacked near the tree, but we kept our diminished food and water supplies carefully hidden from view. Papa slept on the lounge chair or shared the car with the children and the rest of us slept on the ground.

Our "kitchen" was an upturned box used for a work surface, and three stones to contain a campfire. The men spent a small fortune buying three big logs from a farmer. The logs were shoved between the stones, and the ends ignited. Mum controlled the rate at which rice boiled by sliding the burning ends closer to the center of the firepit for more intense heat or pulling them out a little for simmering. She cooked a huge pot of rice just once each day—enough to feed our family and Uncle Ban's. We burned the wood sparingly and extinguished the cooking fires after each use.

Old farm buildings or vacated village huts became latrines. Because the smell near them was overpowering and the flies thick, my family chose instead to dig a trench toilet in the open field behind our camp. We waited for dark before using it, then covered each used section with dirt.

After we set up camp and Tevi began to recover, there was little to occupy our attention. The men went daily to other camps or outlying villages in search of information and to barter for foodstuffs—they usually returned without either. What food they did find was expensive. Leng alone spent over one million riels—more money than most Cambodians earned in a lifetime —in the short time we were camped outside Phnom Penh. Once he bought a scrawny chicken for several thousand riels and received a handful of shelled peanuts in change; another time he bought a dried fish for what once would have been a week's wages.

The old farmer who owned the cucumber patch sold his produce, whatever wasn't stolen. When told by the Khmer

Rouge that the money he took in trade had no value, he refused to listen. Shaking his gnarled fist at their retreating backs, he added in whispered defiance, "Even if it has no value to others, it can light my funeral pyre when I die!"

Farmers farther from Phnom Penh refused riels and even gold. They traded instead for clothing, watches, tarps, medicine, and other practical goods that had not been available in the villages for years. Our silk shirts and beautiful *sampot*s proved invaluable in trade. Unfortunately, most refugees soon ran out of exchangeable goods, and food.

Some rice was finally provided by the new regime about ten days after the takeover, a few days after we reached our roadside camp—just in time to avert starvation on a massive scale. Trucks stopped along Highway 1 near our camp, and soldiers announced that Angka Loeu was once again providing for the needs of the people. An old sweetened-condensed-milk can, with its top cut off, served as the standard measuring scoop. Each refugee in the long queues was ladled one canful of rice as his portion for the day. On days when trucks failed to come, those without food or barter items went hungry.

Many bags containing the gift from Angka showed by their labels that the rice had originally been part of the supplies flown by the Americans into Phnom Penh shortly before the city fell. Angka Loeu fed us from its enemy's larder.

Occasionally, dirty lumps of salt were distributed. Mum dissolved them in a jar of water, allowed the dirt to settle, then poured off the precious saltwater for use in cooking. She also saved the brine in which we had preserved hard-boiled eggs before we left Phnom Penh. As a result, we did not have the swollen feet and hands evident in those suffering from salt deficiency.

Though neither rice nor salt was provided in sufficient quantities, they did extend our rapidly dwindling food reserves and helped maintain our health. Those who depended wholly on

Angka's largess—the poor, with no reserves, and the rich forced out during the first hours of the takeover without time to gather supplies—simply starved at a slower rate than they would have otherwise.

Since Angka supposedly took care of all our needs, trade had to be conducted in secret. Lenient soldiers pretended not to notice trading, yet others strictly enforced the rules by beating offenders and confiscating goods.

My mother and sisters spent part of each day cooking; the men bartered and searched for food; the rest of us had nothing to relieve boredom. Uncle Ban and his children squatted at the roadside, still looking for their loved ones, and I joined them occasionally, hoping I might recognize a school friend or neighbor. I was weary of camping. I wanted to go home, to sleep in my own bed, have a bath, play with my pets, go to school, have something besides rice to eat now that the salted chicken meat and pickled eggs were gone.

While we were camped in the cucumber patch, my father, a cautious man, evolved a rule that we would follow thereafter; we would watch and listen carefully to see what results others had when they tried something new or asked a favor. If those results were good, we followed suit. We lost opportunities by not taking the initiative, but we were saved from fatal mistakes. Our family's guiding rule became "Never do anything first." "Only a fool tests the depth of the water with both feet," says the Chinese proverb.

With the end of the forced march, city residents who had camped as close to the city as allowed were again on the move, seeking food in outlying villages. They filed listlessly past our camp each day, joined by peasants who moved more purposefully. The peasants were determined to reach their old villages in the delta. In addition, dark-skinned, heavily tattooed tribesmen, who had sought refuge in the city, were now seeking routes back to their remote mountain hamlets. In school, I'd read about these hill people, but I'd never seen them until they passed our camp. Under our Khmer Rouge masters, we city dwellers, our delta village cousins, and the primitive mountain tribesmen would soon have much in common. The Communists promised equality. Indeed, we were rapidly becoming equal—equally hungry, equally homeless, equally fearful.

It seemed an eternity since we'd been expelled from Phnom Penh. Though we had traveled fewer than ten miles from the city, we had entered another world.

Chapter Three

Two and a half weeks after eviction, a call was issued for men in certain categories to return to Phnom Penh to begin the reconstruction. Those encouraged to volunteer included former government leaders, military officers, doctors, lawyers, business leaders, educators and professional men, and skilled workmen such as engineers, plumbers, electricians, and mechanics. Families of these men were to remain in the temporary camps a little longer.

A wave of hope rippled through the crowd as the truck-mounted loudspeaker blared this announcement. Former government officials, especially, felt the need to show support for the new regime and many stepped forward. Mothers and children urged their men to register so Phnom Penh would be ready before the monsoon rains came, for already the winds were shifting from the northeast to the southwest, bringing occasional showers. Within the month, much of the delta would be a quagmire.

Papa and my brothers-in-law wanted to sign up, yet felt constrained to wait. They had no desire to volunteer for what might be prison, exile, or execution. During the past few weeks, we had witnessed a level of dishonesty, brutality, and capriciousness that defied understanding. Such behavior, coupled with our aversion to Communist philosophies, made us suspicious. The men were in a quandary. Was the call to rebuild genuine, or was it merely a means of identifying certain men for reprisals?

Though Keang, Papa, and Leng decided to wait, they continually took stock of their alternatives. Every day they watched the army of recruits file toward Phnom Penh. Once Papa noticed an important colleague's familiar blue Peugeot station wagon inching its way along the congested road toward the city. Hoping at last to get reliable information, he hurried through the crowd, trying to attract his friend's attention. The man sat in the front seat next to a Khmer Rouge driver.

A brief look of recognition crossed his somber face, then his terror-filled eyes looked straight ahead. Papa glanced from the man's stricken face to his lap and saw that he was hand-cuffed. In the rear seat, a soldier held a pistol to his head. Papa melted into the crowd, his questions answered.

Two days later, a Voice of America broadcast reported that eighty-five government officials had just been executed. We learned much later that bodies of thousands who had answered the call to rebuild were stacked in public buildings such as Toul Sleng High School. They had been tricked to their own executions.

After the men had left, allegedly to restore Phnom Penh, portable loudspeakers blared the awful truth—there would be no return to the city for us.

"Leave!" they ordered. "Go find a place in the villages. . . . Cities are evil; technology is evil; money and trade are evil. . . . The strength of a nation is in its working men and women, not in the parasites of cities who live off the labor of the peasant. . . . Everyone must work in the fields. . . . Plant rice so the nation can prosper. . . . Only those who work will eat. . . . All are dependent upon the Organization on High."

With hope of returning to the city gone, we recognized the cruelty of the lies we'd been told. A few weeks under Khmer Rouge rule had impressed on all of us that we were dealing with vengeful, irrational masters. Those foolish enough to challenge the decisions of Angka in public seldom did so twice.

One woman, beside herself with worry, timidly asked an officer how she could send funds to her son studying abroad if the Cambodian riel was no longer recognized. I listened closely, for Uncle Ban also had a son studying in France. Sneering, the officer said it was not a concern of the Angka and would no longer be a concern of hers; communication with the outside world had been severed.

In the new Cambodia, the officer loudly boasted, there would be no modern means of communication. No mail service or telephones. No newspapers. No border crossings. No trains, cars, buses, or planes. The evil ways of the Western world were outlawed, all ties to the past abolished. This was a new era—Year Zero.

Not many occupations would be needed. No merchants, no bankers, no teachers, lawyers, or civil servants, no doctors, dentists, or dressmakers trained in the corrupt ways of the West. No railroad engineers, pedicab drivers, cooks, waiters, maids—not even truck drivers or housewives. These people had been leeches on society, consuming the harvest of the true laborer. "True labor" was in agriculture, fishing, and a few other basic occupations directly related to food production.

Reeling at this latest revelation, we tried to find some logic in the demand that everyone work the land. We certainly did not possess the necessary skills, having been trained in other areas formerly considered important. We could not grasp the full intent of these pronouncements.

Papa reasoned that these rash decisions would be reversed once leaders considered the ramifications. He continued to offer words of encouragement: "If we hold on a little longer, surely we can awaken from this world of unreality where good is bad, right is wrong, and our training is deemed not only worthless, but evil."

Noting the humility and quiet dignity of a passing Buddhist monk stripped of his saffron robes, Papa admonished us to practice our Buddhist teachings. Be peaceable. Drive out hatred, desire, and dissension. Strive for inner peace. Others might be able to control the environment, even the physical body, but not the mind.

A new edict came. Everyone was told to select a village quickly, or else be assigned one. Return to ancestral villages was encouraged, but those forced to the east, as our family had been, were to continue in that direction. My parents were determined, nevertheless, to seek refuge in the Khum Speu area to the north, where Samol's parents lived and where Uncle Ban's and Uncle Suoheang's families hoped to return to their abandoned homes. Keang also had ties to Khum Speu because he'd been a high school teacher there shortly after he married Mearadey.

Uncle Ban, his son Si Ton, and my other cousins were not yet willing to abandon their vigil. They hoped that the renewed movement of the population might give them an opportunity to learn the whereabouts of their missing loved ones. We left supplies, wished them success in their search, and hoped they could catch us en route to Kompong Cham Province. Grandmother Butt bid them a tearful good-bye. It was especially hard for her to leave Si Ton, her twenty-seven-year-old grandson who had always been so solicitous of her. We took turns pushing the car, starting the motor only to ascend the occasional hill. We decided to try skirting Phnom Penh by using back roads along the Mekong River.

We were no longer merely homeless refugees. We'd been given a new designation by Angka—"People of the Emigration" —as if that title altered our homeless, miserable state.

The winds shifted. Cambodia knows only two seasons, the wet monsoon, and the dry monsoon. Hot, moist air blew in from the Indian Ocean, temperatures and rain would increase through June, July, and August, then taper off through September and

October. Six feet of rain would fall in the delta during the six months of the wet monsoon. The rains began.

Slogging through the wet countryside, the beaten populace finally accepted how futile it was to continue carrying heavy items that could not be used in grass huts. One by one, prized possessions were abandoned. Rice paddies filled with TV sets, air conditioners, refrigerators, sewing machines, furniture, bags of money, even cars.

Some citizens could not bend with the loss of wealth and the specter of hardship. A Chinese merchant told us he had saved nothing but two bags of riels. His fortune was good for little more than fuel to cook a pot of rice. He tied the bags around his neck and drowned himself in the Mekong.

Fearing enslavement or death at the hands of the Khmer Rouge, a professor and his wife and children consumed lethal doses of poison, climbed into the family car, and drove it headlong into the river.

The rest of us plodded on toward the years of servitude ahead. Slowly, we learned that the Khmer Rouge had left little to chance in their movement of people. From the very first day, what had appeared to us as mass confusion and chaos had been a single-minded effort to empty the city as rapidly as possible, regardless of cost in suffering or loss of life. The leaders were determined to redefine society overnight. Their bold and truly diabolical scheme was beyond our wildest imaginings during those first chaotic months. Mass evacuation had been deliberately conceived to throw us off balance and to prevent organized resistance.

The Communists needed this psychological advantage. They were surprisingly few in number for an army that had just toppled our American-backed republic through prolonged military battle. By their own probably exaggerated count, they had only four thousand regular soldiers and fifty thousand guerrillas to control a population of approximately eight million.

Without deception and swift action, the Khmer Rouge could never have subdued so many of us with so few. If we had guessed that eviction from our homes was something other than a temporary necessity, or that slavery and starvation were to be our fate, we would have resisted more desperately. But our awareness came too late; we could no longer muster effective resistance.

Feeding us a series of lies, keeping us on the move, overwhelming us with the effort of mere survival—all these Khmer Rouge tactics were similar to those of the Nazis in dealing with the Jews. But never before had such strategies been turned against an entire nation; never had a country enslaved its own people so thoroughly; never had a society without cities been attempted on so grand a scale.

Within weeks, Angka Loeu was able to break down societal structure and all but the closest family ties. Weaker members of the population, those who would have burdened the regime, died quickly. And military leaders, government officials, and the educated—the greatest potential threat—were either killed or incarcerated. Spies reported minor infractions and kept people from trusting each other. Some men taken to be "searched" never returned.

Soldiers seized identification papers of those they caught in the random searches. In the name of Angka, items on the proscribed list such as radios, pens, medicine, jewelry, watches, money, expensive Western clothing, and even eyeglasses were claimed. Most of these "luxury" items were destroyed on the spot. Like everything else, the purpose of their destruction seemed to be to intimidate, to bewilder, to create debilitating anxiety.

Women were searched less rigorously than men. We took advantage of this in hiding valuables. I hid my gold necklace in my jacket lining. Mearadey insisted on keeping our birth certificates, graduation papers, and other documents, though she knew she was taking an enormous risk. Keang begged her to destroy them, but she felt sure education would someday be highly prized again, and she wanted documentation.

Not long after we left Uncle Ban's family, we were shunted along a side road toward a ferry crossing where boats, too small to carry cars or many possessions, transported passengers. Here additional belongings would have to be left behind before boarding. The Communists would later claim that everyone had been free to discard or take what they chose.

Step by deliberate step, our Cambodian way of life was stripped from us without our full realization. We reluctantly believed each lie. Even the soldiers didn't seem to understand any better than we did what the leaders had in mind.

When we reached the ferry crossing, we were cautious, but as yet still naïve. Not only did we fail to grasp that reducing people's possessions was a deliberate plan, we failed to understand that these boat rides were designed to separate individuals into small, controllable groups for registration and identification. We were also unaware that all across the nation people were being directed to such river crossings.

Ultimately, we had no option but to board a boat. Nonetheless, we camped near the Mekong for almost a week, and carefully observed what happened to others who boarded the ferries. Uncle Ban and my cousins, unsuccessful in their quest to find my aunt, joined us within days of our arrival at the river.

Papa clung to the hope that Angka would yet change plans and allow everyone to return home. Perhaps the order to move people about was only a misunderstanding on the part of a local commander. When the mistake was discovered, it would be corrected.

Ironically, Papa's vain hope of a Khmer Rouge change of heart could well have come to pass, as we learned much later. Before the takeover, there developed a major ideological split in the thinking of the new leaders. The more radical wanted to eliminate cities entirely, while moderates urged a controlled form of city life, and even acceptance of some aspects of Western technology. The fall of Phnom Penh was so rapid that it surprised even the Khmer Rouge, and the war ended before agreement was reached on how to put their abstract ideas for the perfect society into practice. The radical faction maneuvered to arrive in Phnom Penh first and began eviction immediately. During the weeks we camped in the cucumber patch, the moderates were levered from positions of power. Angka Loeu was then composed of radical, like-minded leaders, related by blood and marriage as well as ideology, Pol Pot being one of them.

By the time Uncle Ban had joined us at the riverside camp, we knew that boats were taking passengers north as far as Prek Po, the district my father had represented in the National Assembly. In this new society without money, boat rides were, of course, free. Angka provided them. There seemed to be no possibility of returning to Phnom Penh, so we decided to take the boat. From Prek Po, where my family had lived before I was born, we would walk to Khum Speu while the muddy roads were still passable.

Our departure became a matter of urgency after Uncle Ban overheard two soldiers discussing us, taking inventory of our suitcases, clothes, radios, watches, pens, and the fact that we had a car. These indications of wealth made us suspect. Considering what we'd left behind, we felt stripped, but to the backward foot soldiers, we appeared laden with valuables.

It had seemed only natural to grab suitcases when we left the city. Now we realized that they marked us as "tainted by the West." To go unnoticed, we needed to look more like villagers. Quietly we rid ourselves of the damning suitcases, tied possessions in long skirt lengths as villagers did, bundled up our shirts and pants, and donned traditional village clothing. Leng even took the spare tire from the car and made sandals for the men. His first pair was crude, but soon he mastered the art, and the sturdy rubber shoes looked like those of Communist villagers.

We spent hours deciding what to take on the boat and what to leave behind. Leng had seen medicine being confiscated, so we took care to hide what little we had. In the bundles, we also hid our gold, jewelry, five radios, Mum's two small silver bowls, some nice clothes, cigarette lighters, and Leng's expensive watch. We saw other people take motorbikes on board so we kept our two.

Leng wanted to keep his pellet gun to shoot birds and small game, but when two soldiers approached just as we started to bury it in a bag of rice, we panicked. Thinking quickly, Rasmei slipped the gun under her loose-fitting *sampot*, sauntered to the river and waded in as though to swim. She let the gun sink to the muddy river bottom. To avoid suspicion, she swam for a while before climbing out. By the time she reached the bank, we'd finished packing and were headed for the boats.

Prodded by impatient soldiers, we joined others on the rain-soaked dock while Papa registered us for Prek Po. He was asked to list our family's name, destination, and number of people in our group. Since both "Choun" and "Butt" are common Cambodian names, he did not bother to use an alias. He was not asked for his occupation or other personal information. He felt confident that our background wasn't suspected.

The boat for Prek Po began loading shortly after noon. It was larger than most, but we could see it would be filled before our turn came to board. With heavy downpours, the heat and humidity increased during the long hours we waited; the children fretted and climbed listlessly on the lumpy bundles. Mum grew impatient. She approached an official and asked if we could board since we had small children with us and a frail old woman.

At first he ignored her, then asked our name. He glanced at his register, and agreed to Mum's request, but by the time we hauled our rain-soaked possessions to the ramp, the boat was full. To our surprise, he ordered a special, small boat for us, our relatives and neighbors, and a few others who waited to go north. Family members carried bundles on board while I helped the children. Si Ton assisted Grandmother. More than half the passengers were our family or friends. It was not easy for forty people to find room on deck, but by late afternoon, we were under way.

Phnom Penh stood silhouetted against a radiant orange sunset. Though we were a quarter of a mile from the riverbank, I could see movement in the abandoned city. Soldiers were unloading furniture and books from trucks and adding them to burning heaps along the Mekong. Litter and smoke blew through the deserted streets. The city receded in the gathering darkness.

"Who is that tall, skinny man? I think I know him," a soldier asked Leng. Leng glanced in the direction indicated and saw he meant my father.

"I don't know him," Leng replied casually, then tried to steer the conversation in another direction.

The soldier persisted. "I think that man is Choun Butt. He used to represent my district. I'm sure that's him."

As soon as he could without causing suspicion, Leng made his way to my father and told him he'd been recognized. We all felt a flutter of concern. Questions flooded our minds. Why had the officer at the dock allowed us to board ahead of others? Why had a special boat been made available?

The boat made three stops. Passengers were free to disembark at any village they chose. At Roka Kong, the second scheduled stop, my parents seriously considered having us get off and walk the remaining distance to Khum Speu. We weighed the alternatives, then decided to stay on board. The extra distance upriver seemed advantage enough, in light of increasing rains and Grandmother's poor health. Shortly after midnight, the boat docked at Prek Po. As soon as he stepped onto the wharf, Papa was greeted warmly by several former constituents. The passenger list was taken to the local Khmer Rouge headquarters. They sent for my father.

"Couldn't this wait until morning?" Papa asked. "It's after midnight."

"Orders, sir."

I was the last to know that Papa had been summoned. I was on board keeping an eye on bundles and sleeping children while the others shuttled back and forth, transferring gear to the dock. Keang and Leng, coming back for the final load, told me the disconcerting news. There was nothing to do but wait for my father's return. We settled sleepily at one end of the deserted dock, nervous but not unduly alarmed.

Early in his career, my father had been a customs officer. Later, his work with the Land Registry Office of Sihanouk's government took him to Prek Po, where he cleared the deeds of people wishing to buy or sell land. Under the direction of his supervisor, Lon Nol, he had traveled throughout the district and knew the people well. When he was elected deputy minister, we moved to Phnom Penh.

Papa had tried to bring responsible government to the people, and had been widely supported. Four years later, Sihanouk refused to allow elections and instead had appointed the same seventy-seven deputy ministers to a second term. When the people were next allowed to vote, they reacted by removing my father and the other deputies from office. The vote was more a statement against the prince than against the deputies, however, and my parents had continued to maintain close ties in Prek Po.

About an hour after my father accompanied the soldier to headquarters, the same man returned with a note to us from Papa.

My Honey and All My Children:

At this time the High Organization has to keep me here, we have to be separated for now. So you and all the children should continue on to your goal in Khum Speu. If I have a chance, I will go and find you as soon as the Angka allows it. The officials say I have done nothing wrong, but I will only be taken to be retrained and to learn. I don't know how long it will take.

Please send me two trousers, two shirts, a lighter filled with gasoline, all the remaining cigarettes, my shoes, Leng's watch, one blanket, and a mosquito net.

Your husband and father, good-bye for a while.

—*Butt Choun*

I pocketed the letter that had slipped from Mum's hand to the dock as she sank onto the pile containing the last of our worldly possessions. Mearadey and I tried to comfort her while the others quickly sorted through our bundles for the items my father had requested. Because Papa had asked for Leng's watch, we sent it, though we doubted it would reach him. We did hope he would at least get the cigarettes. They would be valuable for trade. The soldier took the little bundle, but when Leng and Keang tried to follow, he informed us no one was allowed to accompany him or permitted to speak with my father.

Another soldier approached to say that a place had been located for us to stay while Papa was gone. Not knowing how long he would be detained, we were anxious to remain in Prek Po.

The next morning, Keang and Leng found out that local Khmer Rouge had been instructed to detain all former Lon Nol regime personnel. They had been told to send the men to the Angka to be retrained and reeducated, and had merely obeyed orders.

Each day, we were assured there was nothing to worry about. Papa would return when his training was completed. It was only a matter of time—a few months, perhaps. Mum was furious. The local leaders were evasive. Either they were as uninformed as they seemed, or were hiding their true intent and putting us off with lies. She did not trust them, yet she knew it was foolhardy to let her anger and frustration show.

If only we had gotten off at Roka Kong, where we weren't known; taken a different boat; used an alias; stopped at some other village; chosen another road. But in truth it was futile, wishful thinking. Papa was too well known. Angka would undoubtedly have located him wherever we settled, and the rest of us would have been in even greater peril had he remained with us. We waited.

Prek Po District had been under Communist control for years. The people worked like slaves and private trade was punished harshly. In theory, Angka was the sole owner of property and would provide for all needs. As a matter of necessity, barter continued to be discreetly practiced by anyone with objects of value. Good clothes, gold, or diamonds often spelled the difference between starvation and survival.

The utopian society instituted by the Khmer Rouge had little endorsement from the masses. No one intended to starve for some vague ideology, not if it could be helped. People were willing to work extremely hard, but if hard work could not provide for their needs, they would barter or steal. Even old women and young children were forced to toil in the fields. Anyone expecting to eat in this village had to perform physical labor. If we stayed, the same would be required of us.

In Prek Po we saw for the first time the new Khmer Rouge money. Garish posters advertised the colorful bills, which depicted idealized soldiers in combat, peasants harvesting rice, and various scenes of "true laborers" at work. Khmer Rouge money was not intended for private citizens, however. Angka paid it to village heads in exchange for locally produced rice, which was then sent to China to pay war debts. Supposedly, local leaders would be able to buy equipment, food, and clothing for their communities, but there was nothing available to buy, and people had little interest in this garish legal tender.

We quietly disposed of what little foreign money we held, though we still kept our old riels. It was especially dangerous to own American dollars. Possession of dollars was equated with being a spy for the Americans. The Khmer Rouge routinely accused people of being agents for the West, the right-wing Khmer Seri resistance group, or even other Communist countries.

We wanted to stay in Prek Po until my father returned, but my mother's old friends in the area urged us to move on. Rumors regarding the fate of detainees concerned them. They even suspected Papa's detention was a ploy to keep Keang and Leng where they could be watched. This fear, and the fact we could learn nothing more about Papa, convinced us to leave.

Trucks provided by the Khmer Rouge transported refugees from river ports to other villages. However, those who used them could not select their destination. Since it was vital that we settle in a place where Papa could find us, we rejected truck transport and took another boat to the Mekong's western bank a few miles upstream.

We had calculated it would take less than a week for us to walk from there to the village of Khum Speu, even with the heavy rains and our slow pace. However, this was the first time we had traveled without a car or boat to hold our possessions. We found it impossible to carry our bundles and still help Grandmother Butt and the children, so we stopped at a riverside village, traded two silk shirts for lumber, and built two carts, using the wheels from the motorbikes.

Grandmother rode atop the bundles of Si Ton's makeshift handcart, while he steered to avoid the largest puddles along the muddy, rutted, back road. The rest of us pushed and pulled the other cart, assisted my distraught mother, and carried the tired children.

"Halt!" someone shouted.

Terrified, we turned in unison as a young soldier emerged from a grass hut.

"This is a checkpoint, and the comrade *neary* wants to search your carts."

Dutifully, we waited in the drizzle for the tough young woman to approach. While her youthful companion stood with his AK-47 at the ready, she ordered one, then another, bundle opened. Since she did not ask to look through everything, it was evident the main purpose of the search was to intimidate.

The only bag of rice she probed was one in which Samol had hidden an old army shirt. He'd picked it up in a Phnom Penh bazaar for a good price. Leng had tried earlier to get him to throw the shirt away, warning that he might be mistaken for a Lon Nol soldier in hiding. Samol, however, had lived under the Khmer Rouge before he'd escaped to Phnom Penh, and knew the value of a sturdy workshirt. As the *neary* pulled it out, fear gripped us.

"Why are you hiding this?" she demanded sternly. We held our breath. She explained there was no problem owning a useful shirt, but if it was kept hidden, some less understanding soldier might get the wrong idea. Samol gratefully retrieved the shirt and resolved to dye it black as soon as he reached his mother's house.

The comrade *neary* casually checked several more bundles and found nothing. She even fingered my jacket, but failed to notice the little Buddha. Then she spied Mearadey's packet of birth certificates, graduation papers, and other documents. Those papers revealed more about our family than we wanted the Communists to know. How we wished Mearadey had destroyed them. Among the papers was notification of a grant Keang had received just before the takeover. He'd been awarded a trip to France in connection with his newspaper work, but the war had prevented his leaving. The possession of a paper written in a foreign language could be a death warrant. The *neary* studied the notification letter and we thought we were doomed, until we realized she was holding that document and several others upside down. She said she'd have to keep the papers.

"They will be given to you in your village later," she stated authoritatively, though she never asked where we were going. Without further ado, she returned to her guard post, followed by her youthful cohort with the big gun.

We hastily repacked and hurried down the puddled track, urged on by the fear that those documents might yet be delivered to someone who could read; that somehow those papers might be traced to us.

Chapter Four

Cambodia is shaped like a battered pie pan: roughly circular, with a flat center ringed by sharply rising mountains. Two hundred and fifty miles from north to south and three hundred miles from east to west, its huge delta—the pie pan's flat center—is crisscrossed by meandering rivers and man-made canals. In the southeast corner, the many-branched Mekong, Bassac, and Tonle Sap rivers create a floodplain and wend their way to Vietnam and the South China Sea.

Our river journey and trek toward Khum Speu took us through much of this lush delta, where the nation's exports of rice, rubber, and coconuts had grown. Now, endless miles of overgrown rubber plantations and untended coconut groves lined our route. There was no export. Wealthy owners had fled years before when the Khmer Rouge took refuge among the stands of trees and government forces tried to dislodge them with bombs.

Fallow fields and spindly crops stood where once farms had flourished. Broken dikes bordered muddy, weed-filled rice paddies. This was the season when sugar palms produced the sweetest sap, yet the trees had not been tapped. Where were the noisy ducks and fat pigs? What had happened to the big, black water buffalo and placid oxen? In this rice bowl of the nation, it seemed unbelievable that we could not even find fish or crabs for a meal.

We traveled northwest, passing through poverty-stricken districts the Khmer Rouge had controlled for five years. Rutted roads took us into disease-ridden villages where peasants lacked sufficient clothing to cover themselves decently. It was customary in Cambodia for old people to shave their heads, but in these villages, people of all ages had very short-cropped hair to keep lice in check. Lethargic children with bloated bellies, bowed legs, and weeping sores begged for food.

These once-contented villagers had been reduced to degradation and destitution. They needed food, they needed freedom to go about their own quiet lives, not slogans, famine, fear.

Until we traveled through these delta villages, we had no idea that life under Angka could be this bad. Nothing here reminded us of the stories my father had told of his visit to Communist China. He'd described life there as spartan but decent; there had been hope. We had expected the same of the Communists in our own nation, but there was no hope in these villages where people cringed like beaten dogs.

Equal to the shock we felt was the shock the villagers bitterly expressed upon seeing decently clothed, healthy city residents who still possessed consumer goods. They'd been told that because of the corrupt Lon Nol regime, all Cambodia had suffered as they had. With thousands of well-fed people filing past their doors, the villagers realized they had been deceived.

From these people we learned that the Khmer Rouge had uprooted and moved not only city residents, but also peasants. Some villages had been emptied regularly every three months. As a result, no one repaired huts, maintained ditches, mended dikes, or farmed properly. Former fishermen had been forced to till the soil, while capable rice farmers were turned into unwilling fishermen.

Villagers resented having to share the little they had with newcomers, so rather than impose on their limited resources by eating in their communal dining halls, we stopped at night in deserted villages whenever possible and ate from our limited stores of rice.

One such village was Prey Tortung, where two thousand government soldiers had been massacred by the Khmer Rouge in a famous battle two years before. The Republic had retaliated by bombing the village heavily, killing both villagers and the Khmer Rouge who had sought sanctuary in the compound of a Buddhist temple.

Camped in this abandoned village, we were painfully reminded of the day, shortly before the war ended, when my brother-in-law, Leng, had put on headphones at the airport and listened to a similar government-directed attack on a village only twelve miles from Phnom Penh. The ground spotter near the hamlet reported that villagers had taken refuge in the local temple, and pleaded that the sacred shrine not be bombed. Despite his urging, the compound was mercilessly destroyed. Leng had listened in agony to the unheeded pleas of the distraught spotter. Sickened by such attacks on innocent civilians, some pilots, near war's end, actually turned their planes around and bombed their own air bases.

In the ruins of Prey Tortung, we hunted for firewood in the temple rubble and found piles of whitened bones. Moments after Tevi and my nephew, Rota, went in search of clean water, they dashed back to our camp looking terrified. A skull in the pond had grinned up at them when their bucket broke the water's smooth surface.

As we sat around the campfire eating dinner and preparing for bed, gaunt, hollow-eyed peasants from a nearby village stood in the shadows that ringed the temple enclosure and stared at us like hungry vultures. Though the brick floor of the roofless temple compound offered a cleaner, drier place to sleep than the surrounding fields of rice stubble, none of us could sleep in that eerie place and we broke camp early the next morning.

We tried to travel faster, knowing that soon many roads would be completely impassable. It had been two months since we left Phnom Penh; in former times, we had often made the trip to Khum Speu by car in five or six hours.

It seemed inconceivable that we could ever adjust to the kind of life we saw all around us: that we, too, would till the soil for a livelihood, or have our existence determined by the seasons. Yet it was in this wet, poverty-stricken, rural world that we, and the other millions of displaced city dwellers, were required to make our home. We could look forward to nothing but hardship.

My mother, so recently plump, young-looking, jolly, and self-assured, had lost weight. Her hair had turned prematurely gray. As her health deteriorated, Mum looked to her daughters for comfort and left decisions to her sons-in-law. Without help from Keang and Leng and the other men, Mum and the children would not have survived the exodus from Phnom Penh and the trek to Khum Speu.

Samol planned to return to his parents' home in West Khum Speu. Since his mother was Mum's only sister, we decided to settle there as well. We would have to say good-bye to Uncle Ban's and Uncle Suoheang's families. They were headed for their homes in Svai Teeup, a village in a nearby district. Grandmother Butt had to decide which family to join. It was a wrenching choice, but she finally settled on going with her son-in-law, Uncle Ban, since he had no wife to run his home.

At the crossroads, my two uncles, and their families and Grandmother turned left and we turned right. We would see them often, we thought, since our villages were only a few miles apart.

West Khum Speu was eight miles farther to the northeast. Broken clouds filled the sky, and we quickened our pace to reach the village before we were caught on the road by nightfall and another storm.

We had been uprooted since mid-April. In those two months, I'd had to grow up. As we approached our ancestral village, weary and wet from the long journey, we longed for a sense of home.

Chaos met us on arrival. The inexperienced leaders of Khum Speu District had been overwhelmed by multitudes of uprooted people seeking food and shelter. The High Organization had yet to provide for resettlement or issue detailed directives. People wandered from village to village, not knowing what to expect or what was expected of them.

Fortunately, we had relatives to assist us. Two of Mum's brothers were farmers in nearby villages in the district. Samol's parents, also farmers, took us into their West Khum Speu home and eased us into village life. Otherwise, our arrival as "new people" was hardly welcomed by the locals.

"Old people" had lived under Communist control for years under conditions of great austerity. They had few possessions and had been reduced to wearing patched, faded clothes. In their eyes, "new people" were soft, useless, wealthy, filled with Western notions—corrupted. People from Phnom Penh were especially suspect for being "tainted" by Western ideas, and the Communists ruthlessly hunted down anyone thought to be hiding a suspicious background.

Educational differences further divided "old" from "new." Many from the city felt superior to the darker-skinned, "ignorant" villagers.* For their part, old villagers had no respect for people so deficient in common sense that they knew nothing

---

*Dark-colored skin was considered inferior, even by villagers. It was equated with manual labor, village life, and the cities' poor. However, the generally lighter color skin of city residents was also due to a difference in racial mix. For generations, Vietnamese and Chinese immigrants had intermarried with Cambodians from the cities more often than with villagers.

about planting rice or building homes from bamboo, or managing for themselves in the countryside; these people from the cities who felt so superior because they could read and write didn't even know which plants were edible.

Khmer Rouge leaders played on this resentment and convinced residents that city dwellers really had been society's parasites. Waiters, taxi drivers, secretaries, big businessmen, librarians, filing clerks, or office boys had never been needed in the villages, so peasants felt the Communists were right in exposing such people as nonproducers and, therefore, unnecessary.

To a limited extent, old villagers mingled with the Communist comrades. They might even chance a few infractions of the rules; new villagers were treated harshly or threatened with a visit to Angka for all mistakes.

Our relatives quickly taught us as much as they could about local customs, so that we would not attract undue attention as upper-class outsiders. They vouched for our loyalty when doubts were raised. They even lied to their neighbors to keep the Khmer Rouge from discovering the positions Keang and Leng had held in the fallen regime.

Shortly after arrival, each new family was assigned a twenty-foot-square plot of land. Without providing building materials, instructions, or tools, local leaders expected us to build adequate shelters. Again our relatives came to our rescue. Soorsdey, Mum, and I built a rustic hut with help from Keang, Samol, and Samol's father. Our eight-by-ten-foot shelter took up half the land we'd been allotted.

In delta country that often floods, it is best to build a home on stilts to keep out floodwaters and snakes, and to allow cooling breezes to circulate under as well as around the house. Our first hut, however, was built directly on the ground. With bare hands, sharp rocks, and a few homemade tools, we dug holes and felled large bamboo poles. Between downpours, we anchored the poles in the ground to form the hut's corner supports. With vines, we tied a bamboo frame to these support posts and slender bamboo poles were then secured to the frame at six-inch intervals. While we worked, the children gathered grass that Mum tied in bunches. Starting at the bottom and working upward, we layered the grass over the poles to create a thatched wall. After two weeks of hard, wet work, the hut was built. Mum's sister gave us our only piece of furniture, a homemade bed. Once again, Soorsdey, Mum, and I had a "home"—a room with a dirt floor and a little lean-to side room in which we kept supplies and occasionally cooked in secret.

Keang, Mearadey, Tevi, and Moni built a hut similar to ours except that this one was on stilts. Its elevated floor was made of bamboo crossbeams covered with woven, split-bamboo mats. Both huts were crude, and they leaked when strong winds and rain parted the thatch, but we were grateful for their shelter and privacy. In fact, we were quite proud of our first attempts at building and being "useful."

Most old villagers had sturdier homes with several rooms, and larger yards. However, their furniture, like ours, was usually handmade or nonexistent.

Bamboo, our main building material, grew in abundance around Khum Speu, and was used in many ways. Tender young shoots were eaten. Baskets, mats, umbrellas, and hats were made from it; buckets and drinking glasses were fashioned from its hollow sections. Bamboo formed fences, hedges and irrigation pipes, fishing rods and rafts. It could be fashioned into lethal weapons or used in torture. When moral lessons about strength, flexibility, or tenacity were needed, bamboo was often alluded to.

No one actually ordered us to wear plain, black or gray, high-necked, long-sleeved, pajamalike clothes, but we noted that all "respectable" old villagers did. Though we'd ceased wearing Western outfits back at the river crossing, we felt the need for even more compliance, so Mum's sister helped us remove all trim, and we sewed pockets, two to a side, on all jacket fronts to duplicate the Mao-style uniform. We added patches to make things look old. Then we put the shirts and pants in a pot of water to which the mashed fruit of the poisonous *mockleuah* plant had been added. With repeated soaking and drying, this natural black dye darkened the clothes. The dye faded fast, but that, too, was an advantage; clothing then looked well used. Samol's army shirt was one of the first things put in the vat.

Any unusual or stylish feature of the black "uniform" could bring criticism. A comrade might approach and say, "Oh, you are a rich man. You have a very nice shirt." That was not a compliment. That was the kind of attention that brought the wearer trouble; the kind of attention we were determined to avoid. Although many old villagers, secure in their position, and even foolish new residents continued to wear colorful clothing, we never did. To the family rule of "Never be first" was added "Always fit in, don't be different." Acceptance of the Khmer Rouge style of dress seemed to the leadership to imply acceptance of their doctrines. We dressed the part.

Our relatives gave us other practical suggestions to help us cope in this unfamiliar world: Always work harder than required. Never cause trouble or complain. Never make your home look nicer than others. Never appear to have knowledge of any subject. Always be quick to do whatever you are told. Speak as little as possible. Never dress as well as allowed. Never be caught cooking.

Cambodians have a flair for colorful, bright scarves and beautiful clothing. Though our best silk clothes were now considered decadent, we held on to them, hoping that some day we would feel free to wear them. It was not just vanity, however, that prompted us to save them. To old villagers, clothing was a desired trade item, as we'd already learned before arriving in Speu. Therefore, we carefully hid clothes in our huts along with our radios, gold, silver bowls, extra food, what little medicine remained—and our riels.

Unfortunately, Rasmei, Leng, and their children were sent to Prey Tayo, a village across the highway, and had to build a hut without family help. Shortly after they moved, Leng secretly traded his radio for forty pounds of rice, a bag of corn, some medicine, and one blanket. The $150 radio had been sent from Hong Kong by a friend shortly before the Khmer Rouge closed Phnom Penh's airport, and Leng had been unable to send payment out of Cambodia after the package came. He felt guilty trading something he'd not yet paid for, but it seemed unlikely he'd ever be able to repay his friend as long as the Khmer Rouge were in control. No one in the villages would accept our riels in trade any longer; and, of course, no foreign government would honor our money.

We saw Communist money once or twice after our arrival, but within a month it disappeared from circulation as silently as people did. Withdrawal of this money seemed further evidence that the ideas of the most radical faction dominated the Khmer Rouge leadership.

Within a few weeks, it became illegal in our district to keep a private food supply. Cooking was entrusted only to "old village" workers who ran central kitchens. Across the road in Leng's district, however, it would be months before the "no private cooking" rule was enforced. Since Highway 21 was the boundary between our district and Leng's, villagers on each side of the road were aware of how the other district lived, though visits back and forth were prohibited. Those from Khum Speu District could watch villagers in Prey Tayo cook in the open doorways of their huts. We were bitter over this discrepancy in enforcement of rules, but we knew complaint would be counterproductive. We had to find secret ways to add more food to our inadequate diet.

Mum had grown thin and haggard. Her system could not

tolerate the tasteless rice gruel made in the central kitchen. Day by day she grew weaker, until Soorsdey and I began boiling a little rice for her whenever possible. We kept the fire in the hut small, and Mum mounted watch for any passerby whom we did not know or trust.

To avoid drawing attention by her absence, she dutifully lined up at the communal dining hall twice a day to be ladled her allotted bowl of rice. We were fed at midday and dusk, but Mum ate little of what was served. She slipped the rest to Soorsdey or me. Seated at rows of rough-hewn tables we hungrily devoured the watered-down porridge.

Work crews were disorganized and not very efficient at first, but within a few weeks, endless rules were established and rigorously enforced as village leaders received explicit instructions from Angka. Mearadey was sent with a women's crew to transplant rice. Soorsdey and I were assigned to a brigade that included able-bodied widows without young children and unmarried girls aged twelve to twenty. Our crew and Keang's planted rice, repaired dikes, and cleared jungles for new building sites and fields. Poor health exempted Mum from work at first. We worried about her, but at least her illness allowed her to remain in the village and look after Tevi and Moni.

Across the highway, Leng and Rasmei were also forced to join work crews in their village, but there was no one to look after five-year-old Rota and two-year-old Chenda Poong. My sister had no alternative but to put Rota in charge of his inconsolable little sister, to fend for them both as best he could for ten to fourteen hours each day. Absorbed in play with the other boys, Rota often forgot to watch the toddler.

It wasn't until about eight months after our arrival that men and women too old or ill to work, plus women in the last stages of pregnancy, were assigned to supervise village children. Also, "schooling" and indoctrination sessions were eventually organized for youngsters from the ages of eight to twelve.

When we first arrived in Khum Speu village, men and boys had joined wholeheartedly in soccer matches after a hard day's work, but soon these games were prohibited. Players were told that if they had energy enough to play, then they had energy enough to work longer hours. Angka claimed that it was wrong to waste "the water that comes from the skin" when it could be expended instead in productive labor. Sweat was to be spent in useful work, not decadent play.

One of my first duties was to transplant young rice shoots from the crowded nursery beds to the main rice paddies. Most refugees were new to this work, yet no instruction was given. Apparently, crew leaders were watching to see who could not or would not perform menial tasks, or perhaps they were naïve enough to assume that everyone knew how to plant rice. Either way, I was determined to appear familiar with the task.

Edging near an old villager, I watched stealthily and tried to duplicate her actions as she gathered a bunch of young plants and moved toward the flooded paddy. Wading into that muddy water was one of the most frightening experiences of my life. I knew the paddy was infested with venomous snakes and blood-thirsty leeches, but I did not dare show my terror or refuse to work. More than snakes and leeches, I feared being asked to "visit Angka" for refusing to do as told.

Lines of doubled-over women backed in unison across the paddy, planting rice shoots every few inches. I hurried to keep up. I hated to thrust my hands into the murky water that lapped our blouse fronts when we stooped to force plants into the mud.

I had almost succeeded in overcoming nervousness by concentrating on the task at hand when a woman working near me screamed. She had straightened up for a moment and discovered a leech, swollen to the size of a man's finger, clinging to her chest. It took all the courage I could muster to go back to work as though nothing out of the ordinary had happened. The old villager next to me simply smiled to herself and continued planting.

It was almost impossible to exterminate leeches. If cut in two, each half regenerated, making twice as many as before. They had to be minced before they were incapable of regrowth, and that was too time-consuming. Villagers merely pulled them off and tossed them into another paddy. At first, new residents collected them in bags to burn. However, the repulsive odor of burning, blood-filled leeches was not well received by old villagers, who believed the bad smell beckoned evil spirits of the forests into the village. The only real solution to leeches was to learn to tolerate them, since they were an inevitable part of our life. We soon learned to wrap our pants tightly around our legs when we were working in the paddies and to wear high-necked, long-sleeved blouses that fit tightly at the wrist. My sisters and I constantly reminded ourselves that we had much more reason to fear our leaders; they watched for those who were squeamish.

Loss of blood due to leeches was not life-threatening, but their bite, though painless, often became infected and occasionally caused blood poisoning. The real leech danger we faced was from a less-prevalent thread-sized leech that burrowed under the skin, attacked vital organs and caused internal hemorrhaging. This leech could kill, and there was no effective way to keep it from striking.

Laboring in the rain day after day, stiff from rigorous work, bone weary at night, everyone eventually learned to take leeches and snakes in stride. We had neither energy nor time to expend being fearful about things we could not avoid.

Work began at 5:30 A.M., seven days a week, with never a day off. Even acute sickness offered little reprieve. We were not allowed to talk while we labored; talking was not a productive use of energy. High humidity and oppressive heat sapped our strength. Every able-bodied person stayed in the fields until about 11:00 A.M., then we ate our first meal of the day and had a short rest. If the work was some distance from the village, most of our rest time was spent walking to or from the field. Occasionally, rice was brought to where we worked to save us the midday walk. By 1:00 or 2:00 P.M., we would resume work for four or five more hours of muscle-straining labor. Work ended after dark, about 6:00 P.M. On moonlit nights, we were sometimes required to work two or three more hours before we went to the evening meetings.

To Angka, we were simply machines, and not very efficient ones at that. If a person died from exertion or heat prostration, the leaders seemed unconcerned. Someone else was assigned to fill that place, and the work continued.

My sisters and I had never worked hard in our lives. Heavy physical labor or even strenuous exercise had simply not been part of our routine in Phnom Penh. Yet we knew that if we did not work hard, we would call attention to ourselves. To be considered lazy was a serious charge.

We slept at home when work was close, but assignments to clear jungle areas for new village sites often took us far from Speu. Then we camped near our work for days or weeks at a time. We were given larger portions of rice in the camps than we got from the central kitchen, so our hunger pangs were lessened, and we were exempted from nightly indoctrination sessions. Still, I hated to be away from the village because I worried about my mother.

Men and women plowed, dug ditches, cleared jungles, and built dikes. Since we were more expendable than tools and equipment, we dug with bare hands if shovels weren't available. In place of the highly prized oxen, we were hitched to heavy plows. When plows weren't available, we used pointed sticks to turn the fields.

In addition to plowing and clearing, Leng's and Keang's

65

crews were assigned to tap the sugar palm trees. With bamboo tubes tied to their waists, they laboriously pulled themselves up each rough-shingled palm, hand over hand, with bare toes gripping the trunk. They slit the base of each flower bud and attached a hollow section of bamboo to collect the sap, all the time praying that the frayed safety straps would hold their weight. Each day, they replaced the filled bamboo tubes with empty ones, then carefully inched down the tree, heavily weighted with fourteen sap-filled containers.

At collection stations, the men poured the sap into larger bamboo tubes and carried them several miles to the village. Tubes of "sweet water" hanging from a pole balanced on a man's shoulder often weighed as much as 180 pounds—more than the weight of most of the men.

Palm sugar was a treat that we looked forward to each year. The sap could also be made into a mildly alcoholic drink, illegal under the Communists, but often indulged in, since wine and other intoxicants were no longer available. Village leaders made their own supply for "medicinal purposes."

A few weeks after arriving in Speu District, every villager had to file a biography. We followed the suggestion of Samol's father and requested a scribe that had been provided for the illiterate.

We could not deny that we'd come from Phnom Penh or that my father had been in the former government, but we could claim we'd had little schooling. Cambodian women, especially, were often uneducated. Outside the family circle, Mum, Soorsdey, and I spoke as little as possible, communicated with grunts or short sentences, and refrained from using foreign words.

Despite the fact that Keang and Leng had humble beginnings, they'd risen to positions of great responsibility in the Republic, though both were only thirty-one years old at the time Phnom Penh fell. Each was a self-made man with more education than most Cambodians. If their full backgrounds had been revealed to our captors, my brothers-in-law would have been marked men.

Their government positions and education were seen as threats to the Khmer Rouge. The knowledge they had of national and international affairs plus their experience in judging people and situations were precisely what Angka Loeu feared—precisely what my brothers-in-law must keep secret if they hoped to survive under the Communists. Fortunately, when they were young, each had developed a wide variety of practical skills they could now fall back on to help them fit into village life without drawing suspicion.

Born in 1944, both Keang and Leng came from broken homes, were raised by hard-working mothers, and as young boys had learned to spend long hours doing a variety of menial tasks without complaint. Keang helped his mother run a small open-air food stall. Leng had found work where he could.

As was common, both men began their formal education in Buddhist monasteries, learning from and serving the monks. For poor boys in Cambodia, the pleasant year or two spent in the monastry was the only schooling most received. Even sons of the wealthy were boarded for a while with the monks to gain discipline and a respect for our culture. City dwellers usually sent their sons on to regular school if they could afford it; most villagers did not. It had required great effort, commitment, and sacrifice for both Keang's and Leng's mothers to keep their sons in school at a time when few families saw the importance of education.

Despite broken homes, long school days, and hard work, Keang and Leng often spoke of their boyhood years with fondness. There was enough of the tomboy in me to envy their freedom as young boys in Cambodia. They and the other boys had played tag, hide-and-seek, and marbles; tossed rocks at tin cans; spun homemade tops; swum in the muddy Mekong and fished. Leng was adept at fishing with a net, and enjoyed that sport even as an adult. Store-bought toys were rare, but they had usually been able to acquire an old bike for a foray into the nearby jungles to stalk small birds and game with slingshots. While there, they had gathered edible roots and fruits, spices and savory leaves, for their mothers. Cambodian girls, on the other hand, had never been as free to roam.

When my brothers-in-law started school in 1951, Cambodia was still a French protectorate. Although three years later Prince Sihanouk gained our independence, Frenchmen continued to serve in government posts for years, until Cambodians could be trained. Even at the time of the Khmer Rouge takeover, twenty years after independence, Frenchmen still owned many of the nation's rubber plantations and factories, and French continued to be our second language.

Keang and Leng spoke fluent French, and each had picked up a smattering of other languages useful in their work. In addition, Keang spoke Chinese, which he'd learned in his childhood home; his grandparents had come from China to escape civil war. And as an adult he'd taught himself to read Japanese.

Mearadey's husband, Keang Ngak, was the better-educated of the two men, having gone to school almost twice as long as Leng. After college and marriage to Mearadey, Keang had taught literature and history in Khum Speu's high school. Three years later, he and Mearadey had moved to our home in Phnom Penh so he could go back to school. Keang received his law degree in 1973. At the same time, he worked as an interpreter and reporter for the Khmer Press Agency and later as a translator and writer for government papers and magazines. He moved rapidly into positions of leadership in the Cambodian National Broadcasting System.

Leng, on the other hand, with only ten years of formal education, had risen in six short years from baggage handler to manager of the International Airport.

Both men were were highly intelligent, of slight build, light-skinned and good-looking. And though my brothers-in-law shared similar childhood backgrounds, their personalities were very different. Of the two, Keang Ngak was more ambitiously assertive, a natural leader. Leng Hong was a quiet, reserved man who kept his thoughts to himself. He had the uncanny ability of putting less-educated people at ease, a talent he would further develop in rural Cambodia.

In the biography he dictated to the scribe, Leng stated only that he had lived with the monks for a year and had been an airline porter. He did not mention his additional nine years of schooling or his advancement from porter to head of Phnom Penh's airport. He claimed he had worked only at the domestic air terminal, since work at the international terminal often required foreign-language skills.

Many Khum Speu residents remembered that Keang had been a teacher in their district years before. However, outside our circle of relatives, few knew he had changed occupations when he moved to Phnom Penh. In his biography, he made no mention of foreign languages, his work with the Ministry of Information, or his legal training. He listed himself simply as a Cambodian history teacher who had been raised in Kratie Province.

Under the Khmer Rouge, Keang and Leng became stoop laborers. Each wet season, they plowed and planted. Each dry season, November through April, they were often given the tedious assignment of pumping water into parched rice paddies. It was much like sitting on a bicycle, pedaling hard, yet never moving. Sections of the ever-versatile bamboo were cut to form cups. These were attached to a conveyer belt woven from vines. When a man, perched atop a rickety bamboo crossbar, pushed the squeaky drive wheel with his bare feet, the belt rotated. Empty cups dipped, filled, then rose from the ditch and dumped their contents one by one onto the thirsty field. Round and round the bamboo cups went, hour after weary hour under the scorching sun. Empty. Full. Empty. Full.

Everyone worked hard, but no one worked efficiently, especially during the settling-in period. No organizational or supervisory training had been given to the simple rice farmers who were now village leaders. We suspected that most of the work assigned during the first wet weeks was simply to keep everyone occupied while our leaders figured out what to do next. Later, much of this original work was redone or abandoned, confirming our suspicions. At first, we didn't begrudge the heavy work or even the lack of proficiency. We might be opposed to the Khmer Rouge ideology, but if the High Organization could really do as was claimed, bring productivity and prosperity, equality and peace, to Cambodia, we were willing to work to bring about the new era.

We understood it would take time to get everything running smoothly as inexperienced leaders using unskilled laborers endeavored to usher in a new society, but we could neither understand nor forgive their propensity for veiled threats, brutality, and murder. We resented being treated like prisoners of war with no rights. We could not understand their obsessive distrust. The Khmer Rouge didn't seem to realize that most of us—reduced as we were—would work with the new government to rebuild the nation if given a chance.

By the end of June, four or five million uprooted people —well over half the population—had settled somewhat into the austere routine of rural communal living. Sometimes an entire village was emptied of its old residents, as had been the case near Prek Po. Usually, new residents were not allowed to occupy the empty houses, but had to build new huts on land cleared at the village's edge, as we had done. Inexplicably, many old homes stood vacant.

"The High Organization" that had orchestrated the expulsions from cities and circumscribed our daily lives became

70

omnipotent and omniscient in everyone's mind. Angka blessed us with food, clothing, and purpose. We were to turn to Angka for our every need.

Although orders came down from Angka Loeu, local leaders seemed as ignorant as the rest of us about who made up this inner circle of leadership or where it was located. Broadcasts over loudspeakers in the village square came from Phnom Penh we were told, but Angka was only voices over the airwaves.

Keang and Leng made educated guesses about the makeup of the Communist hierarchy from what they heard over the loudspeakers and what they knew about the leadership of the underground Communist party during previous years. However, without free movement or news media to aid them, it took my brothers-in-law some time to discover which leaders had wrested power from their comrades. Even listening furtively to Voice of America broadcasts brought little enlightenment, since no one outside Cambodia knew what was going on either.

Piece by piece, it took years to learn that The Organization was controlled by six or eight of the most radical leaders from the earlier Communist movement. These men and women deliberately strove to remain faceless and nameless. Their premeditated anonymity served them well; the decisions of individuals could be challenged and questioned more readily than those of the mystical Angka Loeu. If the populace did not know who the leaders were, there was no one to complain to, find fault with, or target for reprisals. Many Khmer Rouge leaders chose an alias or otherwise obscured their former identities and personalities to become collectively Angka Loeu—a new unassailable deity.

Soloth Sar, alias Pol Pot, soon became the most well-known Khmer Rouge leader, both within and without Cambodia, though we did not learn his real identity for years. He became prime minister of Democratic Kampuchea following the takeover in 1975. Throughout our captivity, Pol Pot seemed to main-

71

tain control regardless of which government position he held, and his name became synonymous in the minds of most Cambodians with the nightmare we lived through daily.

As a young man, he had gone to school in France, where he was more Communist party organizer than student. Upon return to Cambodia, he had devoted himself almost exclusively to party efforts, though he was known by name and reputation to Keang as a teacher and a journalist.

He and Ieng Sary were married to sisters, Khieu Ponnary and Khieu Thirith. These women were important Communists in their own right. Both held powerful positions in the new government.

In 1963, Pol Pot, his brother-in-law Ieng Sary, their wives, and many other Phnom Penh Communist party members had disappeared from public view when Prince Sihanouk sought to destroy the Communist party in Cambodia. Rumor had spread that the prince had had them killed, but in fact some had joined the guerrillas in the jungles while others had gone to Hanoi or Peking to get further training. Ieng Sary was put in charge of foreign affairs when the leading Communists surfaced as Angka Loeu in time to usher in the Khmer Rouge regime.

Several Cambodian Communists had held important government positions in both the Sihanouk and Lon Nol regimes; Khieu Samphan had been my father's colleague in the National Assembly. He had also held a cabinet post under Sihanouk. Keang considered Khieu Samphan the "brain" behind the Khmer Rouge movement and Pol Pot the "power." As a student in Paris, Khieu Samphan had been active in the Communist-dominated Khmer Students' Association. Unlike Pol Pot, he was a serious student; and his doctoral thesis, *Cambodia's Economy and Industrial Development*, written in 1959, seemed to be the blueprint for the course the Communists followed after they took control.

Khieu Samphan's thesis stated that the strength of Cambodia lay where the bulk of the population dwelt, in the villages. He adhered to and developed the concept that city residents were parasites, draining the lifeblood from the country. Cities consumed more than they produced. Cities held only 10 percent of the population, yet claimed the lion's share of goods and services. He felt that former regimes had squandered resources to impress the outside world, leaders had amassed personal fortunes at the expense of the peasants, and that the population's desire for modern conveniences had kept Cambodia from meeting the country's real needs. He proposed concentrating on agriculture, with multiple yearly rice crops, as the best way to put the country on a firm, equitable footing. Secondary industries would come later.

Much of our work under the Communists for the next four years would be to clear the jungles and build or repair the irrigation systems needed to produce two or three crops of rice annually. In an effort to fill impossible quotas, untrained local leaders haphazardly ordered construction projects. Our capable engineers had been killed or forced into hiding.

Sometimes dams were located so poorly that fields remained flooded too long or water drained off just when it was needed most. Instead of the accustomed single bumper crop of rice, there were now two or three poor crops grown with less total yield and much backbreaking labor. Rasmei worked on one such ill-conceived dam. She spent months away from her family as part of a long, antlike file of black-clad women who carried basketloads of dirt for the dam on their heads.

Just as Hitler's *Mein Kampf* served the Nazis, Khieu Samphan's dissertation became Angka's theoretical guide for action. The major deviation from his original thesis was that actual implementation would be by ruthless use of force. "Peasants must be treated with patience and understanding," he had written as a student. In practice, that process was too slow for the impatient leadership. Angka adopted a merciless, dogmatic

73

line that allowed it to lie, starve, brutalize, and kill in order to impose its version of utopia on us.

After the 1970 coup, which toppled Sihanouk and formed the Republic under Lon Nol, Prince Sihanouk had joined forces with his former enemies, the Khmer Rouge, perhaps hoping to regain control by cooperating with them. Until 1975, the Communists used his name to win support from the peasants, and to gain credibility and international backing for their cause. In September of 1975, almost five months after they came to power, the Khmer Rouge actually did allow Prince Sihanouk and his wife, Monique, to return to Phnom Penh; we learned later that they were kept under virtual house arrest. The prince was head-of-state in name only. After the takeover, he occasionally traveled abroad on diplomatic missions for the Khmer Rouge when it suited their purposes, but his family was forced to remain behind to ensure his cooperation and return.

Angka's inner circle was united by ideology and background, and more than half of its members were also related to one another by blood or marriage. Each had been educated in France in the 1950s, had been active in the Cambodian student organization there, and had spent much of his or her adult life abroad. Convinced that they had laid plans for the perfect society, these radical theorists were now enslaving their own countrymen to put untried notions into practice. As adults, none of them had been involved in manual labor, yet now they glorified it. Educated themselves as lawyers, economists, and teachers, they feared education for the masses. While enjoying the advantages of the middle and upper classes, they extolled the virtues of simple village life.

Pol Pot and others had many characteristics of the classes they vilified: light skins, potbellies, and a desire for comfort, fine food, and ease. Not all of these traits were shed once they headed a Communist nation. While requiring that we live in primitive conditions, those who represented Angka Loeu lived in

TO DESTROY YOU IS NO LOSS

relative comfort. They used Western medical technology for treating their own ailments. We, their subjects, were forced to rely on primitive practices, witch doctors, and herbal cures. They rode, we walked. They issued orders, we followed. In this world turned upside down, their most successful strategy was a capriciousness and inexplicability that defied comprehension.

Chapter Five

We were often reminded that "Angka is like a pineapple. Its eyes look in every direction at once." And Angka's eyes were the "leaders" at every step in the organization. Leadership positions were consistently given to the poorest and least-educated villagers—even to the local drunks. Those formerly without advantages and position were elevated, while those of us formerly favored were forced to the bottom. As far as Angka Loeu was concerned, illiterate villagers made ideal leaders. They obeyed without question and posed no threat to the central organization. Eight men from Bun Tear Chey, by far the district's poorest and most backward community, became village chiefs in our district.

Cambodia had long been divided into provinces, counties, and districts, but Angka further tightened these political boundaries and divided the population into subdivisions in order to maintain absolute control. In addition to forming work crews according to age and sex, Angka divided each village into *krom*s, with a *krom* chief to supervise ten families.

Every community also had a village chief and several assistants. Each assistant supervised a specific aspect of village life, such as food distribution, spying, or leadership of a work crew. If a village was large, separate kitchens and dining pavilions were set up for every two hundred people.

Khum Speu District had only eight villages; the standard was ten. A group of districts was organized into a *srok*— roughly equivalent to a county—with one large village serving as the *srok* headquarters. Angka could easily send directives down through this network and reach into the smallest unit. Two or three soldiers were stationed in each *srok* village to enforce orders. They left headquarters only when it was necessary to resolve specific problems. Thus, a few thousand well-placed uneducated soldiers effectively controlled millions.

We were conscious of Angka's multilevel chain of command, but our day-to-day existence depended most on the *krom* leader and the work leader to whom each of us reported. These two were the most likely to bring a person to the attention of higher leaders for disciplinary action.

I preferred to have a male *krom* leader rather than a female or a husband-and-wife team. Women tended to be more critical and inquisitive, which made it harder to cook privately without their knowledge.

The food supplied to us was simply not enough for survival, and *krom* leaders knew it. Almost every family kept hidden three fireplace stones, and supplemented the central kitchen meals as best they could. Any curious passerby could see at a glance almost everything inside the doorless huts, so everyone depended on *krom* leaders to look the other way.

Many *krom* leaders, work leaders, and even village leaders participated in illegal trading. Since they supervised the harvesting and storage of food, they had ample opportunity to pilfer a little, just as those who cooked for the village managed to hide small quantities of rice in their baggy clothing. Food could be acquired in our district as long as a person had gold, and didn't get caught.

Leadership was intoxicating for those who had once been despised village nonentities. These new leaders vied with each other in carrying out duties and executing assignments diligently. Thousands of leaders and subleaders effectively diluted the power held by any one person and guaranteed that no one could control a unit capable of challenging the central organization.

Each leader was expected to spy on every other leader and resident. Each was jealous of his corner of responsibility and watched to see that no one infringed upon his authority. Fear of falling from favor with Angka kept new leaders in line.

Everywhere, even in our work brigades, old villagers were favored. I tried to please my crew and *krom* leaders because I did not want to be targeted for punishment. If a new girl didn't work harder than an old villager, she ran the risk of being charged with laziness. For laziness, you could have your rations reduced or even be sent "to see Angka," meaning exile to another village or a labor camp—or perhaps worse. All I knew during the hot, wet summer months of 1975 was that a person sent away seldom returned, and I did not want to be separated from my family.

I hadn't been working long before I realized that I owned something my crew leader coveted. It was a small plastic bag; the sort of thing that in Phnom Penh I would have thoughtlessly tossed away. Though I wanted to keep it for my own use, I decided it was best to offer the bag to her. In exchange, I hoped my life as a worker would not be so hard. It helped.

Work crews were strictly segregated by sex as well as age under the Khmer Rouge, with men always supervising men, and women supervising women. As I grew more observant, I noted that my leader was jealous of any girl in her crew who was more attractive than she was. New girls who tried to look nice were constantly given extra work or harassed in other ways. Personal vanity carried a high price tag, so I withdrew from any competition.

In addition to my plain clothing, I cut my hair just below

the ears in the blunt, unattractive Communist style that was approved for both men and women. This style of haircut was not mandatory—the Communists didn't make such rules; they didn't have to—but it was common sense to conform when it mattered so much to those in charge. Besides, there was never enough time to care for hair properly. It took no great effort to look or feel unattractive when I was constantly hungry, tired, dirty, and dejected.

Our family had been prepared to face a few months of hard labor and political unrest while Angka established authority and adjusted to peace. However, conditions got worse the longer we lived under the Khmer Rouge, despite endless promises of a bright future.

Radio Phnom Penh broadcast three times a day: before work, during the midday break, and again at night. These broadcasts, carried over the centrally located loudspeakers, incessantly proclaimed how contented the people in other villages were—how busy, productive, and happy. How *happy* we should feel to be free of our old exploiters, the former government. What *joy* each should sense in building the new country. What *pleasure* it was to sacrifice for the good of all. The broadcasts made it sound as though a carnival atmosphere had gripped the nation. By decree, we were living in the midst of utopia.

What little hope I'd had that life might get better gradually faded as the reality of the situation became increasingly apparent—why bother to make us happy or improve our lot when Angka could simply decree that we were happy already?

The implication in every broadcast was that if we didn't share the general joy, the fault lay with us. We must work harder to erase our old, false notions and continually weed out selfishness, laziness, and desire.

Throughout the heat of summer, we completed the planting and tended the crops. Heavy rains continued. The huts leaked. Dirt floors turned to mud. On nights when winds were high, rain came through the thatch and everything in the hut got soaked. We worked all day in wet clothes and came home at night with nothing dry to change into. Some nights we could not even sleep because of the rain that leaked in; Mum, Soorsdey, and I sat up in bed all night huddled under a small square of plastic.

By mid-July, our rations were cut; Angka had run out of rice and was unable to import enough from China. Until the next harvest, the nation would have to tighten its belt. Rations in many parts of the country were reduced to less than a cup of rice per person per day. This provided fewer than four hundred calories even when other things were added to the rice. Those not working—the children, the old, the ill and crippled—got less. Kompong Cham Province was better off than some areas, but still we were always hungry. Central kitchens boiled the same amount of water, they simply added less rice to it. My ladled share sometimes contained only a few grains in the bottom of a bowl full of milky-white hot water. As a result, we dipped heavily into our gold reserves to buy rice or corn whenever we could.

One tunic I'd brought from Phnom Penh had to be altered. My newly developed arm muscles made the sleeves too tight, but the real problem was my bloated belly.

Since our midday rest time was often taken up with coming from and going to distant fields or waiting in the food line, we had only minutes to eat. If we ate slowly, leaders claimed that we weren't hungry, and we got less food the next time. I learned to gulp down the gruel. Forced to trot back to work, I could hear my stomach rumbling in protest. Though *people* dared not speak out, the Communists couldn't stop these complaints.

New villagers began to make up carefully phrased songs and sayings that expressed our dislike for the regime that controlled our existence. We shared these little ditties with each other, or just hummed them under our breath. Often Communist leaders and old villagers, ignorant of the double meanings, didn't even know that an insult was intended. Little children loved to chant one particular singsong rhyme as they ran around the village. One child chanted the first line, and a second answered. It rolled around their tongues in a satisfying way, but it wasn't the nonsense verse it appeared to be:

> Where is Angka Loeu?
> Angka Loeu is under the tree . . . and buried.

The hidden message had to do with two people speaking about someone summoned by Angka. The first was asking where the guilty party had been sent. The answer implied that Angka must live underground, since so many sent "to see Angka Loeu" had been buried.

I developed several casual friendships with members of my work crew. However, I was cautious about joking with my new friends, and careful to reveal little about my past. Any person, anyone at all, with knowledge of my family was capable of betraying us. Outside the family circle there were only three I grew to trust during my first year under the Khmer Rouge. One had been a second-year business major at college. Like Soorsdey and me, the other two girls had been high school students. The fathers of these girls had been killed by the Communists, which was a further bond between us. We were afraid of drawing attention to ourselves if we spent much time talking together. Each of us, however, treasured the friendship of others from Phnom Penh who understood the adjustments we had been forced to make.

I was so overwhelmed with the task of simply surviving that I didn't miss Papa too much at first. When the family did discuss him, it was often with thankfulness that he had been spared the degradation and slave labor to which we were now subjected.

Sometimes I took out Papa's letter for the family to re-read, though I knew it by heart. I had hidden it in a hollow section of bamboo in a corner post of the hut. It was necessary to hide the letter, because it revealed our "fondness for the past," which we learned was also a crime. For this reason, we hid our religious objects, family pictures, and heirlooms. We even hid pencils and paper, since the possession of these indicated literacy.

Leaders made sporadic, cursory searches of our huts. Those who used special belongings openly often had them confiscated and were sharply reprimanded. A favorite form of discipline was to deny the person his two meals for the day. Repeated reprimands led to an "indoctrination session" with Angka.

We used our precious paper to forge passes to other villages upon occasion or to send secret notes with friends to Leng and Rasmei across the road. Passes to visit villages within the district were often granted, but passes between districts were seldom issued to new villagers. However, these "official" passes were nothing more than handwritten notes. They were easy to duplicate, especially since many of those who checked them could not read, but we didn't chance forging them often.

We even had to use our plastic tarps discreetly. Possession of large sheets of plastic or other useful objects, though technically allowed, might cause an envious neighbor to find an excuse to report the owner for some infraction. As punishment, the item could be taken—to end up in a leader's home.

Our best clothes, wrapped in plastic, had been secured between layers of thatch in the hut's rafters. We stowed our riels in the roof thatch, too, and hid some pieces of jewelry in hollow sections of bamboo and buried others in the dirt floor. My gold necklace remained in my jacket lining.

It was particularly dangerous to keep a radio, tape recorder, or camera. The Khmer Rouge automatically assumed that the owner was a spy for the United States, another offense worthy of death. Despite this, Keang kept one radio, and traded the others for rice. To hide it, he dug a hole in the floor in one corner of the hut that Mum, Soorsdey, and I shared. He buried a large bowl in the hole and put the radio in the bowl to keep it dry. The bowl was covered with a lid—the only part showing above ground. Old clothing and household objects tossed in the same corner kept the lid from appearing unusual.

To power the radio, Keang used a generator for a bicycle light. One of us cranked the generator while Keang, with his ear pressed to the speaker, strained to listen through the static to Voice of America or BBC broadcasts. The rest of us tried to look casual as we stationed ourselves at the door and around the hut, ready to sound a warning if someone came.

Through these occasional broadcasts, Keang learned that escapees to Thailand from highland provinces near the border reported not just hunger, but severe famine. The sparsely settled provinces had never produced much rice, and now they contained a large percentage of ill-prepared new residents. Their stored food was gone, and the next harvest was still a few months away. Meanwhile, they were starving to death.

For the first time, we felt fortunate to have selected a village that had long been under Communist control. It was not as poverty-stricken as those border communities or the war-torn river villages we'd passed through on our way to Speu. Local Communist leaders in our province of Kompong Cham were reportedly more ruthless than those in some other areas, but we could still get a little extra food as long as barter items held out. The only advantage highland villagers had was their nearness to Thailand. Without food, most did not have the strength to escape, though countless numbers died trying.

Where we lived, near the center of Cambodia, there was little possibility of escape. People caught out of their villages without travel passes were shot, no questions asked, no explanations accepted. Perhaps a lone person could chance escaping, but not a family.

Throughout the remainder of 1975, neighbors usually did not inform on others because they, too, needed extra food whenever they could get it. Most local leaders continued to turn a blind eye to our cooking as long as we did not appear to have a large supply of rice, or make our preparations obvious. A leader had to protect himself in case someone reported him to his superiors, or those superiors observed for themselves such infractions. The hypocrisy became almost a game that could be indulged in, if not flaunted.

Repressive measures brought out our ingenuity; we devised ways to provide for our needs without arousing undue suspicion or animosity. Mearadey thought of a clever way to avoid being caught cooking stealthily in the back corner of the hut: she cooked openly in front of her house. Khmer Rouge leaders allowed wash water to be heated or tea steeped over a fire in people's front yards. The tree-bark tea was one of the few pleasures allowed, and had beneficial medicinal properties that controlled diarrhea. A large bark-filled pot in front of a hut was a common sight and caused no suspicion.

Mearadey occasionally lowered a container of rice or corn into the pot with the simmering tea, then quickly replaced the lid. No one questioned the kettle's contents; the outdoor fire could be much larger than a clandestine one, so more rice could be cooked at a time. Despite the various ways we contrived to provide extra rations, we still went hungry more often than not.

At times we indulged in wishful thinking about items we might have brought from Phnom Penh: such simple articles that it had never occurred to us to bring them. Who could have guessed the value of a plastic tarp or a used plastic bag? Matches, thread, rubber bands, thumbtacks, wire, and nails. Umbrellas, boots, stockings, shoelaces, string, rope, bandages, aspirin. We wished we'd brought more plain clothing with high necks and long sleeves, that Mum had bought more gold jewelry with our inflated riels. Keang longed for a camera to record, for posterity, the horror of this regime. Without visual proof, he feared our stories would be discounted as exaggerations—assuming we lived long enough to tell them.

Whenever we let our desires run wild, someone in the family was sure to remind the rest that we wouldn't really want to have most of those objects; such things would just label us as wealthy, cause jealousy, or be confiscated.

Sometimes we chuckled over the absurdity, in retrospect, of people carrying air conditioners, refrigerators, or TV sets on their backs as they trudged from the city. In the village, a community-owned generator ran for a short time each day to provide energy for the loudspeakers and a few lights in the center. Other than that, there was no electrical power. We had no windows or doors, much less air conditioners. And no one would have food to put in the refrigerators even if electricity were available. There would be nothing to see on TV screens either, since there were no television broadcasts.

Some smaller things we had carried so persistently all those weeks had proven just as worthless: our riels, can openers, serving dishes, nail polish, high-heeled shoes. But we wished we'd brought a few special mementos of our former life, photo albums, gifts with sentimental value, an address book with names and addresses of relatives both in and out of Cambodia, and especially objects to help us remember my father. Of course, these things might have been confiscated by the *neary* who took our diplomas and documents, and even if we had been able to bring them to the village, they might have caused trouble for us. Still, we missed them sorely. If we ever had the chance to write to relatives in France or America, how could we do so without addresses?

What little pleasure we had was found in our moments together. The more the Khmer Rouge worked to break down family ties, the harder we tried to strengthen our bonds of love. We had to hide our humanity, but we refused to surrender it to Angka. As long as we could laugh, our captors had not won.

I missed food more than useful items or nostalgic souvenirs. Because I was always hungry, I spent a lot of time thinking of ways to get more, or dreaming of delicious meals I'd once had. It became almost an obsession. Food shortages were particularly acute in the months before harvest. People in the poorest areas of Cambodia ate anything that might provide nourishment: insects, rats, snails, algae, worms, snakes, lizards, roots, grubs, leaves, bark, when the area was depleted of fish, field crabs, wild fruit, birds, monkeys, and larger animals.

Many plants in Cambodia are poisonous, and in ignorance these were also eaten at first. Before long, it became standard for new villagers to observe which plants the water buffalo or oxen avoided and to do the same. A practice evolved: if something was not poisonous, we ate it. Tasting good had ceased to be relevant. To extend our rations, Mum scraped bark and cooked it to a paste. It reduced the gnawing in our stomachs, though it held little nourishment.

Youth brigades guarded banana and papaya trees. We couldn't wait for the fruit to ripen, so green bananas were cooked in the central kitchen with the day's ration of rice gruel. They turned the contents of the huge caldrons into an unappetizing, slimy, black gel, which tasted absolutely awful but they added bulk to the porridge, reduced intestinal cramps, and kept the liquid from sloshing around in our stomachs. I was grateful for those foul-tasting, filling bananas.

When green bananas were harvested, there were usually more than could be consumed at once. The extra fruit was grated, then dried in the sun for three days. Stored like rice, it was added to the central kitchen's rations as needed throughout the year.

Cooked green papayas, in contrast to green bananas, were delicious, or so I thought at the time. Again, because the papayas were likely to be stolen, they were harvested before they ripened. The person preparing the green papayas would always develop painfully raw, red hands from the papain enzyme—the same enzyme used in Western meat tenderizers. Green papayas digest the protein in skin and tongue just as an excessive amount of fresh pineapple does. Once cooked, the enzyme was no longer active and we could enjoy the green fruit.

One day I was working in the fields with my crew when we saw a huge python. Usually, snakes slithered away when people approached, but large pythons are slow, especially when they have recently eaten. My friend grabbed the snake by the tail and pulled the creature backward. She yelled for some of us to help her and for others to run and get some men to kill it. We hungry city girls, who just six months before would have screamed and run at the sight of a snake, to say nothing of touching it, now saw it as meat. We grabbed the tail and pulled with all our might. My friend explained, as she tugged, that she used to go into the jungle with her father. From him she'd learned that if you approached these giant snakes from behind, grabbed their tails and moved backward, they were quite helpless. The snake would only try to get away by moving forward in a straight line and would not attack to the rear. Snake meat is delicious, and the entire village praised us for this welcome addition to the gruel.

Everyone anxiously awaited the first harvest. Angka's promises of abundance once the crops were in had kept us from complaining too much about the heavy workload and reduced rations. But just as the harvests were in full sway in December, many villagers were relocated. They were denied the satisfaction of eating the fruits of their long months of labor and had to beat down the desire to shout curses at Angka.

We had been tricked once more. Would we never learn? Angka Loeu was determined that there would be no sense of ownership, not even from the labor of our own hands. The rice we ate was ours only as a gift from Angka. Much of the rice we had struggled so hard to produce was shipped to China to pay war debts.

I did not find out until much later that in October of 1975, an order was secretly issued by The High Organization that all former Lon Nol soldiers and government workers would be expendable after the harvests were in. The actual order from Angka to underlings was not so blatant. Local leaders, as ignorant as we were of Angka's intent, were simply told to assemble former soldiers, government men, and any troublemakers on specified days. Trucks would arrive to relocate them to new camps and villages where they could better be educated in Communist ways. Village leaders were not expected to be responsible for reeducation; that was a job for Angka.

Three months later, on January 26, 1976, in Mongkol Borei District, a Khmer Rouge official stated, "To rebuild our Cambodia one million men is enough. Prisoners of war"—meaning those expelled from cities—"are no longer needed, and local chiefs are free to dispose of them as they please." Taken literally, that pronouncement meant millions of Cambodians were expendable.

Throughout the harvest that year, men from the Khum Speu villages were called "to other assignments."

In some cases, relocation actually took place just as we were told. Some new villages had been built during the year, and people were moved into more suitable huts. We personally knew of people who were moved to our province from villages near the Vietnamese border. Some men actually were taken to help construct further housing in newly cleared areas, but for most men, we would later learn, "relocation" meant something else.

Occasionally, someone from our village would come upon a few decomposing bodies when they strayed off the path into a jungle clearing or wandered into restricted zones. Initially, it was assumed that these were isolated incidents of brutality or the site of traitors' deaths.

Apparently, soldiers in some regions bragged about their part in multiple executions, but this was uncommon in Khum Speu. In Battambang Province to the west, killings took place closer to the villages or were witnessed by peasants. In our district, murders were carefully concealed.

Chapter Six

I was tired of constantly being admonished to emulate the docile water buffalo. Water buffalo made no demands. They worked hard all day, yet never complained and seldom got sick. They subsisted on grass. Unthinking, they did the bidding of their masters. These dim-witted animals were more highly esteemed by Angka than any villager.

I was also weary of being compared unfavorably with bamboo; so versatile, pliable, and useful. And I resented being likened to a single grain of rice—insignificant.

According to Angka Loeu, each person should aspire to be like one grain of rice in a huge bowl—no different from any other grain and insignificant by itself. No one was to esteem himself above another. No one was irreplaceable. Only in being part of the whole did one have value. Remove one grain of rice and the bowl would be just as full.

Unsubtle allusions to the "eyes of the pineapple" insured that everyone would endeavor to remain indistinguishable from all others. No one wanted one of Angka's many eyes focused on him.

Though talkative and friendly by nature, I had become wary and silent since coming to Khum Speu. I mentally reviewed everything before I spoke. It was best to play dumb. I tried never to stand out except by working extra hard. I never volunteered for anything or complained where it could be heard by those outside my family, or my closest friends. I took no initiative. Whenever I was asked a question, I answered, "I don't know," even when I knew the answer or had an opinion. I acted impressed by everything the leaders told me, as though their thoughts were profound. I dutifully sang the Communist songs, did my work in silence, watched old village girls, and tried to act as they did.

I found that it was not even wise to show any intelligence about Communist matters. When a passage was read from Chairman Mao's "Little Red Book," I just looked blank and asked, "Oh, what does that mean?" Even when the meaning was readily apparent, village leaders preferred to believe that only they could comprehend the deep meanings of this profound manual.

If the Khmer Rouge praised cowlike behavior, I vowed to appear as docile and unthinking as the oxen that plowed the fields. I tried to will my mind to shut down, so that I could go about my work like a dim ox. My mind refused.

I'd catch myself reliving childhood scenes or deriding some inane slogan. I, too, joined in the dangerous habit of singing insulting ditties under my breath.

Communist leaders who understood the play on words in an innocuous lyric still had difficulty justifying punishment of those who sang it, especially the punishment of little children. Many old villagers, ignorant of the second meaning, sang the words aloud in all innocence as they worked.

One song would not leave my head; it popped unbidden into my thoughts whenever I was not on guard. I feared Angka's leaders could sense when I was thinking this song, or that out of carelessness I would sing it out loud where they could hear. They seemed to have the uncanny ability to know everything about a person. On the surface, it was a song about planting, but *ling-go,* meaning *sesame,* is similar to the word for *stupid,* and *kor,* the *kapok tree,* also means *silent* or *mute.* The song's lyric said: "You know you must plant trees./To do well you must plant *ling-go* and *kor.*" The double meaning was: "You know you must plant trees./To stay alive you must be stupid and mute."

Slogans. Endless, endless slogans were repeated over loudspeakers throughout the day and in the evening at the interminable meetings. I wanted to clap my hands over my ears to shut out the unwelcome words. "Forget all you learned. Hate the former regimes. Hate American imperialists."

Even China and Russia came under attack for faulty implementation of communism. Lon Nol and Prince Sihanouk were vilified. Yet, in the same breath, we were told that hate was evil and had no place in the new society. Angka was the people and now that everything belonged to Angka, hate and envy should cease. We were free; we were happy.

"Give your whole life to Angka." "Be prepared to sacrifice yourself." "Be like the water buffalo; contribute but make no demands on society."

It was hard to keep track of time; life was the same from day to day, month to month: work and fear. In dry weather, I labored on dam projects with my youth crew and often lived away from home. In the rainy season, I worked closer to Speu. There were few days or experiences that stand out.

During evenings when we camped at the dam site, I wove hats from palm fronds for my family or as barter items. Usually, however, I was too spent to do anything not required. At least away from the village we were not subjected to nightly indoctrination sessions. They were far more oppressive than work. To come back to the village muddy and exhausted after a long day in the fields, I dreaded the nightly meetings where the entire village of several hundred people met for three or four hours of numbing speeches and confessions. I dared not be absent, nor let my head nod or my eyelids droop as I sat on the hard, backless benches in the communal dining pavilion.

Meetings began with a few rousing Communist songs, that no one dared refuse to sing with gusto. In Phnom Penh, I'd loved to sing along with records or the radio. I'd known all the popular American and English songs by heart. Now I limited my singing to the requirements of evening meetings or to humming a satiric refrain while I worked.

After the songs, evening meetings settled into the first order of business—*kosang,* a formal warning that a person had displeased Angka. Anyone could charge another with real or supposed failings. Old villagers had some opportunity to discuss their alleged crimes before being punished. New villagers were expected to "confess" without knowing the charges. It was a dictum of Angka that in our society of comrades, the faults of another were only pointed out to help that person improve; therefore, the "guilty" were expected to submit to the humiliation of a *kosang,* then "reconstruct themselves" into good people by confessing and repenting. Most often it was new villagers who needed reconstructing.

For a minor infraction, a *kosang* usually brought denial of food for the next day, reduced rations, or extra work. A person was "called to see Angka" or sent for "reeducation" if they committed a "serious crime" or after they'd received several *kosang*s. Prisons and work camps for intractable citizens were almost nonexistent. Either a person was an asset, or he was an expendable liability. Old villagers were usually deemed capable of mending their ways; new villagers were often ruled incorrigible.

Children were encouraged to report failings in their parents and other adults; their word was taken as fact. An envious neighbor, or one harboring a grudge, could cause trouble or even death by accusing his enemy of failure to live by some Khmer Rouge rule. Seldom did anyone receive more than a couple of *kosang*s of a serious nature. The most common serious crimes were stealing food, keeping a private hoard of rice, or dwelling on the past. Even asking to stay home when ill could bring the serious accusation of laziness.

In addition to facing accusations by others, we were expected to confess areas in which we had failed to do our best for Angka. If a person did not stand up often and admit his own failings, he could be certain others would point them out. My family actively sought for trivial things we had failed to do well, so we would have something to confess that would not bring serious repercussions, yet would show that we were trying to improve.

During the final part of the meetings, we were bombarded with local lectures or broadcasts from Phnom Penh. Often our illiterate leaders, not expected to think for themselves or offer original ideas, simply spewed forth strings of Communist sayings about the need to increase production.

Another favorite lecture theme was renunciation of personal desires for group goals. Renunciation of material goods, wealth, education, family ties, and religion were all recurring subjects. Angka wanted all villagers to cease to be concerned with themselves, to strip away pride and envy. Individualism was to succumb to collectivism.

Sometimes there were theatrical performances by children at evening meetings. We were expected to give these productions our solemn attention. These embarrassingly amatuer plays depicted gory scenes in which loyal, valiant Khmer Rouge were beaten and tortured by diabolical Lon Nol soldiers, with the Khmer Rouge always triumphing in the end. Villains wore black moustaches and made awful grimaces to indicate their wicked nature. Other revolutionary themes were similarly treated. I had no firsthand knowledge regarding the inhumane treatment of Khmer Rouge soldiers or villagers by Lon Nol's army, but the barbaric acts they committed in these plays were identical to those the Khmer Rouge perpetrated against us.

I joined a group of villagers one evening in a jungle clearing to watch a propaganda film extolling the close ties between Cambodia and China. It featured Pol Pot and other leaders who had traveled to Peking, and I was curious to see just what the men behind the awesome Angka Loeu looked like. To my surprise, they were ordinary-looking men, about the age of my father. I felt an emotional letdown when I saw how unexceptional they looked. The incessant propaganda had led me to believe that The High Organization was composed of superhumans. Looking at these grinning men, it was hard to imagine any of them willfully ordering the backbreaking labor, suffering, and death I saw each day.

No matter how hard we worked, we never received any praise for our efforts. Respite and rewards were nonexistent. Lack of punishment was the most we could hope for. There seemed no way for a new villager to win favor, no way to negotiate the system, only punishment for any infraction no matter how minor. Fear for my life was so constant that I had to force myself to block it from my mind. More and more I felt I would welcome death.

I probably would have killed myself if I hadn't known my family would be punished harshly for my act. Suicide was considered criticism of the regime. Angka reasoned that if a person killed himself, he had a negative attitude, which was most likely shared by his family.

I decided I would will myself to live at least until Mum died. When Soorsdey married, there would be just the two of us in the hut, so it was not likely that my sisters and their families would still be considered part of my family.

A favorite slogan of the evening meetings was "You are responsible for yourself." "Self-responsibility." The innocent words had a sinister implication under Angka.

Work crews, for instance, were divided into several small

units. Each unit, of four or five people, was given an assignment for the day, along with the admonition that we were responsible for ourselves, meaning work did not end until the assigned goal was reached. Excuses were not accepted, and supervision was unnecessary. Either we remained in the fields until completion of the task or suffered the consequences.

On one work assignment the first year I was in the village, my crew of five girls was camped near a dam site and given an assignment to transport five cubic meters of dirt to the dam each day. If we finished early, we were through. If not, we remained until the work was done, no matter how long it took. Though I was very ill at the time, I dared not quit or slow my pace. I did not want to be called lazy and reported for a *kosang*. Besides, everyone in this crew was a friend, and I did not want to let them down or they, too, would be in trouble. I knew that the girls wanted to finish early so we could sleep during the heat of the day. However, if we finished early consistently, our leaders assumed our workload was too light and added more.

It was hard to do my share the first day that I was sick. I had a slight fever, and although I was ravenously hungry, I was unable to eat. All through the next day, I fought fever and nausea. At night, I took a bath in a jungle stream. At first, the cold water felt good, then chills set in. I was extremely ill and unable to sleep. I'd just dozed off when it was time to work again. My crew wanted to beat the unbearable afternoon heat by starting at 2:00 A.M. A full moon lit our way as we hauled dirt.

I had asked the "nurse" for some medicine to settle my stomach and reduce my fever, and was given a routine folk cure. After the second full day of work, still unable to eat or sleep, I was desperately ill. Returning to the nurse a second time, I obtained the poisonous *sleng* seed that served as our antibiotic. Throughout the day, I worked and nibbled on pieces of this bitter seed, finally taking five sections of it at once. I would either be cured or killed in the process and didn't care which.

Still the fever rose. The third day was the worst. Much of

the day I worked in a state of delirium. I thought I would be dead before nightfall, but at least it couldn't be called suicide.

Day after day, I worked in spite of the fever, eating piece after piece of the seed. Eventually, my illness subsided. I never lost a day's work, thanks to friends who made up for my slowness by working extra hard themselves.

Since thousands of doctors and medical personnel had been found and liquidated, the "doctors" and "nurses" now available were untrained. They were merely soldiers who had been assigned these titles and functions. The nurse I went to see was a sixteen-year-old village girl turned soldier. She could neither write, nor read to know what was in the bottles she dispensed. Reading was not essential, however; under the Pol Pot system of medicine, each patient diagnosed his own symptoms and requested a specific treatment. The nurse unquestioningly gave it. Medicines for stomach upsets, diarrhea, and fever were most in demand. Angka's doctors and nurses administered intravenous feedings using green coconut milk for serum; needles were reused repeatedly without sterilization.

The only other source of medical help available to villagers was the *krou* Khmer, who used a combination of herbal cures and charms to treat patients and exorcise ghosts. At least these native doctors had spent years as apprentices to learn the collected wisdom of past generations. The longer we lived in Khum Speu, the less we scoffed at the *krou* Khmers' potions and chants. However, people in most villages did not even have the luxury of a well-trained witch doctor to consult.

Angka scorned Western medicines, claiming that herbal cures were sufficient—except, of course, for high-ranking leaders. Angka retained fully qualified doctors to treat top leaders, using modern antibiotics and techniques. The attitude seemed to be that the average peasant should either be strong enough to function without medical attention or, quite properly, should die, and thus relieve the state of supporting a nonproducer.

The second time my fever flared, I was so faint that I

couldn't walk, and had no alternative but to admit to my illness openly. I was sent home. With several links from her gold belt, Mum purchased some exorbitantly expensive medicine on the black market. I was soon better, but each year I continued to have recurring bouts of debilitating fevers.

Gradually, most of us learned to treat ourselves, or to consult a shaman, in order to avoid medical attention by Angka's doctors and nurses. Medical folk wisdom spread among those of us new to village ways. To clear up infections, the root of the *ch-kii sreng* tree was burned until only charcoal and mineral ash remained, then an ash-and-water poultice was applied and kept in place for several days. To settle stomachs and control diarrhea, we all drank tree-bark tea and everyone tried to keep a few of the potent *sleng* seeds on hand. *Sleng* seeds contained a quininelike substance. The strength of the drug varied from seed to seed; if it was too potent, it killed rather than cured.

If a person contracted malaria, he often died unless he purchased quinine on the black market—the *sleng* seed was only partially effective. One ounce of gold bought four quinine pills, and many pills were required to effect a respite. Most people lacked the required gold, so they watched in silent agony as loved ones sickened and died.

Folk treatments of a more dubious nature were common. Pregnant women were treated with a potion made from a bat. The entire bat was roasted at high heat in a pan until only black ash remained. The patient would drink this ash mixed with water.

Many Khmer Rouge believed a useful medicine could be made from human bile ducts. Consequently, some victims killed for crimes against the state had their bile ducts cut out and dried for use in treating others. Bile ducts were also used to impart courage. When Khmer Rouge soldiers were first introduced to cold-blooded murder, many could only participate after becoming drunk on home-brewed palm wine. They believed, however, that by eating the bile duct of a victim, they would become staunch enough not to require wine. Dried, powdered bile duct was therefore added to their alcoholic drinks. Eventually, some soldiers were able to kill without being intoxicated. Some even learned to relish it and bragged about it afterward.

An entirely new malady was *chhoeu sattek*, "memory sickness," suffered by those who longed for the past or complained about how bleak life was now. Anyone with photos or heirlooms could be accused of memory sickness. A special symptom was failure to report for a full day's work. Rather than force a person to work against his will, or to work in poor health, a solicitous leader simply dropped by the person's hut and casually said, "Don't worry. Worry only makes you get worse. If you worry, you might think about the *old days.*" The implied threat that the person might be accused of memory sickness was usually enough to get the worker back on his feet and into the fields —sometimes only to die on the job. Those with acute or chronic memory sickness were sent to see Angka.

There was no harm in keeping photos that depicted old village ways, but if they showed a person wearing Western clothing or indicated other signs of "wealth or contamination by the West," it was dangerous to have them. What few photos we had certainly were damning by Khmer Rouge standards. Possession of family letters, such as the last note from my father, showed an unhealthy concern for the past. In addition, it obviously indicated that we could read. Also, the items my father had asked for identified him as a "wealthy" man, and a traitor to Cambodia by virtue of having been detained. Yet we refused to part with these cherished, damning objects of remembrance.

Except for annual bouts of nausea and fever, I was seldom seriously ill. The supplemental food, which our carefully husbanded resources allowed us to buy, maintained my basic health. Only one further serious illness plagued me. It was brought on by the poison spray I was assigned to spread over cotton fields. A strong wind blew the day I worked in the fields and no face mask or protective clothing was provided. I became violently ill. From that time on, respiratory problems plagued me. It was a common complaint for those of us who came in contact with the spray.

Needless to say, when we had so few options for treating our physical ills, medical attention for mental illness or depression was nonexistent. Chronic depression was commonplace as the reality of our situation became apparent, but sometimes even depression might be an asset: to appear stupid and docile, simply following orders like a dumb ox, passed for loyalty.

Though I knew that the only way to survive was to give in to a system too powerful to defeat, I could not force my mind to bend. How could I believe the propaganda spouted at evening indoctrination sessions? "Reflecting on my life" and "learning from my work experience" only taught me to hate the system more. Out loud I said, along with the rest, "I must put my whole mind on my work; I belong to Angka," but inside I denied it. I dutifully repeated, "I will not wear any color but black," while I thought rebelliously, This blouse only *looks* black. Under the dye it is really bright red! I desperately needed the satisfactions these silent forms of defiance provided.

Some slogans of the Khmer Rouge were the same as those I'd been taught all my life as a Buddhist. I willingly chanted, "I must not drink alcohol or gamble." "I must not play around with women," we intoned. Mentally I substituted "men." Envy, jealousy, laziness, and stealing were denounced as well, but compared to the executions that Angka condoned and decreed, these sins were nothing. Hypocrites! I wanted to scream.

"Playing around with women" was one of the more serious crimes. Under Angka, all sex offenses were serious but almost nonexistent. Unmarried couples were forbidden to speak words of endearment. Homosexuality was virtually unknown and condemned if discovered. Rape was beyond comprehension.

Premarital or extramarital sex brought the death penalty. Not many were killed for adultery; most people were too tired to find or be a willing partner.

Repeated quarreling with a spouse brought enforced separation or possible death. But there wasn't much quarreling either. All a person wanted was to eat and sleep after an exhausting day of work. It takes energy to fight or make love, and few had the stamina for either.

Along with the awesome words "Angka Loeu," which had come to imply some godlike creature who capriciously meted out death and seemed to know my every thought and action, there was another phrase that filled me with fear and a sense of helplessness.

The dreaded phrase was *lut-dom*. *Lut* is the part of metal processing in which a rod of metal is placed in a fire until it is red-hot and pliable. *Dom* means the hammering—when the hot metal is put on the anvil and pounded into shape, any shape desired. *Lut-dom* described the way people were expected to be molded by Angka into the pure Communists of the future. If, after heating and hammering into shape, they still refused to conform, they were either "reheated" in the fire of evening political meetings and everyday struggle, or disposed of.

Whenever leaders referred to the Wheel of History— implying that the inevitable era of communism had arrived—I could not help but conjure up the awful image of a huge wheel grinding me under as it rolled slowly but relentlessly forward. "The new Cambodia is like a train gathering speed," we were told. "Nothing you do will stop it. If you try to step down or stop the rushing train, you will be crushed under its powerful wheels." I had become unwilling baggage aboard the train of this alien ideology, yet I could find no way to get off. After almost two years under Angka, the future seemed a gaping, black tunnel rushing to swallow me.

Dreams were my escape—a way to bend without breaking. Every night, I relived happy family parties, school events, or childhood games. The worse my daylight existence, the sweeter my dreams.

I seldom thought about the future; it seemed nonexistent. However, while I worked in silence, I often dwelled on the past —a sure sign of "memory sickness."

I mourned the passing of time. The Communists were robbing me of the many occasions that traditionally had marked a girl's developing maturity. It made me sad that unlike my mother and sisters, I'd never learned to cook. Under the Khmer Rouge, only trusted old villagers were allowed to prepare food, though it took no special talent to boil huge vats of gritty rice that was often raw on top and burned on the bottom. Cooking had lost all semblance of the art my mother and sisters had practiced.

The best meals I ate after we arrived in Khum Speu were some my work crew helped provide. There was the snake we grabbed and the time we caught some fish. In the process of building dikes across the tributary of a small canal, we had created a pond. Forming bucket brigades, we passed bamboo buckets down the serpentine lines and dumped the water across the dike into the stream below. Hour after exhausting hour we bailed. By evening, the pond was almost dry. Schools of small fish were trapped in the remaining water. The leaders had allowed us to catch the fish for the communal kitchen. Some were eaten that night; others were pickled, then soaked with rice for several days. After aging, the fish were fried as a special treat to accompany the usual portion of rice. In memory, I savored those delicious meals.

Some days as I worked I thought of cheese, a food foreign to the Cambodian diet. When Papa had taken us to a French restaurant, I had sometimes tried it. Mum had even bought the rubbery stuff from an import shop once in a while. It was a funny, chewy food, but I had liked it for breakfast on French bread with a little sugar sprinkled over it. Knowing I would most likely never taste cheese again, I found myself thinking of it often. I constantly thought about food, or its lack.

Several times a year, when I was young, my father had rounded up our family, his two sisters' families, and any other relatives that were handy and had taken everyone to a nice restaurant for a grand banquet. Oh, how I missed my father, who had loved to please and surprise us.

Each New Year's Day, he had played cards with all the children: his own as well as nieces and nephews and his friends' children. He'd stacked a pile of riels on the table and paid the winner of each game. He paid the loser; he paid the second best; and before the day was over, he found an excuse to let every child win a hundred-riel note for his very own.

Ironically, as the days became more nightmarish, my dreams became increasingly delightful. I often dreamed of times Papa had taken us to ballets, where beautiful girls with long fingernails executed intricate movements. Their graceful bodies swayed to the music like bamboo in the wind. In dance, they told the eternal stories of good versus evil—stories from our Buddhist scriptures. These professional dance troupes were remnants of old court days, when dancing girls were trained from infancy to entertain the god-kings.

By the time I was born, those days of opulence were already dying out rapidly. Prince Sihanouk had moved from his father's sumptuous palace and lived in the government-built official residence of Chamcar Mon. After the coup, Lon Nol also had lived in the Chamcar Mon villa. The old royal palace had been turned into a national museum, filled with jewels, gold-covered Buddhas, and beautiful thrones. My school class had gone there. The Khmer Rouge had looted and vandalized the beautiful building shortly after they entered Phnom Penh.

When I was about twelve years old, the villa of Chamcar Mon had been bombed by a disgruntled military officer—the lover of one of Prince Sihanouk's relatives. The officer had hijacked a small fighter-bomber and attacked the villa because he felt his career was being thwarted. My school was about a mile from the villa, so when we heard the bombs explode, all the girls had run up to the rooftop patio to get a better look. Most of the bombs had fallen on Chamcar Mon's manicured grounds. Lon Nol suffered only superficial cuts, but forty-three people had been killed in the attack. By prearrangement, the pilot had flown to a part of Cambodia controlled by the Khmer Rouge.

That bombing incident had been the first time I'd focused on the Khmer Rouge. I'd decided then and there that they must be bad people to have allowed that pilot a haven after he'd killed so many people. I had joined the national outcry for his return.

Oh how naïve I had been—we all had been. Obviously, the death of a few dozen people had little meaning to Pol Pot and his colleagues, who not only bombarded us nightly with a full repertoire of frightening slogans and veiled threats, but who actually killed people over minor infractions of their impossible rules. We'd almost grown accustomed to being told:

"To keep you is no benefit. To destroy you is no loss."

"Even the slightest infraction can lead to disappearance."

"We may have to send you to see Angka."

"I wonder if you are suffering from memory sickness?"

I tried to accept the fact that life might never revert to the ways I'd known. If so, the only school certificate that I would ever earn had been the one the *neary* took away—the one that showed I'd graduated from grade school. Because of my father's plan for me to master English, I'd been transferred to an English school when I was ten. The transfer put me two years behind other girls my age. We'd now lived under the Khmer Rouge for almost two years, which put me further behind my age level, and there was no indication that schools would reopen soon, if ever.

Discouraged over my lost education and bleak future,

there were moments when all I wanted was to slip into oblivion. But then my will revived, and I would refuse to think of myself as merely an indistinguishable grain of rice whose personal desires did not matter.

Chapter Seven

Cambodia was becoming a country of women and children. During the civil war, thousands of men had been killed on both sides; since then, many husbands and fathers had been taken, allegedly to be retrained or to serve as soldiers. As efforts were increased to hunt down educated men, more widows were created. Other women were alone because they had been polygamous wives; Angka allowed husbands to keep only their first.

Unusual pressures were placed on men and women who had never married to do so and produce children—grist for the mills of Angka Loeu. However, life for a single woman under Angka was no more difficult than for a married woman, and many people would have preferred to remain unattached.

In fact, there were certain advantages to widowhood. At least widows were never required to marry again against their will. With so many more women than men, they weren't considered as desirable—which suited most of them just fine. If they hadn't liked their marriage partner, at least they were not stuck with him any longer, and if they had loved him dearly, they were now spared further concern for his safety. Caring deeply about another human is a handicap in uncertain times. My mother certainly had no desire to remarry.

Though she lacked formal education, Mum was an accomplished woman. In the days of her youth, village girls were rigorously schooled at home in feminine skills, and each one prided herself on mastering some specialty that would make her a desirable marriage partner. My mother had gained an enviable reputation through her skill as a weaver. Under her grandmother's tutelage, she had been able to complete three to four inches of silk cloth on the loom in one day. This was better than average, and occasionally she'd been able to weave as many as five or six inches—a remarkable feat. It took months to make a silk *sampot.* Years of practice had given my mother mastery of dye techniques and great skill at hand knotting the delicate silk threads into elaborate geometric designs. This ability, learned as a girl, now saved her from work in the rice fields with other women her age.

When my mother had partially recovered her health and the rains had ceased, she was assigned to weave cotton material for the black uniforms that were standard issue for everyone when their own clothes wore out. Mum was assigned to look after small children as well as to weave, and she was saddened by the wretched waifs under her care. The little ones looked at her with solemn brown eyes deep-set in wary faces. Many were malnourished or ill, which made their eyes look even bigger. Some whimpered or sat dejectedly rocking back and forth in the dirt at her feet as she spun. Flies gathered around their eyes and mouths; they were too listless to brush them away.

My mother had continued to supervise Moni and Tevi, but unfortunately Tevi had just turned eight. She would soon have to move from her parents' house to be trained with the other eight- to- twelve-year-olds in the atheistic, Communist ideology and taught to spy on the villagers. It troubled Mum greatly that all her grandchildren would be raised in dormitories.

At fifty-seven years of age, it was not easy to discipline herself to sit all day and spin lumpy thread out of poorly combed cotton, then weave it into coarse material. She worried as she worked, her thoughts as snarled as the lumpy thread at her feet. Worry for her family churned inside her as though it were a living creature.

Constant worry, more than hardship, aged her. She had not known such sorrow and anguish since the first years of marriage, when she and my father had lost their first three babies.

No, it wasn't the work that aged her. As the oldest of five children in a rice farmer's family, my mother was no stranger to work or to village life, although by village standards, she had been raised in a middle-class household. Education had not been sought, nor was it readily available in rural Cambodia when she was young, so my mother had never gone to school. Her youngest brother had been one of the few children from Khum Speu to get any schooling in that era. He became a forest ranger; Mum, her sister, and two other brothers had stayed home and helped farm.

Her "baby brother" was the one who had begged us to join him near the Thai border when Phnom Penh was under attack. Just before the Khmer Rouge takeover, we learned that he had escaped to France with his wife and two children. Every time we thought of them, we regretted that we had turned down their invitation.

Recently, Mum added her sister to her worry list. My aunt was crippled, yet she was forced to work in the fields, and her twenty-one-year-old son, Samol, might soon be drafted.

Another of Mum's nephews had been forced to join the army in 1973. He had planned to flee to Phnom Penh when Samol came to live with us, but had been conscripted before escape was possible. As a soldier for almost three years, he lived in constant fear, not so much of fighting, but that some *neary* would convince his commander he should marry her.

Soldiers were encouraged to marry early. If they were too slow, commanders assigned them a marriage partner.

Whenever stationed near home, Mum's nephew begged his mother to arrange a wedding with some respectable girl. Each time, however, military assignments took him away before arrangements were completed. He never knew when or if he would return. It was necessary to serve as a soldier to keep reprisals from his family, but he did not want to be saddled with a *neary* for a lifetime partner. It was hard to decide which was worse, the girls themselves, with their filthy uniforms and unkempt hair, or their espousal of an abhorrent philosophy.

The Khmer Rouge usually required a draftee to take a new name—to help him break with the past. It also effectively kept families from inquiring after their soldier sons and daughters, since the Khmer Rouge didn't know them by family name. If a soldier's family was relocated while he was away, he had no means of finding them when he returned. Mail service was nonexistent and deaths went unreported. Later, when the murders committed by the regime became widely known, soldiers who had been involved feared retribution and didn't dare return home. All this aided Angka's design to disrupt family ties.

Mum also feared more and more for Keang and Leng. The Khmer Rouge continued to rank society's members according to those most worthy of emulation and those who were the greatest enemies of the people. According to that system, our family was on the enemy list.

"Federalists," the first category of enemies, included members of the royal family, all government workers, even policemen on the streets—anyone with "authority." These were considered unredeemable and all were to be killed. Papa had been in this category, as were Keang and Leng, if it were but known.

Traitors in the second group were "Capitalists and Speculators": businessmen, intellectuals, students, teachers, professionals such as doctors and lawyers, plus technicians and skilled laborers. In this category, most were to be eliminated, but some were deemed capable of reeducation and could be spared. According to his biography, Keang belonged to this group.

Of the three categories of farmers, big plantation owners generally were killed if found. They had farmed many acres, owned equipment, and employed others. Especially damning was their employment of others. It was self-evident "exploitation."

Middle-level farmers had owned land and equipment, but had not used the labor of others. Mum's oldest brother fit this description. She especially worried about him because he was an outspoken critic of the new regime. Many in this group, however, were not killed, just stripped of possessions and humbled. Poor farmers were classified with factory workers and manual laborers as the proletariat. Leng's biography listed him as an unskilled laborer; everyone sought that classification.

Mum worried that Mearadey and Rasmei would be widowed if the backgrounds of her sons-in-law were discovered. Above all, she agonized about her "precious Ne and Da"—the nicknames by which Soorsdey and I were known within the family. We came home each night so exhausted we seldom spoke. Our existence consisted of working, eating, and sleeping. But Mum's worst fear was that Ne or I would be forced to marry a soldier as some friends' sons and daughters had been made to do.

It was considered unpatriotic to refuse a soldier's marriage proposal. It was possible to turn away the first few offers, but if refusals continued, a girl was accused of feeling superior and might even be put to death. Since Angka didn't allow divorces, a person could be trapped for life with an unwanted partner. Already Mum had turned away hinted proposals, especially for Soorsdey. But it was only a courtesy that she was even asked. Parents no longer had to be consulted. Ne was almost nineteen and I had turned sixteen in August, four months after the takeover. We were considered good-looking, desirable girls, despite our efforts not to draw attention to ourselves.

Mum's poor health brought her into close contact with old people in the village; she worked with them. In addition to weaving, spinning, and baby-sitting, the ill and elderly made bamboo baskets, braided rope, and performed other tasks around the village. Though life was physically less rigorous for them, it was equally bleak. They had grown up in a society that revered its old. Now the Khmer Rouge made them feel useless. Traditional family attention and pleasures of their twilight years were denied them. They'd expected to spend old age as wise, senior members of loving family groups, free to visit Buddhist temples regularly, and contemplate the next world. Instead, their days were filled with long hours of toil, and their wisdom was scoffed at by their captors. They were treated like flotsam, serving no practical function in a society that cared only for "useful" objects.

One pleasure remained to them. Pol Pot had not denounced the chewing of betel nuts and leaves. This pleasant-tasting, mildly narcotic plant dulled the pain and loneliness of many, especially old peasant women. My mother, like most women from the cities, shunned the teeth-blackening, lip-staining habit, and was repulsed by the bright red spit. But now my mother understood the need old people had to drug their senses, so she never condemned those who found solace in the betel nut.

One way we could get Mum's mind off our current troubles was to start her talking about the past. The deep lines around her mouth and eyes would soften as she reminisced about her youth, her marriage, and life as a young woman in Phnom Penh. She treasured the memories of her traditional upbringing.

When she was young, a great fuss had been made of village girls when they were first "in their shade." With the start of menstruation, my mother had been expected to leave her childhood behind; she could no longer run and play at will with other village children. She had entered the exciting world of womanhood and was expected to spend her time indoors, learning women's work and skills. Each month while "in her shade," she stayed indoors, especially when outsiders came by.

During those years of preparation, when Mum learned domestic skills from her mother and grandmother, and developed her art as a weaver, she also learned techniques of skin care and makeup—which roots to grind in preparing the yellow powder to give her skin a delicate glow. She learned proper behavior and bearing. In the company of men, she was always chaperoned.

Since parents contracted marriages for their daughters with young men of promise, they felt it was wise to keep girls segregated as much as possible. They didn't want their daughters to fall in love prematurely with unsuitable partners, so parents assumed the duty of guarding their children's affections. This was one reason why girls in Cambodia had been discouraged from gaining an education. Many parents had thought that once a girl learned to read and write, she would spend all her time sending and receiving secret love letters. My great-grandfather, however, had been very progressive. During the two years that Mum's grandmother trained her in weaving, her grandfather taught her the rudiments of reading and writing.

Mum had had several suitors. Her father favored one; her mother, another. She was sent to live with her grandparents in another village until the issue was settled so that no suitor could kidnap her and make her his bride before her parents decided who should be her future husband.

Before the matter was resolved, a new well was completed, and the village planned a celebration. A government official was to be present for the special occasion. On a whim, my mother and a friend decided to dress in their best *sampot*s in honor of the dignitary. The girls spent all morning giggling, dabbing yellow powder on their skin, and brushing their long, black hair until it shone. Pleased with their efforts, they had hurried to the village square with their parents.

To my mother's and grandparents' delight, the dignitary had been accompanied by a handsome young assistant—Mum's distant cousin, Choun Butt. He had not seen Ean Bun since she was a child. Apparently, she made a great impression on him that day, because soon thereafter his mother paid a call to discuss a wedding.

Samol's mother had recently given us some old photographs of my family. One picture was of my parents shortly after they wed. Mum had been just eighteen; my father, a year older. That was unusual. Young males usually had to work for several years before they could afford to marry. My father's education had made it possible for him to earn a good living while he was still young.

Marriage changed my mother's entire destiny. It lifted her from the ageless village life of Khum Speu and dropped her into the twentieth century. She had to learn to entertain important guests, manage a complex social life, and mingle in society. As a wedding gift, my father had provided his bride with a serving girl, and she was never without one again until our expulsion from Phnom Penh. The last serving girl joined our household when she was only nine years old. Her parents had been too poor to keep her and had arranged with my mother to take her in, feed and clothe her, give her a small wage, and teach her skills that might advance her in the world. Just a year younger than I, she was almost like a sister. Mum loved all of our serving girls and they returned that love. Most of them remained with us until they married, and often it was my mother who arranged desirable matches for them.

Mum's first serving girl had been invaluable: she had helped the young bride learn the necessary skills to help her

113

promote her husband's rising career, and had kept my mother company when my father's work called him from home.

While Papa had been away on one of many short trips, their four-year-old daughter contracted cholera. She was sick only one day; by night she was dead. The servant had offered comfort to my grief-stricken mother and cared for the new infant daughter, my parent's third child. They had already lost their only son, who died shortly after birth.

The baby girl, then their only living child, seemed healthy until she was about a year old. Then she, too, fell ill and died a year later. Shortly after, Mearadey was born.

To have their first two daughters and their only son taken had been a severe blow, and my parents devoted all their love and attention to Mearadey, fearful that they might lose her as well. But she remained healthy, and Mearadey's birth had been followed two years later by Rasmei's.

A picture packed by Tevi in her little satchel showed Mearadey and Rasmei as young children standing by the side of my seated parents. Although the photo was folded and cracked, we kept it safely hidden with the other pictures salvaged by Tevi. Our few photos were the only visual reminder we had of our former life.

A snapshot taken of Soorsdey with our servant girl and me, inside our home in Phnom Penh, had been played with by the children so often that the lower-right-hand third of the photo was obliterated. Still, it was kept with the other treasured reminders of our life, and Tevi was praised for her foresight in saving it.

Among the photos preserved in Tevi's bag had been one of our house in Phnom Penh. It showed the balcony of the main living quarters and the lower apartment where Mearadey and Keang's family lived. Although of poor quality, it was prized.

Mum had been inordinately proud of that home, so unlike the thatched village house where she grew up or the little hut

we occupied now. She had supervised its construction and selected the furniture. Every modern convenience from toilets and
sinks, to our overstuffed furniture, TV set, and refrigerator, had
had to be imported.

My sisters and I had had an upbringing very different
from Mum's. None of us had ever participated in the ancient
rites of passage into womanhood, and each of us had received
an excellent education. My two oldest sisters spoke fluent
French, and my father had made sure that both Soorsdey and I
had special instruction in English. He had felt English, not
French, was the language of the future.

Mum worried that Tevi, Rota, Chenda Poong, and Moni
would never have proper schooling, that they would grow up
illiterate and, even worse, incapable of independent thought and
without religion.

Mum treasured a picture her sister had given her that had
been taken in Speu years ago in front of Po Preng temple. It had
been a special day when she and Papa returned to their ancestral
village to present the monks with the gift of a radio. As guests
of honor at the religious festival, they had joined a parade
through the village streets with waving flags and antique cere-
monial canopies held high; there had been fabric flowers and
bright parasols everywhere. Most of the villagers in that photo-
graph were relatives; the rest were close friends. Papa stood out
because he was the tallest man present and the only one in dark
glasses. Mum's brothers had held the radio proudly. Five-year-
old Mearadey, thumb in her mouth, had sidled up to Papa for the
picture, while Rasmei had clung to my mother's skirt.

From the loom in front of our hut where Mum worked,
she could see down the road to the spot where the temple had
once stood. All that was left was a mound of rubble. Behind it
stood Po Preng prison. It incensed all of us that the prison had
been named after a sacred edifice. Known for generations as a
place of worship and tranquillity, it was now a place where men

were incarcerated; to the rear of the temple rubble was the military prison headquarters. And in the forest beyond the once lovely grounds, posted signs warned against trespassing. We had seen more men enter that prison than could possibly be housed there. Rumor spread that the sacred woods were the scenes of slaughter.

Shortly after we had arrived in Speu, old men and women strong enough to work had been assembled in front of stately Po Preng temple. Some were told to build a bridge nearby. No one had minded being asked to build the much-needed bridge, until they learned that the building stones would come from their beloved temple. Several refused to tear down the structure and were told, "Don't worry, just go home." That night, while the village slept, soldiers came. The elderly who had refused to work were told that Angka wanted to see them. The next morning, the old people were again assembled at the temple and given the same instructions. Some of their friends, they noticed, were missing. Again they were told they were free to work or go home. This was repeated several mornings. Before long, those who remained agreed to build rather than disappear. Fortunately, Mum had been too ill at that time to build bridges. She doubted that she could have agreed to take part in the desecration of a temple where she had worshiped for much of her life.

Later, the Khmer Rouge announced that Angka had not torn down the ancient temples. The elders of the nation, they claimed, had chosen to do this as their acknowledgment that religion had drugged the people.

Initially, after the takeover, monks had been allowed their saffron robes and monasteries. But by 1976 they were forced to lay aside their sacred robes and live as others did—or be killed. Many chose the latter. Monasteries were dismantled or turned into granaries.

The Khmer Rouge had destroyed the temples and decimated the monks, and they had punished worshipers, but they had not been able to stamp out faith. Many followed my mother's practice of maintaining an altar in their homes. In a corner of our hut, Mum had set up a little shrine. It could be dismantled or covered on a moment's notice so it would not draw attention when leaders or their spies went by. Here my mother often retired in quiet prayer and meditation.

We had taken religion for granted before the Khmer Rouge victory. It had been as much a part of our lives as the air we breathed. We'd questioned Buddhist principles no more than we questioned the certainty of seasonal change. Though most young people weren't actively religious, the Buddhist tradition was a fact of life.

My mother had loved the teachings and the ceremonies that went with being a Buddhist in Cambodia. Now the inner peace and serenity Buddhism teaches its adherents was often the only haven she found in the raging storm tearing asunder the life she had known. She did not fear death. In fact, it would have been a welcome relief, but she knew that her existence was all that kept me from giving up.

When Mum became angry about the injustice and indignity in which we lived, she let her fury be dispelled in rows of uneven weaving. Quickly regaining composure, she passed the shuttle back and forth across the loom in monotonous, smooth motions. Some hapless soldier or villager would be forced to wear clothing born of her wrath. She did her best to create quality material of poor-quality thread. Only small sections of the cloth on her loom showed where she had momentarily lost control of her feelings.

When it became apparent that Mum and her sister were about to lose the privilege of choosing partners for their children unless they acted quickly, they arranged a wedding between Soorsdey and Samol, to which the couple readily agreed. My sister and cousin had known each other all their lives. In addition, Samol had lived with us for two years after he fled his village. "Ol" had added fun to our household, and was the first close contact that either Soorsdey or I had had with a young, unmarried man.

Ne and Ol were formally engaged in mid-January 1976, but not before seeking official approval from local leaders. In theory, anyone considering marriage had to consult the leaders first. In practice, previous family arrangements were simply kept quiet until official approval was granted. Even Angka's dicta couldn't change the customs of centuries overnight.

Following the hasty marriage arrangements that we hoped would keep Samol out of the army and Soorsdey from being claimed by a soldier, we were surprised to learn that Angka had not yet authorized marriages for civilians. Soldiers could marry when they desired, because of their favored status and the fact that they were often sent away on short notice, but local leaders hadn't yet received instructions regarding the rest of us. During the war years, villagers under the Communists had contracted marriages with little interference. But times had changed. Soorsdey and Samol would have to await Angka's pleasure.

Mum was delighted. Soorsdey and I didn't have to be married in order to avoid unwanted proposals, we merely had to be engaged. Since she wanted only to insure that we would not be forced to marry against our wishes, she hoped Angka would take plenty of time. Her attention shifted to me and how she could arrange another long engagement.

In Phnom Penh, Soorsdey and I probably would not have married until after we graduated from college, although both Mearadey and Rasmei had married without finishing secondary school. Mearadey had completed all except her final level of certification. Rasmei still had the last two years of school to complete when she left her studies to become a bride. Except for the few girls who went on to college, most, especially those in the villages, were married by the time they were nineteen.

Dating was not part of our culture, and we'd had little opportunity to know any boys well. In the lower grades, boys and girls attended separate schools. In secondary school and college, the few girls who attended sat apart and seldom talked with male students. Higher education was mainly a male pursuit, necessary in order to find good employment, and attract a wife from the more prosperous families.

It was customary for a young man to ask his mother— who, of course, had been looking over young female relatives for years—to select a bride. Sometimes he suggested a girl he might be interested in, as had been the case with my father. Before a final selection could be made, it was necessary to be sure the astrological signs were compatible.

Keang, after teaching for a while, felt capable of supporting a wife, and, like my father, had asked his mother to arrange a match with someone he had in mind. His mother was my father's cousin, and Keang was interested in marrying Mearadey, seven years his junior.

Mearadey had seen Keang a few times at family gatherings, but they had never spoken to each other until engagement plans were made. During their one-year engagement, they talked a few times in the presence of chaperons. Mearadey had been pleased with the prospect of marriage to her handsome distant cousin. My parents later arranged for Rasmei to marry another cousin in much the same way.

Mearadey and Rasmei, like other Cambodian girls, had the right to reject their parents' choice of husbands, but girls seldom did. Proper young women spent most of their time at home and did not talk to young men, so they had little opportunity to find husbands on their own, and it did not occur to them to try. Not only were parents given the responsibility, they were also credited with the wisdom to make a wise selection for their child.

Although, under the Communists, the criteria for the selection of partners had changed, Samol and Soorsdey also trusted their mothers to make a wise selection. And since young couples had traditionally remained engaged for a year before marriage, Ne and Ol were not upset with the delay while the Communists established rules governing weddings. They didn't have to wait long.

As the first anniversary of the Khmer Rouge victory approached, Angka decided to halt the harvest long enough to allow a celebration. Since victory fell only three days after the traditional Cambodian New Year in mid-April, these two events were combined into a three-day-long holiday—our first days off since we arrived in West Speu. As part of the celebration, a day was set aside for weddings. Soorsdey turned nineteen during this holiday. Samol was twenty-one. They had been engaged for only three months.

Angka announced this first scheduled wedding date mere days in advance. I remember how cheated we all felt without quite knowing why. After all, there were no arrangements to be made on our part. No invitations to write, no banquets to prepare, no gifts to buy, or special clothing to make.

In contrast to Khmer Rouge nuptials, traditional Cambodian weddings had been grand affairs that lasted two days. Both Mearadey and Rasmei had been given elaborate wedding parties that included all our relatives and friends and important government colleagues of my father's, including President Lon Nol. For a week before the actual wedding, relatives began converging on our household in Phnom Penh. By the time everyone arrived, most of the guests had to sleep on the floors and verandas. It was a wonderful time in which everyone stayed up late to catch up on the news since we'd last been to a wedding, funeral, or graduation. The women brought food and helped cook for the crowd. Similar gatherings took place in the groom's house as his relatives arrived for the celebration.

As children, Soorsdey and I had loved the bustle and excitement and looked forward to the time our own turns would come for grand wedding parties. A couple of the young men in attendance might someday be our grooms.

The time-honored Cambodian wedding ceremony had begun early in the morning as the bride and groom were helped by family members to dress in elegant, gold-trimmed, traditional silk robes and gold jewelry. The bride wore six to ten gold bracelets on each arm and several heavy gold ankle rings. The groom was dressed in the customary silk wedding *sampot*, deeply pleated in front, and topped with a long brocade shirt and a knee-length robe edged with mirror-cloth. At each step of the five-part ceremony, articles of clothing were added or removed as custom dictated.

The first portion of the lengthy ceremony was a formal presentation of gifts to the bride's family by the parents and close relatives of the groom: traditionally, about thirty gifts. The quality and quantity depended on the wealth of the groom's family. These gifts were given in pairs to symbolize the new family unit about to be created: two platters of assorted fruit, two bottles of wine, two silver bowls, two *sampot*s, and so on. After this gift-giving ritual, a wedding breakfast was served.

The second ceremony was the cutting of hair from the bride and groom. Little was actually snipped. The ritual symbolized that the old life had been cut off and a new life was to grow to replace the old. Lunch followed.

Then a Buddhist monk, often a relative, spoke of the new life the young couple was to build; he performed the actual marriage rites. In the evening, the party shifted to a restaurant for a banquet. The meal was followed by the thread ceremony.

One by one, guests approached the seated bride and groom, draped a brightly colored string over the couple's extended arms, and made a wish for them. By the time every guest had added a thread, the couple's arms were covered with bright-colored "wishes" for their happiness. A Cambodian orchestra played all evening and sometimes there was dancing. At Mearadey's and Rasmei's weddings, Western music was played as well—a recent innovation.

The fifth and final ceremony took place the next morning. With everyone assembled in the bride's parents' home, each guest approached the young couple and asked a question or made a request. Questions were framed in an effort to trick the bride or groom into answering "I" instead of "we." This had been a lighthearted conclusion to the festivities, meant to reinforce in the mind of each that they were now one. Each would no longer act alone, but must consider the partner in every decision. By noon the party was over. So it had been for centuries.

Chapter Eight

Even though she had been given very short notice, Soorsdey was pleased at the thought of being Samol's wife. Many prospective brides had been denied even a few days' warning. Often a girl would be informed that her wedding would take place the next day. Or, worse yet, a girl or boy working in the fields would be summoned to the community hall and told that the time had come to marry; there would be no time to request permission for even close members of the family to be present. Sometimes a girl would only discover which groom had been assigned to her as she stood in the thatch-roofed, open-sided community dining hall, where the ceremony took place. Many were not pleased with their assigned marriage partners. Soorsdey and Samol were lucky.

For Soorsdey's wedding, Mum loaned her a beautiful shawl to make the occasion a little more festive. Wearing their cleanest black clothes, Samol and Soorsdey joined other waiting couples in the dining hall. Grooms sat on one side, brides on the other, guests in the rear. Samol's family and ours were both in attendance—that, too, was a privilege denied many families. Work in the fields was more important; but fortunately for us this wedding day was part of the victory celebration, when most people didn't have to work. This was Khum Speu's first group wedding, so no one knew what to expect of the ceremony.

It was a very simple, impersonal affair. The district commander gave an hour-long speech. The hundred couples were admonished to be good workers, perform better in the new year than they had in the past, and to be more dedicated to the cause of building Cambodia—more unselfish.

Following the lengthy harangue, each couple took their turn in front of the district leadership. They then "married themselves" by saying "I am happy to have this comrade for my spouse. I will be a good worker and help produce more rice in the coming season."

Finally, Soorsdey and Samol's turn came. They sat down in the two chairs, then took turns standing to speak, promising to be diligent workers. It was over. Comrade Soorsdey and Comrade Samol were now man and wife. After that, we returned to West Khum Speu and ate with the other villagers in the dining hall. Each village celebrated the anniversary of victory and liberation by killing one pig for each kitchen and serving extra rice.

In the evening, we had our private family gathering at Samol's mother's hut, since it was larger and more secluded than ours.

We tried to make the occasion less dismal by our forced gaiety. Mum had secretly procured a scrawny chicken, and relatives brought what fruit and other food they were able. Guests took turns entering my aunt's hut to eat a little chicken and rice, while the rest of us kept watch outside. We noticed that the tea, taken from the big caldron in front of the hut, had a decidedly stewed-chicken flavor.

Years before, Samol's parents built a room at the side of their hut, where Mearadey and Keang had lived when Keang taught school in Speu. This one room was to be the new couple's home. They would be spared the degradation of spending their wedding night with other couples in some requisitioned "honeymoon cottage."

All the larger homes throughout the district had been

claimed by the Khmer Rouge for the night, and the displaced families had to move in with relatives. Each newlywed couple was assigned a room. Some of these couples, unfortunately, had not wanted to marry each other in the first place. Perhaps they had procrastinated too long in making their own selection or had incurred a leader's wrath and were being punished. Soldiers patrolled that night around the honeymoon cottages to insure that each couple consummated their marriage. Built on stilts, the thin-walled huts offered little privacy. Spies listened through the thatch to hear whether the couples would reveal how they truly felt about the Khmer Rouge. Later, the spies and soldiers made rude, suggestive jokes in front of the newlyweds. It was a humiliating start.

Many Cambodians share the same names, and in these group weddings the wrong person occasionally came forward when they heard their name called. If the mistake was not discovered quickly, the bride and groom were stuck—though it made little difference, since they were unknown to each other anyway. One partner was as good or bad as the next.

Not a great deal was expected of a spouse, so there were not many areas in which to be disappointed. A husband could not provide better for his household by working harder or being educated. The wife did not cook, sew, or maintain a home. Little romance was involved. The couple merely shared a little shack or moved in with relatives and spent their nights together, falling exhausted into bed for a few hours' sleep.

It is amazing how well most of these utilitarian marriages worked. Perhaps each spouse reasoned that, since they could not get a divorce or another partner, they might as well make the best of it. Perhaps having someone was better than having no one at all. Forbidden to show affection outside their immediate family, most young marrieds clung to each other. They had expected to have a partner selected by parents under the old system, so now they simply bowed to Angka's decision.

When soldiers married, they could request that their partner accompany them when they were transferred. If they married an old villager, the request was often granted. If their partner was a new villager, the request was usually denied. For many new villagers, separation was preferable, especially if their partner was transferred to Phnom Penh.

Angka Loeu did not want former residents of the city to see the destruction and report back to others. When permission was granted for new villagers to join their partners in Phnom Penh, the families usually never heard from the new villagers again. Eventually, relatives would assume their son or daughter had been killed. Before long, to go to Phnom Penh was viewed by new villagers as a one-way journey.

Although Samol and Soorsdey shared the room built onto his parents' home, they continued to work much as they had done before. They were together only at the midday break and at night. There was little time or energy to build a relationship. The fact that they had known each other for years gave them a decided advantage in establishing a loving marriage.

Now Mum and I had the little hut to ourselves. We seldom saw Soorsdey, though she lived near. It was even harder to keep track of our relatives in other villages. Upon rare occasions, someone in the family forged a pass to visit Leng and Rasmei, only a mile or two away, or to check on Uncle Ban and Grandmother Butt. Since forging a pass was becoming increasingly dangerous, it was not risked often.

My mother was very anxious for several days after Ne and Ol's wedding. She feared the missing chicken would be discovered, and might possibly be traced to her. Each family was expected to raise a few chickens, but not for personal use. When a chicken was killed, it was officially meant for the collective pot, where one chicken served as many as fifty people. To insure that no chickens were consumed privately, leaders periodically counted the birds as they roosted at night in the pens by each hut. Ingenious villagers found a way to circumvent the official count by training a few young chickens to roost in the jungle. These birds, not included in the total, could be consumed or sold on the black market.

Everyone deeply resented being responsible for raising chickens, yet not benefiting adequately from the labor. Somehow, raising chickens seemed more personal than raising food in communal gardens. It was even more galling to have a village assistant claim several chickens for the "community pot," since we all knew that at least one bird would find its way to the leader's hut instead. The chief would make a public show of joining everyone at the communal meal, only to go home and eat again in secret.

The Khmer Rouge enlisted youths, some no older than eight or ten, to keep a sharp lookout while playing in the village, to insure that the rest of us did not enjoy similar clandestine feasts. Tevi was one of those given spying assignments.

Little Tevi—her name means "angel"—had been assigned to live in a hut in the children's compound with nine other girls and was allowed only occasional visits to her family. Mearadey and Keang feared the intensive indoctrination would weaken the bond they had with their oldest daughter.

A major task of youth groups such as Tevi's was to guard against the chronic problem of theft. The Khmer Rouge considered these heavily indoctrinated children the most trustworthy choice for this function. But even they were watched by soldiers or leaders to guarantee that they did not steal the food they guarded.

Tevi patrolled vegetable plots and the central storehouse where rice, corn, beans, and sugar were kept after the harvests. Her crew also took their turn at night duty guarding crops in the large fields that were farther from the village. Children were stationed within sight of each other around the perimeter of each paddy. Snakes frequented the dikes at night, and the young guards were terrified of stepping on a cobra or viper if they walked around the dikes in the dark. Instead, these frightened little sentries stood glued to one spot for hours.

Still, the stealing of food by children as well as adults took place routinely. Hunger drove people to take chances. It was all that kept many of us from starving. Tevi occasionally brought us a handful of rice that she'd concealed in her oversized clothing.

Instead of going to school, youngsters worked the fields, guarded supplies, and attended lengthy sessions meant to make them loyal advocates of the new system. During these indoctrination sessions, they were taught only the rudiments of reading, writing, and numbers. The children were often housed in former school buildings; buildings whose books had been burned and where advanced reading and writing skills were no longer taught.

The younger generation was losing the rich language and culture of Cambodia. Words associated with our cultural and religious heritage were deliberately dropped. Subtly shaded language was no longer needed. Few words were required to tell someone to work hard and do as told without asking questions. Children found that asking questions brought punishment; independent thinking was condemned. They learned it was safest to be silent.

My brothers-in-law often pointed out an obvious flaw in the Communist system of teaching the young. When children are taught to be spies, to turn in their parents, disavow family loyalty, betray friends, kill and accept killing as necessary, then a generation is reared who live by that code of ethics. It is a code of behavior embodying the antithesis of self-sacrifice, love of one's fellow man, generosity, trust—the very qualities Angka Loeu proposed to foster. Angka could not destroy humanity in a people and still hope to draw upon that humanity when the nation was finally "purified." Instead, they were breeding a society that would readily turn against the leaders and the system with no compunction if the opportunity arose, or if members of the society felt personally threatened. We saw it happen, often.

As relatives of children who were subjected to this training, we did our best to counteract the dogma the young minds were being fed. We would not lose them without a fight. We knew we ran the risk the children might report us; still, most families were willing to take that chance. Some paid with their lives.

With Tevi in the youth brigade, Mum had only five-and-a-half-year-old Moni to watch each day while she wove. Moni's name means "glitter," but most of her sparkle had vanished. She was a solemn child and became more so once her sister Tevi was forced to move out of the family hut. Moni and her cousin, Rota, were almost the same age and would be joining the youth brigades in two years.

Rota, though not anxious to leave his parents, was venturesome and looked forward to being old enough to ride the black, lumbering water buffalo, which was often a boy's first task once he left home. He was eager for new experiences. For the first years in Speu, little had been expected of him. He and his friends roamed unsupervised through the village ten to fourteen hours a day. Once he turned eight, however, he would feel important and useful.

Chenda Poong would miss Rota terribly when he moved out. Though he often neglected her, he was all the family she had for the greater part of each day. Once he left, she would be alone, left to shift for herself along with the other children in her village. Her spirits drooped. She badly needed the attention of her family. My mother was endlessly frustrated by the restrictions that kept her from leaving the district to supervise this forlorn little granddaughter.

We were lucky that Tevi accepted her parents' teachings,

and became the family's trusted envoy. Children moved easily through the villages without arousing suspicion. Therefore, they were often trusted to trade a little gold for some needed item through the illegal barter system that developed. Since there was little haggling over prices, children could trade as effectively as adults. Each time we needed rice or medicine, Mum removed a link of her gold belt and gave it to one of her grandchildren to be used for the purchase.

The three oldest children were invaluable to our family's survival in many ways. Though young, they sensed how serious their efforts in our behalf were, and how essential it was to keep family matters absolutely private. A slip of a child's tongue could bring death to parents. No one ever learned about the former prominence of our family from Tevi, Moni, or Rota; they acted ignorant of family matters. For mere children, they played the role of double agent remarkably well.

A month after Soorsdey and Samol married, one dream of Mum's was realized. My cousin Si Ton obtained a pass to leave his district and came to West Speu to ask Mum if I would be his bride. I was honored to learn that Grandmother Butt had fostered this marriage arrangement. A weight seemed to lift from my mother's heart, and therefore from mine.

Mum agreed that we could wed when Angka Loeu again allowed it, which she presumed would be at the end of the next harvest season, a year away. In the meantime, I no longer had to fear unwanted proposals. Being engaged was like having a cloak of protection about me. I felt safer, a little less vulnerable.

After fleeing their home during the war, Si Ton and his family had lived near us in Phnom Penh, where he had completed school. Having received permission to go to Paris for advanced studies in chemistry, his application forms had been in the process of passing through the last of the seemingly endless government bureaucracies; he would have been in Paris and safe in a matter of days. Then Phnom Penh fell.

At sixteen and a half, I was not eager to marry quickly, though I did admire Si Ton greatly. However, my cousin, eleven years my senior, was most anxious for the next wedding date to be announced. Until then, we would seldom see each other because of the difficulty in getting a pass.

A few days of rest and extra food because of the harvests, plus Soorsdey's marriage, and now my engagement, made us feel that life was improving. Hope again began to build as I fantasized my future with Si Ton.

Having grown up under a system in which I was not expected to choose my own husband, it never occurred to me to question the system or worry too much about whom my family might select.

I knew Si Ton was a kind, gentle man, and I was happy with the arrangements Mum and Grandmother had made for me, though I would also have been happy if they had arranged a marriage with someone else. Mostly, I was pleased because Grandmother and Mum were so happy.

Mum relaxed a little. She felt she had discharged her duty as a parent by arranging a good match for each of her girls, and she knew my father would have approved her choices. She assured me that I would grow to love Si Ton as much as I now esteemed him. She teased me with her own version of a patriotic song that said, "You have rice; you can have everything."

"Da, you are young. You might yet have 'everything.' "

One morning in early January 1977, it was announced in Si Ton's district that that day would be a marrying day. Si Ton borrowed a bike from the village chief and pedaled as fast as he could, in order to intercept me on my way to the rice fields.

"Come, Teeda," he urged. "If we hurry we can be back in time for the weddings." I was dismayed. I'd be a bride in a few hours with no time to tell Mum or prepare myself.

Though I was given permission to go, my crew leader advised against it, pointing out that we would have to live in the district in which we married. Couples usually wanted to remain near the bride's mother. Also, Si Ton's district was poorer, which would mean less food. She reminded us that in a month or two a wedding day would be announced for Khum Speu. I favored waiting. Si Ton reluctantly agreed, but pedaled back to his village at a considerably slower pace, a disappointed hunch to his shoulders.

When a marrying day was announced for Khum Speu—and I had adjusted to the idea of being a seventeen-year-old bride—the rules changed: marriage between districts "was not possible." Local leaders did not want to lose good workers to another district through marriage. Si Ton and I would have to wait another year and hope the rules changed back again.

In February, Grandmother Butt died. I grieved that her wish to witness my marriage to Si Ton had not been realized, and I felt doubly guilty for having asked him to wait.

Grandmother's death came as a shock to us. We felt she would have lived for several more years with proper nutrition and medical attention. We blamed her death on Angka.

Most of us were allowed to attend Grandmother's simple funeral, but Mearadey was expecting her third child any day and couldn't walk that far. She was despondent about missing the funeral and the rare opportunity to see relatives.

Mearadey was also dispirited about the impending birth. She worried about the unborn child's health, since her own diet was poor, and she hadn't been seen by a medical doctor during the entire pregnancy. Accustomed to modern medical facilities and practices, Mearadey was apprehensive about giving birth in the old high school where Keang once taught. It had been turned into a crude, though fairly clean, hospital. There was no trained medical staff to handle emergencies, little or no medication was available, and equipment was almost nonexistent. Babies slept with their mothers on the same cot or bamboo mat.

Mearadey's baby was born on February 16, just one week

after Grandmother died. Refusing to trust the Khmer Rouge doctors, she resorted to folk birth practices, on the chance that some might work. Old villagers told Mearadey that it was especially important to appease local ghosts and spirits at the time of a birth or illness, when a person was particularly vulnerable. Certain chants and potions were recommended by the *krou* Khmer, and threads were tied about the new baby's tiny wrists and ankles to keep her spirit in her body.

Keang had little faith in such practices, and secretly traded a gold necklace for tetracycline to safeguard his wife and infant daughter. Our bartered goods bought extra food for Mearadey, to help insure the infant's milk supply, but the baby was so small and frail that we were almost afraid to love her too much.

Babies died needlessly in Khum Speu, though Angka encouraged the production of new workers for the new society. Little allowance was made for children's needs, and without proper nutrition and nurturing, even the strongest weren't really healthy.

Keang and Mearadey named the baby Chenda, her cousin's name, meaning "cute." Her second name, Peach, means "diamond," indicating how precious she was to us despite the unhappy circumstances into which she was born and the extra work she would cause her already exhausted mother.

With the approach of summer, after Mearadey had returned to work, food reserves again dwindled and relocations were once more ordered. Many new people were trucked into Speu District from the eastern shore of the Mekong to get them out of the path of the skirmishes between the Communist Khmer Rouge and the Communist forces of the Vietnamese.

Tevi stumbled into her parents' hut one morning just before dawn, eyes filled with terror. Her teacher, a leader and a former student of Keang's, was dying. He was a kind, idealistic young man who had joined the Communists four years before with a desire to build a new, more just Cambodia. He was from the moderate Khmer Rouge faction and abhorred the violence of the leaders' policies. Those in power who followed a hard line had no use for his kind; he became a victim of the leadership purges.

While talking to his young crew the previous evening, he had been issued a summons to see Angka the following day. He feared that if he left with the soldiers the next morning, he would never return, so at night, while the village slept, he escaped.

A few hours later, he had returned and called the children to him. For him, running was not the answer: "I won't be in this world anymore. You must stay and work hard and study. You must help rebuild Cambodia. . . . Though you must follow, don't respect those who come to replace me and the other moderates. . . . Be careful. Be good. Do not cause trouble or you will be killed. . . . Good-bye, my children." Then he had gone to his hut alone and taken poison. Now he lay dying.

Keang ran to the hut and was with his former student when he died. Quickly and privately, Keang washed and prepared his body in the customary Buddhist fashion. The young man had been kind to Tevi and made life in the village easier in many ways for Keang's family. Keang slipped from the death chamber and returned to his own hut before the leaders knew the man was dead.

In mid-July, Si Ton paid me a second surprise visit, this time at a dam site. He was excited to report that his family was being relocated. All new people from Svai Teeup plus a surprising number of old-time residents were to get better housing. Si Ton and his family felt fortunate to be included, especially since Uncle Suoheang's family had not received such an invitation. Only one of Uncle Suoheang's married daughters and her three children had been listed in the order to relocate. She had registered as a widow, to keep the Communists from learning she had a husband who had gone to America for military training and had been unable to return after the fall of Phnom Penh. She looked forward to better housing for herself and her children.

Si Ton was in a great hurry. He had to be back in time to meet the trucks, due later that day. He wanted me to join him in relocating. Leaders from both villages had agreed to his request. However, since we weren't married, my mother would not be allowed to accompany us. I wanted to go, yet I could not leave Mum alone. I felt torn.

My crew leader suggested that instead of going with his family, Si Ton could request permission to move to West Speu, but he rejected that idea. It would mean deserting his father. Reluctantly, I decided against joining Si Ton until we were wed.

Disheartened, we once more agreed to part. We promised to try to contact each other to arrange a new date, perhaps during the next harvest season, or whenever the authorities might allow. In the meantime, we could compare notes about his village and West Speu before deciding which one to settle in. Sadly, we said good-bye.

A few days later, I received a short, tender letter from Si Ton written moments before he left Svai Teeup. He'd sent the note by a trusted friend who routinely ran errands to West Khum Speu.

Si Ton's sadness at our parting was evident. He wished I was with him and felt sorry life was so hard for me. I was touched by his concern, and frustrated that our plans to marry had been thwarted so often.

I learned much later that Si Ton's group, after waiting impatiently all afternoon for transportation, had been told that, since they were being moved such a short distance, it would be faster to walk to the new village by way of a back trail, through an old plantation. Excitedly, they set off.

The trail wound past a reservoir swollen with the season's heavy rains. Dense groves of neglected cashew nut trees ringed the pond. Men in a nearby work crew listlessly tilled the muddy fields and watched with envy as their excited fellow villagers went down the path toward their new homes.

Four loudspeakers played a military march that resounded through the grove as Si Ton and the others hurried through the trees. Ordinarily, villagers were not allowed inside the cashew plantation. Posted around the perimeter were black-and-white signs, with an *X* superimposed over a skull.

Near the loudspeakers, a registration table had been set up. One by one, people trotted down the shaded path after registering, not even waiting for other family members to sign in. The officer in charge urged everyone to hurry before darkness fell, and they did. As each person rounded a sharp bend in the narrow trail, death fell with the dull thud of a wooden hoe.

The bodies were pushed noiselessly into the blackness of the pond. If the soldiers, who were assigned the fiendish task of clubbing the startled villagers, failed to deal a death blow, the victims would surely drown before consciousness returned.

The last eager villager registered, by the light of a full moon, shortly after 8:00 P.M. Then the officers folded their papers and returned to *srok* headquarters; the loudspeakers were dismantled and brought back to the village; and three very drunk young soldiers—propped against their blood-splattered hoes—sat under the cashew trees and sobbed. The startled workers filed slowly past them on the way home for a late supper.

Chapter Nine

A week after Si Ton left, Keang was ordered to Po Preng prison in East Speu. The date was July 21, 1977.

Though racked with grief, Mearadey and the children looked on with impassive faces when Keang and twenty-six other former Phnom Penh residents were led away. Angka reasoned that no one should feel sorry when a "traitor" was taken. Tears were construed as disapproval of the decision and thus of the regime. To look on with a blank face was a cruel thing to expect of a wife, when she knew that no man sent to Po Preng had ever returned. Men usually remained there for a few days, then disappeared. Mearadey had heard the whispered rumors that the sacred forest behind the prison was where prisoners were clubbed to death as they knelt before an open trench.

Mearadey could not focus on her work during the day and could barely meet the needs of six-year-old Moni and five-month-old Chenda Peach at night. In her mind's eye, she kept seeing Keang, face down in the mud of an open, rain-flooded trench, with his body bloated and his head split open.

I knew nothing of his arrest until my work crew was moved from the dam site to a rice field closer to Khum Speu— a field where Soorsdey's crew also worked, after she and Samol had been moved to another village. Soorsdey's crew was allowed to go back to their village each night because they were married women. This gave her a chance to check on Mum on her way to and from work. Mum told her the awful news of Keang's arrest, and she told me the next day when we met in the fields.

That same week, two friends and I were ordered to gather our things and report to the village. Our families were to be relocated and, until the move, we were assigned work in Khum Speu. Surprised but pleased to be selected for housing, we trotted down the muddy road to the village, chatting happily about our good fortune.

On July 29, we were told that the trucks would arrive the next day to move us. That same evening, Mearadey glanced up from feeding Chenda when a shadow darkened the room. Staring in disbelief, she thought she saw Keang standing in the doorway, his back to the fading light of evening. Overcome with joy, unable to speak, she touched his face to be sure he was not a ghost. He was the only man we ever heard of who returned from that prison.

He'd been interrogated many times during the week he was in jail. On the day of his release, Keang was questioned for four hours by the *srok* leader, who came specifically to interrogate those jailed. Keang told the man that he did not object to the Communists. He had no ill will toward them, and he'd worked hard for them for over two years. He had dutifully read Mao's and Lenin's works and acknowledged that they contained some words of wisdom. The leader asked if Keang was afraid.

Keang answered honestly that, of course, he was afraid, though he did not know why he had been imprisoned. He had done nothing against the Khmer Rouge. He also told the interrogator that many young leaders in the district had been his former high school students, and they could truthfully report that he had never taught against the regime.

The leader replied, "Don't be afraid anymore. Tonight we will get you home."

Keang didn't believe him—it was too much to hope for. But that evening the leader gave him a ride home. Still, Keang and Mearadey thought Keang would eventually be killed—the Communists were good at building false hope. He felt he was living on borrowed time, but knew of no way to extend it. Escape was impossible and would only endanger his family further. He went back to work the next day, just waiting and wondering when and how he would meet death.

Keang never learned the reason for his unique release, but made a number of educated guesses, using scraps of information later assembled. At the interrogation, he'd had to admit that he had more education than most country schoolteachers. He did not divulge his work with the Ministry of Information, however. He'd proved to be a diligent worker, and he'd never caused any trouble, so he hoped his education would not be held against him. He was liked by those in village leadership, but he knew that was not enough to explain his release. Many others who died could have made the same claims.

Searching deeper, Keang felt the *srok* interrogator was the key to his release, but did not know why the man had intervened. The interrogator had been a teacher before joining the Khmer Rouge. Perhaps he had a soft spot in his heart for another former teacher, or thought Keang had the potential for eventual leadership that could be useful to Angka Loeu.

In an impromptu family council, Keang and Mearadey decided to request permission to join us in our move; otherwise, my mother would be left alone while I was away on lengthy work assignments. If they were allowed to move with us, Mum could continue to watch Moni and Chenda, and Keang was most anxious to leave the district. He hoped his whereabouts would be lost to the *srok* leader in the midst of all the relocations.

Since others had been given permission to join loved ones, we were optimistic in making the request. When the village

139

leader said no, Mearadey did something unheard of: she begged him to reconsider. Tears in her eyes, she pleaded.

He hesitated. "No," he finally concluded, "it is not possible. You must stay, and Comrades Ean and Da must go."

He let it slip that he had orders to keep Keang in the district.

We felt sick—Keang's release must indeed be a trap. He would be sent for again. We could think of no other reason the *srok* leader would give such a directive. Meanwhile, the village chief assigned Keang and his family to Tra Pang Sral village. They were to move in two days. We left the chief's hut in utter confusion. Why Tra Pang Sral?

Tiny Tra Pang Sral was where Samol and Soorsdey had been sent. Mearadey was pleased to be moving near her sister —if they were really to move.

Although Mum and I were discouraged by the chief's refusal to let Keang and Mearadey join us, and sorry to be separating from the rest of the family, nonetheless, we were as excited as the other villagers that our turn had finally come to leave the muddy hut where we had known such hardship. It was reported that the recently constructed new village had large, substantial huts and new furnishings.

We spent what remained of the evening making bundles of things not needed in our new home. We gave these to Mearadey and Soorsdey and secretly moved Keang's radio, our valuables, and our soggy riels to Soorsdey's hut in Tra Pang Sral. We hid what remained of Mum's gold belt and some other jewelry in our own bundles.

By morning, Mum and I had decided to make a different request—could we go instead to Tra Pang Sral, too? We would willingly give up a chance for a better hut just to remain with the family, and there was no lack of volunteers to take our place. Many villagers had been told they'd have to wait another season until more housing was available.

Begging favors was hazardous. I feared the leader's wrath, and I feared our fate if we remained, because Keang's "move" might prove to be just a lie. Still, we had to ask.

While we sat in the chief's home, making this last-minute plea, we saw neighbors, laden with bundles, hurrying toward the village square. Relatives from nearby villages had been allowed time from work to give loved ones a proper send-off, and there was a festive air as they and friends rejoiced at the good luck of those who had been chosen.

I heard trucks enter the village while Mum and I anxiously awaited the leader's decision. Wiping sweat from his brow, he paced in concentrated silence. There was no time to consult with *srok* headquarters; he'd have to make his own decision, and suffer the consequences if it was wrong. I knew he felt pressured and confused. He liked me; I was a hard worker, but he did not especially like my mother, whom he considered a complainer. Among other things, Mum had made it plain to him that she resented being called by her first name; it showed a lack of respect.

He was in a quandary, not knowing if the *srok* leader meant to include Mum and me as part of Keang's family in his orders not to move Keang. He finally denied our request—the safest route open to him. He decided we qualified as a separate family group. We must relocate.

Downcast, we left his hut, knowing we'd have to hurry to be ready on time. We rushed to our little home, collected our bundles, and hastened toward the dining pavilion as fast as Mum could shuffle. Breathless, we arrived at the edge of the crowd of well-wishers just as the tailgate slammed in place on the last truck. The vehicles were filled with people wedged in so tightly that there was little room for anyone else.

Pausing at the edge of the square, trying to decide what to do, I caught our leader's eye. He shrugged his shoulders, then made a slight motion of his head toward our hut and a gesture with his hand, as though brushing away flies. As he turned away, I had my first inkling that leaving on the crowded trucks might not be wise. We returned quietly to our hut.

That afternoon, the chief stopped by and said to me, "Comrade Da, if anyone ever asks why you weren't on those trucks, say that they were too full."

I too resented his familiarity in using my nickname— something never done outside family circles. Teeda was considered too pretty a name; most Khmer Rouge names were one syllable.

Two girls on the trucks were dear friends. I expected eventually to get some word from them about life in the new village. Though there was no mail service and movement was severely limited, people had worked out a fairly effective though slow system of secretly sending notes via friends with errands to other villages. Given enough time, most messages eventually reached the intended receivers. Impatiently, I waited to learn from my friends and Si Ton what I had missed by failing to join them.

A weeks later, an old villager, whose story I tried to discount, said that he and two friends had made an unauthorized foray into one of the huge, abandoned colonial plantations, looking for green bananas, when they arrived at a place with an awful stench. Afraid to look, they ran in the opposite direction, only to stumble on a fresh site of executions at a well.

Bodies had been crammed into the well, and more littered the ground. Aghast, the men saw a baby who died as they watched. One woman wore a beautiful shawl that fell apart in the men's hands. They decided these people had been gassed, since other clothing also fell apart when they touched it. They saw no blood and concluded the poison that killed the people had damaged the material as well. Panicked by their discovery, and fearing for their lives, they ran. The old man whispered that he now knew why the miles and miles of old plantations lining Highway 21 were off limits.

I heard a few other such stories, but my first personal exposure came a short time later when my crew was clearing the jungle. We saw a foot sticking out of a mound of dirt, and were immediately ordered to another area.

I was staggered by the scene. Who were these people? What had been their crime?

From other districts, whispered reports began filtering into Speu of body-filled wells, trenches, and reservoirs. Some of the "canals" we'd dug had not been canals at all. Some ill-conceived dams had been put to another use. Still, we wanted to believe that these were isolated incidents, that some explanation would be forthcoming.

In early September, surplus clothing was distributed by Angka to our village. When the bundles were carelessly dumped in the square, I was shocked to see my friend's favorite tunic. I knew the girl would never willingly part with it, old and faded though it was. I also knew I wasn't mistaken. The smock had once been a bright peacock-blue dress with a skirt too long and sleeves too short to be practical. My friend had cut the bottom off the knit dress and whip-stitched the material to each sleeve. With leftover material she'd sewn two huge pockets to the dress front. She then had a practical, though unglamorous, long-sleeved tunic to top her baggy, black trousers. Since it had been her only long-sleeved outfit, she wore it constantly.

Other people also recognized it and identified things that had belonged to other residents. In unison, we made the horrible connection between the whispered rumors and these clothes, between the clothes and the communal graves we'd stumbled upon.

Stunned, we could no longer deny the evidence before us regarding the fate of our neighbors. No leader even dared offer some other explanation for the clothes piled at our feet. In numbed silence, villagers and leaders alike melted from the square.

Village leaders, as ignorant of motives as the rest of us, had merely been told to identify family members whose husbands and fathers had previously been reassigned. If the village quota for new housing allotments was still not filled, they were to select men and their families whose activities or ancestry matched the descriptions on a currently circulated list; included were those with Vietnamese-sounding names, and former Phnom Penh residents (especially if they also had light skin, since ethnic Vietnamese, who had formed much of the technological work force in Cambodia, had lighter skin tones than the average full-blooded Cambodian). Kept in ignorance of the growing threat Vietnam posed to Angka, we didn't question why these people were being moved.

Dissatisfied with our makeshift huts, people were anxious to qualify for better housing. Some even volunteered information about themselves to prove they belonged to the favored groups allowed to move. Over three million took part in this migration.

In the past, people had become suspicious of the calls for workers, since most men failed to return. We had concluded that such calls were often a ruse to permanently remove selected individuals. However, this new resettlement call for entire families was viewed differently; it matched our expectations for a return to normality. Conditions had to be better in newly constructed villages, we'd reasoned. Perhaps families would be reunited with missing fathers and husbands after all. Tossed a crumb of hope, we built a feast of optimism.

Close friends and relatives, who did not want to be separated from each other, had timidly asked to be allowed to resettle with those who had been called to transfer. To our surprise, many had been allowed to leave. Most of us jumped to the conclusion that this new leniency must be a turning point toward a decrease in arbitrary rule.

At last, Angka seemed concerned with the desires of the people. Those who had moved once were the most anxious to move again. Life had improved when they'd been relocated to Khum Speu District from their villages near the Vietnamese border, so it was easy to convince them that the next move would be even better. Their enthusiasm was contagious—they would soon be in fine homes and reunited with loved ones. Told to leave bulky household possessions behind, since the new villages had everything provided, those who qualified had willingly lined up to board the waiting vehicles with only a few personal belongings.

Ox carts, trucks, and buses arrived on the appointed day in each village; the average-sized truck held about eighty people. Each vehicle filled rapidly and pulled out of village squares amid tears and cheering.

Typically, a few miles from the village, the vehicles stopped along a tree-lined road. Greeted by stirring music, blaring from loudspeakers, people eagerly piled out of the trucks and lined up to register. A handful of soldiers escorted the women and children, a few at a time, down the winding forest paths or through the abandoned rubber plantations. Hurrying behind the soldiers, excited villagers wondered aloud about their new village.

Upon arrival in the clearing, they hesitated, then tried to retreat. Before them gaped newly dug trenches, an abandoned reservoir, a well, or an old mine shaft. Horrified, villagers were ordered at gunpoint to line up. Their elbows were tied behind their backs with red cord and they were made to kneel along the open trench. Dumbfounded, most obeyed without complaint or struggle. Soldiers administered a quick blow to the back of the head or neck with a heavy wooden hoe or a machete. Each soldier was able to kill villagers at the rate of twenty to thirty per

145

minute with little noise or wasted bullets. The red parachute cords were retrieved for future use.

After the women and children were dispatched, their husbands and fathers were ushered into the clearings. Seeing their massacred loved ones, their own will to live weakened. Most submitted in mute silence, kneeled, and were clubbed.

The worst deaths were reserved for royalty, former leaders, pilots, and those who attempted to run away; their jugular veins were severed with the serrated edges of old palm fronds. In isolated incidents, some victims were first tortured, babies were torn limb from limb and pregnant women had their stomachs slit open. But in general it took about fifteen minutes to unload and dispatch each truckload of victims. Then the next truck arrived and dumped its human contents to be "registered" and slaughtered.

Thousands upon thousands upon thousands of Cambodians filed into the plantations. Only soldiers returned. These special soldiers, with the assignment to kill, moved efficiently from area to area. They were always in a hurry; their trucks were always due at still another village.

During French colonial rule, hundreds of exploratory mine shafts had been sunk on the plantations as men searched for gemstones. These old shafts were over one hundred feet deep; the bottom could not be seen from the upper edge. Truckload after truckload of victims was dumped into each shaft. When soldiers finished, the shafts, reservoirs, and wells of Cambodia were full.

In the region between the Mekong and Vietnam, people were less often dumped into reservoirs or shafts. Ordered to relocate to the west, they were loaded onto small boats in groups of ten or twelve, ferried to the middle of the river, or around a bend, clubbed and shoved overboard. Villagers downstream were told that the Vietnamese were responsible for the bloated bodies that lined the banks. However, a few victims lived to tell what really happened, just as survivors in our area did.

Throughout the land, this grisly scene was repeated from harvesttime until well into the rainy season, but in any one area, the "killing time" lasted only a week or two. Mass murder in Khum Speu, and most other areas, took place during the wet monsoon.

Eventually, we would learn that each July had been a variation of this same pattern. In 1975, our first July under the Khmer Rouge, high-ranking government officials, army officers, big businessmen, and outspoken villagers were taken away, to "build dams and reservoirs" or to be "reeducated." The following July, any known government employees and soldiers, plus the educated and affluent men, were taken. In July of 1977, families of those formerly taken, plus the Vietnamese, were ordered to relocate. The circle kept expanding. As "July" and "slaughter" became synonymous, we referred to July as "the killing season."

At first, when entire families "relocated," there was less suspicion or resistance to the move, and it was easier to keep the secret of the murders. During the wet monsoon, the Khmer Rouge's ongoing war with the Vietnamese slowed, so Angka was able to concentrate on disposing of its internal enemies. When the mass graves were finally discovered, the justification given us by Angka for killing women and children was that anyone associated with a "guilty person" was tainted.

Keang had information that eventually everyone over the age of twelve at the time of the takeover was ultimately scheduled to be killed—excepting, of course, top leaders. Then there would be left only pliable youth who did not remember the former way of life and had no training or ability to organize resistance against Angka and its plans for a "perfect society."

Just as the Children of Israel were not allowed into the Promised Land until all the older generation (steeped in the ways of the gods of Egypt) were dead, so, too, the hierarchy seemed determined to reconstruct Cambodia with only those

147

untainted by the past. The Khmer Rouge, however, didn't wait for the older generation to die naturally.

These "moves" affected my family in many ways—mostly with tragic consequences.

Mum's brother (the outspoken farmer) and his family were told in early July that Angka wanted to see them. His prosperous farm had been confiscated six years before, and he had been forced to work as a common laborer in a nearby soap factory. He'd once reported with disdain to my mother that in the factory they burned beautiful, expensive hardwoods—wood formerly exported for quality furniture construction. What a waste, to fire soap vats with valuable wood when ample scrubwood abounded. He also resented making soap from coconut oil when people were starving.

My uncle had been one old villager unafraid to speak his mind. We never learned what triggered the request for his family to see Angka. However, his partiality to America was well known and he was critical of many Khmer Rouge farming practices. Two of his eight children were married, and thus not included in the call, but my uncle, his wife, and six of their children were. All eight died.

Leng's mother and sister-in-law were also "relocated" during the killing time of 1977. Leng had lost track of his mother when Phnom Penh fell. Over a year later, she and her widowed daughter-in-law and her grandchildren had been moved to a village not far from Prey Tayo. She knew that Rasmei's relatives were from the Speu area, and through repeated inquiries had finally learned where Leng and Rasmei lived.

Leng managed to see his mother only once. With sorrow, he learned that one brother had been executed; he'd been a captain in Lon Nol's army. He would never learn the fate of his second brother.

Everyone in his mother's village was killed in the July relocations. *Everyone.*

Through a fortuitous intervention, these "relocations" bypassed Leng and Rasmei. Life under the Khmer Rouge had been particularly difficult for them. Not only had they been separated from the rest of us, and forced to settle across the highway, but Rasmei, unlike most married women, was often away from the village for four or five months at a time working as a laborer on a major earthen dam project.

Leng had come to the attention of his village chief as a particularly diligent worker. Even though the chief was illiterate, he did not feel threatened by clever people, and was happy to make use of their skills. The leader did not want to lose Leng to another village, so when the time came to relocate half of his villagers, he did not select Leng's family, though they matched the city-bred, educated, light-skinned description of those wanted.

It was only a few weeks later that Leng's distraught leader learned the awful truth: the 150 people he'd selected for transfer had been sent to their deaths. Logically, Leng's family should have been part of that "transfer," so it was only a matter of time before they, too, would be ordered to relocate.

As we later learned, some people actually did move to better housing; some "relocations" wiped out entire villages, while others were bypassed. Leng's village, though smaller than average, was typical in that approximately half the villagers were killed. From the ten villages in his district, at least fifteen hundred to two thousand people were killed in 1977. Most districts were much larger, so as many as fifteen thousand to twenty thousand were killed per *srok*, and there were many *srok*s in each of the country's twenty-two provinces—all with similar death tolls.

Throughout Cambodia, the stench of death filled the air. Like wildfire, the news leaped from district to district. Reports flashed back and forth across the land, whispered over the human telegraph system: genocide.

Chapter Ten

There is a human tendency to believe that nothing really bad can happen to you—to the other person, perhaps, but not to you and your family, particularly when you've done nothing wrong. When the relocation orders came, former city residents had even felt that their superiority over old villagers was at last being acknowledged. Everyone had cited instances of actual relocations, reassuring themselves that it was a common Communist practice. So, like sheep, we had willingly, happily, assembled in town squares throughout the nation, and impatiently waited for trucks or ox carts to haul us away.

As the magnitude of the slaughter became known, a deep depression overtook me and I questioned my own survival. I, too, would be moldering in the pond if I had joined Si Ton. My clothes, too, would have been part of the mound dumped in West Speu had Mum and I joined my friends. It seemed such an ugly twist of fate that Si Ton, coming from a less prominent family, should be a corpse in a reeking reservoir, yet I lived. No wonder the chief had not dared move Keang from the district against orders.

I had no explanation for being alive except for the leader's lingering doubts about Mum and me being part of Keang's family. Mum was grateful—not for her life, but for mine. She immediately set up her little shrine again in the back of the hut to offer thanks.

I could not bring myself to pray, could not bring myself to believe that it would be possible to continue to remain alive; not when, one by one, my close friends with less prominent fathers were killed with their families. Loved ones on every side had been murdered. Those death trucks had been meant for Mum and me! Angka was stalking us. What was our crime?

A black shroud of speechless horror enveloped me as piece after gruesome piece of evidence accrued. Suspicion. Distrust. Gut-twisting terror. Each person clutched his thoughts more tightly to himself. Everyone worked harder. We dared not complain. We had never before felt so totally beaten, so much like slaves at the mercy of diabolical masters. Each time we had told ourselves it could not get worse, but it had. Like walking dead men, we waited our turns in mute silence. Any person or event out of the ordinary filled us with panic.

Like repeated blows of a hammer, I learned almost daily of the death of yet another relative or close friend, and of the nonexistent new villages where they had supposedly gone. Silently, I berated myself, tortured myself, for being so gullible. *Why* had I allowed myself to believe the lies? Would I *never* learn?

My mind returned again and again to the deaths of loved ones. My fiancé and his whole family were dead; only one brother, studying in Paris, had been spared. Papa was surely dead. Leng's brother and sister-in-law and their two children were dead. Leng's mother was dead. His other brother was probably dead. Grandmother was dead. Mum's brother, his wife, and six children were dead. Uncle Suoheang's daughter and her three children were dead. Many other relatives were dead. My two best friends were dead. No doubt even Blacky and Brownie had long ago starved or been shot. Everywhere I turned there was death.

I mourned for the murder of my fiancé and the marriage that would never be. How flimsy had been the cloak of protection in which I'd smugly wrapped myself as his bride-to-be. How suddenly it had been torn away.

All of Uncle Ban's children had been outstanding students. Now, except for my cousin in Paris, all eight children and their parents were dead or missing.[*]

Up to the time of the first harvests, men had been punished for acts of rebellion, real or suspected, or eliminated because they had held positions in the former government. We had thought oppressive measures would diminish once former officials had been identified, rooted out, and removed, as Papa had been. Despite the frightening slogans and the continued harsh treatment, we had not fully grasped that the lives of this generation did not matter; what mattered was Angka Loeu's "plan" and the future utopian society of which its leaders dreamed. To Angka, we *were* just grains of rice. Insignificant.

Cambodia, we were instructed, could still renew itself, even if all but two Cambodians were destroyed, as long as those two were not contaminated. In bitterness, some whispered that the killings would stop only when Pol Pot and his wife, Khieu Ponnary, were left as the "two uncontaminated Cambodians."

I could not shake the dread I felt every time a soldier or a *srok* leader entered the village. It could only mean trouble for someone. Keang's mentor was dead, himself a victim of the purge. Would Keang again be summoned by Angka? Would explanations be demanded from Mum and me about our failure to relocate? Surely someone would question Leng's continued

---

[*]Si Ton's mother and his four missing sisters had been sent to Battambang Province. After three years of Khmer Rouge control, his mother and one sister died of starvation and illness within hours of each other. Si Ton's three other sisters had married in Battambang and had children. Their husbands had been executed by Pol Pot's soldiers.

presence in Prey Tayo. From one quarter or another, we were sure death would strike.

Before 1977, Keang had held out some hope for the future. Surely the day would come when the leaders would feel secure enough to return some trappings of civilization to the masses. None of us even remotely believed that any longer. None, it was clear, would live to see that day.

Slogans took on new meaning when the incredible plans of Angka to wipe out not only the past, but most of the people from that past, became apparent. If someone complained about conditions, he was curtly told, "To destroy you is no loss."

The message was now chillingly clear. Complaints ceased; we had a claim on nothing, not even life.

Hungry people wanting more food were told to "ask Angka."

"Who is Angka Loeu?"

"Why, the people, of course! It is everyone; it is you. Go ask yourself."

At the nightly meetings there were many analogies to common trees. We were told, "If you are wise, you will plant a hedge of *kor* trees around your hut." Everyone knew this play on words meant that if we wanted to live, it would be well to insulate ourselves with a wall of silence.

Another tree invoked was the banyan. This large tree is subject to disease. If decay is noticed in time, it can be scraped away, leaving the good wood to develop into a full-sized trunk again. But if the diseased part is not cut away, the tree weakens and dies.

Leaders justified destruction of "diseased elements" of the old society, even the killing of people touched by those diseased elements—their families. We were told repeatedly that in order to save the country, it was essential to destroy all the contaminated parts. Society would again become viable only when all corrupting influences were cut out. It was essential to cut deep, even to destroy a few good people, rather than chance one "diseased" person escaping eradication.

Rather than slowing down, each year the purges and paranoia had spread to encompass more and more people in ever-widening circles. There seemed to be no end to those who could be considered an enemy of Angka Loeu; no end to those who might add their spilt blood to Angka's expanding, crimson pool.

The national anthem of Democratic Kampuchea, sung at each nightly meeting, was meant to stir us to increased efforts, dedication, pride, loyalty. Instead, it took on a macabre new meaning and filled me with revulsion.

Bright red Blood which covers towns and plains
Of Kampuchea, our motherland,
Sublime Blood of workers and peasants,
Sublime Blood of revolutionary men and women fighters!

The Blood changing into unrelenting hatred
And resolute struggle . . .

Chapter Eleven

After September of 1977, we could still be killed at will, but we would no longer go blindly to our deaths. The mere sight of a palm-frond saw caused apprehension, and no one wanted to work at any plantation, though, of course, we did as we were told. Despite our growing awareness, Angka found ways to fool us, at least for a while.

Routinely, work crews had been subdivided during the day, so it caused no alarm initially when one or two workers were ordered to go to the next field, or to fetch a stack of bamboo from the jungle. At the same time, other leaders sent a few workers to a nearby project. None were ever seen again. Comparing notes later, we realized that all those who failed to return had belonged to one or two families. After that, we left our crew only with reluctance, though we obeyed—just as we obeyed all commands.

Early in January 1978, soldiers approached my crew. The girl who was ordered to go with them was a distant relative of the royal family; her prominent father had already been killed. Terror filled her eyes, upon learning that she, her mother, and five brothers and sisters were being moved. I bid her a brief good-bye and blinked back tears that would betray how much I cared for this sweet, quiet girl, and how frightened I was for her.

A few days later, a vulgar former monk, who was now one of the district leaders, mentioned that a soldier had boasted drunkenly to him how five of them had raped my friend repeatedly until she died. The soldiers could have been executed for their foul deed, but no one dared report them. The fact that Angka's strict sexual-conduct code could be flouted and discussed openly shocked me.

During a work break, three girls and I sat in the middle of a field, to converse without danger of being overheard—a defensive practice common during the Pol Pot years. We vowed to kill ourselves rather than be subjected to rape followed by sure death. From then on, we each kept in our pockets a handful of *sleng* seeds or small vials of insecticide concentrate.

Wanting to make sure the poison would kill, not just make us sick, I poured one drop on a worm. Stiffening, it turned black and looked like a shriveled twig. The poison would do.

Working day and night, living in continual terror, knowing I would be killed sometime, but not knowing when or how, was worse than death. Life was of no use to me. It only benefited the Khmer Rouge, and I often considered swallowing the poison. Yet its mere possession gave me some sense of control over my life. For the half year since I learned of the mass murders, I had dwelt on death, especially death that would not look like suicide. My friend's horrible fate reinforced my depression.

I can't bend anymore, I told myself. This storm is too fierce. It lasts too long. I just can't bend anymore! I'm not bamboo.

For weeks after my friend's tragic end, and my own decision to poison myself if the need arose, I could not cast off a sense of impending doom. The murder of Si Ton and my other relatives continued to haunt me. I felt dead inside, and found myself fingering the little bottle several times a day.

Then, unexpectedly, on my way to the rice fields one morning, I glanced up, just as the sun rose over the paddies. The sheer beauty of heavy ripening rice silhouetted against the glorious orange sky took my breath away. A massive, plodding buffalo moved across the scene, giving a sense of the continuity of life from former times to now—an instant lesson in patience and perseverance. All nature affirmed that some things were beyond Angka Loeu's power to control. Neither sunrise nor storm, neither cloud nor wind nor bamboo, nor I, would be controlled by Angka. Angka Loeu was not omnipotent. I felt—for the first time in months—that life might still hold something worthwhile.

I realized I could no more cease to fight for life than I could will my mind to remain in neutral. This knowledge lifted my spirits. This newfound hope was reinforced a few days later when my village leader was ordered to shift some people to Tra Pang Sral, and Mum and I were among those chosen to fill the quota. In April of 1978, we moved into Keang and Mearadey's crowded hut during the Victory Day celebrations.

I hadn't seen Mearadey's baby for several months, and was shocked to see how frail she was. Chenda Peach surveyed us suspiciously with solemn eyes, from the safety of her mother's lap. She had refused to take comfort from anyone but her parents after they left Khum Speu nine months before. Instead, she had lain whimpering listlessly in the grass by their hut each day while Mearadey worked in distant fields. Concern for this nearly starving child tore at our hearts. She screamed whenever I came near, but within a few days, my mother was able to win her affection once more. I continued to be away on work details too often to be considered a friend.

Despite Chenda's reserve, we had a joyful three-day holiday before we began work in this new village. We didn't even bother to go to the annual victory celebrations in *Srok* Chamka Lear.

Other years, some of us had walked the ten miles to our *srok* headquarters village for the festivities. Mum couldn't walk that far, so she had never gone. However, most people went to Chamka Lear if they could. There were no parades or fireworks —just speeches and patriotic songs. Even folk dancing had been dropped as an unnecessary waste of energy. But there was extra rice and a little meat, and it was on these occasions that we were allowed to mix freely with villagers from other districts in our *srok*. At these yearly holidays, we learned of our relatives' marriages, and births, and deaths.

A year before, at the *srok* celebrations, a new holiday schedule had been greeted with enthusiasm. We were to work nine days and have every tenth day free. That routine had lasted only six months. Technically, it was still allowed, just never observed. Leaders "donated" those leisure days in the name of their villagers to help fill production quotas. Though we resented it, no one dared complain or refused to work. Radio Phnom Penh regularly broadcast announcements about villages throughout the country that made similar "gifts" of work or donated rice, or of districts that "volunteered" to go hungry in order to build the nation.

After the 1978 celebration, I was assigned to work with the older women in my new village, until the girls returned from a project. One woman in the crew was a middle-aged widow named Satah, whom we had met two years before when Soorsdey and Samol married. Her half sister had married in the same ceremony but was killed a year later.

The widow Satah had been moved to Tra Pang Sral just before the killing season of 1977. We never learned why the vehicles hadn't gone there, but they stopped coming to our district after they left West Khum Speu the day I had barely missed inclusion. Perhaps they had deadlines to meet elsewhere. Perhaps enough victims had been sacrificed for the season, or people had become too suspicious and likely to resist. Perhaps the soldiers had been needed to fight the Vietnamese.

Whatever the reason, Satah had been spared, though she was not well liked by the leaders because she complained about

158

conditions. Satah had grown up in a wealthy, polygamous family, and her husband had been a rich railroad executive. He, like my father, had been detained at a river crossing, his elbows tied behind his back with a red cord.

Two half sisters had traveled from Phnom Penh with Satah and her son, Nye. Also in the traveling party had been a distant relative, Mey Kamphot, and a half brother's teenaged sons, Vitou and Sarakun. The two boys had lived in Satah's home off and on ever since their parents divorced when they were young. Because the young men and her son were near my age, she often told me about them.

After her husband's detention, Satah had decided to proceed to his ancestral village to await his return just as we had done, but she and her family had been less wary: they had gladly accepted a truck ride when local leaders offered to drop them off near their destination.

Instead of turning right onto Highway 7 at Skoun, as promised, the trucks, filled with families of important detainees, had rattled north along Highway 6. No amount of protest had altered the direction. By midmorning, the vehicles halted at Phum Prey, and the drivers evasively claimed they had instructions to bring the 150 people to the old Buddhist temple complex. They knew nothing more. The empty trucks drove off, leaving behind a bewildered, anxious crowd.

Satah had no intention of remaining to see what was in store for them. She had quietly arranged with a local farmer to take her family to Khum Speu District in his ox cart. At the end of one long day, they were safe in Bun Tear Chey village. All who had stayed at the temple died that day.

Satah had urged her nephews to live apart from the rest of the family, so they would not be identified with her "suspect" background. Having no other relatives in Bun Tear Chey, seventeen-year-old Vitou and sixteen-year-old Sarakun had built their own lean-to, and quickly blended into the local population.

Satah told me about her relatives during work breaks or

when she stopped by to visit my mother and me in the evenings. Soon she and Mum became good friends. Satah had spent the war years in California with some of her children who were students there. She fretted that there was no way to let them know she was alive. I loved to hear her descriptions of America, and to practice my almost-forgotten English, but we were careful that our conversations were never overheard.

In the course of our chats, we discovered several connections between our two families. Her nephew, Sarakun, had recently married my friend, Naly, from the Khum Speu girls' crew. Satah's relative Mey Kamphot was in Keang's crew, and their friendship developed as they worked together in the fields. A few weeks after my arrival, I met Satah's other half sister, Kunteara, in the girls' crew.

By the time I joined the girls' crew, there was a shortage of food, as there was every summer. This year, even the workers away from the villages were allotted only one cup of rice per day, so I was always hungry.

Tra Pang Sral was much smaller than the village I had just come from, and everyone ate in one dining hall. At times, only widows and children occupied the village. Seldom were more than half of the population of four hundred in residence at any one time. Most of us stayed there only between work assignments.

Late June of 1978 brought another short but intense killing season. Phnom Penh widows and their children disappeared at an alarming rate. Surprisingly, once again my family was bypassed. The fact that we were diligent workers who never caused trouble probably saved us.

There were marked changes in the killing pattern in 1978. Subtlety and subterfuge were less often evident in eliminating the unwanted citizens and hiding the evidence. Usually the murders were discovered within a few days. Not as many people disappeared at a time, but it was not uncommon for crew members to find bodies when walking to work through the paddies and overgrown nut groves, or when clearing land for new fields.

A major difference in the killing pattern was that village leaders and local guards now executed their own residents. Keang suspected the loyalty of local leaders was being tested, since they now knew the fate of those they had "relocated."

One day, five of us had been sent to a stream to bathe. When we saw two guards approaching, we were terrified. In work assignments, strict sexual segregation had always been maintained, with male and female crews bathing at different times or different places. We thought our moment to die had come. Not until the soldiers put down their guns and began stripping did we realize they were just girls who had come for nothing more sinister than a cool bath. Because people didn't always bother to undress to bathe, we might never have guessed their sex.

There was so little time to rest that we often just waded into the water and washed our clothes and ourselves at the same time, then fell exhausted onto the grass, and tried to sleep while we dried off.

In Tra Pang Sral, one of the more prosperous villages, every hut had its own well, but even with the luxury of our own water supply, there was never time or energy enough to keep our clothes or ourselves properly washed, or the huts really clean. When we returned from work, all we wanted to do was sleep until time for dinner and the evening meetings.

Seven of us shared Keang and Mearadey's one-room hut, which was even smaller than the one Mum and I had shared in West Speu. Though Tevi, and later Moni, were usually with the children's crew and I was often away, it was still crowded. Keang and Mearadey and their three children slept on the bed, the only piece of furniture. Mum and I slept on the floor. Bundles of clothes, cooking pots, and other objects were kept well hidden under the bed.

Under these crowded conditions, a husband and wife were

seldom alone. The lack of privacy and a perpetual state of near-exhaustion greatly hampered husband-wife relations. Nor was it safe for a couple to seek solitude in the forests, since they might be shot if found by the Khmer Rouge before they had time to explain themselves. Besides, people feared the woods. Unfriendly spirits, malaria-bearing mosquitoes, snakes, and other creatures made it an unattractive place for a tryst.

Contraceptives were not available—or necessary—under the Communists. Abstinence was the common form of birth control.

In June, when I was home between work assignments, I saw that Satah was upset. Her two nephews had been sent to a labor camp the month before and were lucky to still be alive. Sarakun had stolen a five-pound bag of rice so his bride wouldn't be hungry. Vitou, to lessen Sarakun's guilt, had assumed part of the blame. This saved them, because Vitou played an important role in his village. He and three others were full-time hunters for Bun Tear Chey during the summer months when rations were at their lowest. Their efforts supplemented the village's nearly exhausted food reserves, making it possible for this otherwise backward village to eat better than the rest of us.

In his hunting capacity, Vitou had won the respect of the village leaders, who depended on the young man's hunting exploits, and did not want one of their best hunters executed over a few pounds of rice. So, with repentant pleading on Vitou's part, he and his brother had been spared death.

Four months later, Satah was relieved to learn that Vitou's and Sarakun's brains had been adequately "reconstructed," and they were released from the plantation labor camp. Not only had they survived months of hard labor during the hottest, wettest season of the year, they had won the respect of their guards. Upon return to the village, Vitou was sent immediately to resume hunting, for what little remained of the wet season. Their aunt, however, feared both her nephews would soon be drafted.

The previous December, Chinese-backed Democratic Kampuchea officially broke diplomatic relations with Soviet-supported Vietnam, and the two nations had been in open conflict for the past nine months. Pol Pot's forces were battling for existence and were pressuring everyone available to join the cause. Even former city residents were wanted in the army.

A façade of invincibility had hidden the High Organization's troubles. But despite efforts to disguise it, that façade was at last crumbling. In a desperate bid to remain financially solvent, Angka initiated last-ditch economy measures. Food rations were cut further, offices ran on scraps of paper or recycled school notebooks, and even furnishings from Phnom Penh villas were sold to other countries to help pay for the war effort and buy weapons abroad.

Unable to correct shortcomings or provide us with urgently needed goods and services, Angka pretended the needs didn't exist, and continued to bombard us with slogans and ideological lectures attesting to the nation's strength and prosperity. Three times a day, broadcasts spewed out vilification of the outside world, especially Vietnam, and continued to boast of "gifts" of labor and rice donated by villagers.

During this time, Keang began picking up a few clues that all was not well with the High Organization. One was Prince Sihanouk's reemergence from "retirement" after a year's forced absence. His public appearances were aimed at gaining local, as well as international, support for the Khmer Rouge.

Peasants resettled from northeastern Cambodia brought tales of fierce fighting between the Vietnamese and the Red Khmer. Voice of America and BBC broadcasts reported border clashes with Vietnam, but these dispatches lacked firsthand information.

With no foreigners allowed in, and none of us allowed out, there was no way the world could know what we were suffering. The outside world was in almost total ignorance concerning what had been happening inside Cambodia during the four years since the fall. The atrocities were unknown. Accounts of the few escapees, who were city residents and Lon Nol supporters, had not been believed.

The West was finally beginning to take notice of our plight only because recent refugees from the mountain tribes were former supporters of the Khmer Rouge. These hill people were repeating the same stories of horror that had been told by earlier refugees.

The escape of these emaciated tribesmen graphically exposed Angka's failure to help the very people it claimed to have freed from the Republic's yoke of oppression. They had suffered even more than the new villagers. These stoic people had never required much from any government, but they had expected enough to eat, and freedom of movement. They had subsisted on a slash-and-burn form of agriculture. Under Pol Pot's reign of terror, the tribesmen were confined to one region, worked to exhaustion, starved, and brutalized.

The Phnom Penh broadcasts continued to report Angka's experiment with "pure" communism in glowing terms: flourishing schools, ample food, happiness and contentment, and high-yield, multiple rice crops.

Keang watched carefully for each indication of trouble in the government, for any crumb of rumor from people who had been moved from the war zone. Our family's survival depended on some break in Pol Pot's stranglehold on the country, but there was little in what Keang learned that offered any hope.

We felt we had barely survived the last killing season, and were sure we could never make it through another. Village by village, every new resident was being removed, no matter how loyal. Svai Teeup, Si Ton's old village, was the first in our area to be cleansed of all its "diseased elements" from the cities.

Shortly after his release from the labor camp, Satah's nephew Vitou and a hunting companion discovered a terrified woman from Svai Teeup crouched under some bushes in the cashew plantation near the old pond. The starving woman was covered with infected scratches and insect bites. The boys gave her food, though they knew it might cost them their lives to aid a runaway.

Along with other new villagers, the woman and her three daughters had been taken from their hut one night, and forced to stand at the edge of an empty reservoir in the nut grove. Hundreds of bodies lined the bottom. When the drunken soldiers came to club them, the three girls had encircled their mother and clung to each other. Their bodies took the brunt of the blow meant for her, and they fell into the pit together. Other bodies landed on top of the stunned woman, covering her. She lay motionless. In the dark, she went unnoticed, though soldiers later climbed into the reservoir with lanterns, and clubbed any they thought might not be dead.

Slowly and painfully, the dazed woman had pried herself from the tangle of arms and legs, crawled over the bodies and made her escape. She had subsisted on grubs and roots since then. For five days, Vitou and his friend had risked detection by bringing food to her.

When it became known in the village that several victims had survived, and were hiding among the nut trees, the leaders first threatened death to any villager who aided them. Then, four days later, loudspeakers in hand, leaders walked through the plantation, announcing amnesty for anyone who wished to come out of hiding, if they did so quickly. A few came, but the woman refused to budge.

Vitou pleaded with her. They would continue to provide for her, but she had to know she was consigning them all to death sooner or later. They could not go undetected for long.

Realizing he was right, she agreed to return, but on her terms. She did not believe the leaders would really allow the returnees to live for long, when they could tell others what had happened to them. She had a plan, but would not reveal it.

When Vitou and his friend returned to the village that evening, they saw her wandering aimlessly. When anyone spoke to her, she stared with a blank expression. Within a few days, she was assigned to a crew and labored diligently, but she never talked. And the woman had been right. One by one, the other survivors disappeared. Several weeks later, when Vitou left to hunt elsewhere, the woman was still in the village, still speechless and still alive.

Cambodians throughout the country knew of mass executions, yet we never heard of any uprisings. When our turns finally came, perhaps we, too, would just kneel in passive silence, simply because resistance might only serve to make the mode of dying worse.

In the fall of 1978, I worked on distant projects and seldom returned to the village. Girls were now employed in heavier and heavier work as more men were drafted to fight the Vietnamese. Girls were not required to serve in the army, but many volunteered. Soldiers got more food, and it seemed a better life than hauling dirt.

One balmy, moonlit evening in late October, when my crew was between projects, my family discussed what we would do if the Khmer Rouge should ever be defeated by the Vietnamese. We decided unanimously that we would attempt to leave the country.

Momentarily, I let myself get caught up in speculations about escape, then faced reality as I saw it; we would never be free. Angka Loeu was too powerful. Western nations were far from ready to rush to our aid, and they were the only force strong enough to break our chains. I refused to get excited about the possibility of escape. It only made our situation more unbearable to dream of freedom. Months before, I had been emotionally lifted by a beautiful sunrise, and had let my hopes soar. I no longer believed I could outlast Angka. My suicidal depressions had left me, but not my fatalistic attitude. The Communists would never change. My life would never change. I would be a slave until I died.

Keang discouraged talk of that sort and urged us to continue to be hardworking, noncomplaining. He warned us to vent all our frustration in the privacy of the family, never outside it. In Tra Pang Sral, we had a reputation as hard workers who did just what we were told. If others complained about some task, the leaders could assign it to us, and it would be done. We never volunteered, but we never refused. We never tried for the better jobs or put ourselves forward in any way. The only hope we had of staying alive and together was for none of us to be singled out for relocation.

Keang's grasp of history told him that no regime lasted forever, and some toppled when least expected. He never really thought we'd break the yoke we were under in his lifetime, but the intuitive will to live was still strong in our family, and he wanted to keep it, and us, alive as long as possible.

It was evident, when I returned to the village for those few days, that Mum was worried. Village leaders had demanded to know why she continued to reject marriage offers for me when I no longer had a fiancé.

"Why do you always say no? Do you think the boys are not good enough for Comrade Da?"

I hadn't known she had been subjected to such direct pressure. There was little time to comfort her before my crew was ordered to another project, but before I left, I mentioned a ploy used by some girls and their mothers. A worker could not ask for time off, but if her mother sent a note stating she was needed at home to discuss wedding plans, it was possible to have a leave. That way, Mum and I could have some time together.

It wouldn't arouse suspicion, since Angka had announced that there would be another marrying time in December or January. This was a few months earlier than normal, because so

167

many villagers were scheduled to leave for the front. Some wanted to marry before they left, while others hoped to postpone military service by marrying.

Not long after I told my mother about this trick, Keang, delivering a load of corn to a granary, passed my crew, and stopped long enough to tell me to observe certain fellows who worked in crews near mine. He named a few who wanted to marry me. I suspected some just wanted to postpone being drafted, but others may have genuinely wanted me for a wife. Keang said it was too hard for Mum to choose, so I was to select one I could be content with. I refused to give it serious thought. None of them pleased me.

In the meantime, without my knowledge, Satah suggested to my mother that I marry her son, Nye, who was seven years my senior. Mum rejected that proposal because the astrological signs weren't right. Then she and Satah decided I should marry Vitou.

Satah had pestered her nephew about marrying ever since his younger brother's marriage eight months earlier. When Vitou returned from hunting in October, she redoubled her efforts. He put her off.

Vitou lacked the most effective means for survival in the villages: gold or fine clothes to barter. Instead, he had developed enviable skills needed by his captors that made life easier for him than for most other villagers, new or old. He was sought after by many as a husband for their daughters, but he preferred to remain single—the future was too uncertain.

By November, however, it became apparent that Vitou must either marry or be drafted within weeks. He certainly didn't want to fight and die for a cause he didn't believe in, yet to marry simply to avoid being drafted seemed inadequate, even cowardly, to him. It didn't seem right to marry just to leave a young widow. Nor did he wish to produce children he couldn't provide for better than those he saw in the villages. He would never deliberately bring a child into the world to live like that, he told his aunt.

Satah argued that marriage to me would be beneficial to both of us. My leaders had decided I would marry the next time it was allowed. Either I chose or they would. Satah pointedly reminded Vitou that he would, no doubt, be in the same situation unless he soon made his own decision to marry.

At least Vitou and I came from the same general background. If we lived through this bondage, there was some chance of future happiness. If he was forced to marry a *neary*, not only would they have nothing in common in their backgrounds, education, or interests, but they would have opposing political views. There seemed no chance for happiness with a wife like that. Marriage to an old villager would offer little more.

He had become a man of some importance in little Bun Tear Chey and among the leadership. True, it was because he could do something for them that they could not do for themselves. But if that was the way to survive in this society, that was what he would do. Local cadre had no idea of Vitou's negative attitude toward their ideology and methods. He kept that to himself and had learned to parrot their sayings, sounding much as they did. They considered him one of the few promising young men from among the new villagers.

Vitou recognized that his aunt's arguments made sense. Besides, it would please her for the two families to be united. She had grown fond of my family in the six months she had known us. Vitou's distant uncle also advised him to accept the marriage arrangements. His sister-in-law, Naly, favored the match as well. He realized he even knew which girl it was that his aunt had in mind. He had seen me once when he went to the fields. Though I wore baggy clothes and had a blunt haircut, he had decided I was cute. His young aunt, Kunteara, from my crew, also had complimentary things to say about me.

Vitou finally told his Aunt Satah to arrange the marriage

—if I desired it. Since she had made most of the arrangements already, she was delighted at his agreement, however belated.

A few days after he talked to his aunt, my crew leader gave me a note from my mother. I was to return home to discuss wedding plans. The girls nearby began to giggle. I felt smug, knowing they thought I was really going to choose a husband. I was sure it was just the plan Mum and I had discussed the last time I was home. With the permission slip clutched tightly, I walked the fifteen miles back to the village, very pleased with myself and delighted that Mum had called for me so soon.

When I arrived, I was shocked to learn that there had been more marriage proposals, and the time had come to consider them seriously. A day later, Vitou and his aunt came to visit Keang and my mother. I had not been told he was coming or that he was one of the suitors. Only after Vitou left was I told that a marriage had been arranged, if each of us approved. My mother and Satah wanted us to see one another before making a final decision.

I knew it would please Mum if I married Vitou. Perhaps I would then be allowed to work closer to the village, and thus be able to care for her. That would please me. Keang, Soorsdey, and other family members had met Vitou, and they all approved. I liked Vitou's Aunt Satah and his Aunt Kunteara. Keang admired his uncle. My friend, Naly, was married to his brother. There really was no other suitable partner; I voiced no objections to the marriage.

Chapter Twelve

Vitou Mam.

Would he fit smoothly into our extended family? Would I like him? I had agreed to marry him, but I had not yet made up my mind to like him.

I began my own evaluation of Vitou, adding to it whenever he came to call. I suppose he was doing the same with me. I couldn't pretend he was any more eager to marry than I.

From Satah, Naly, Kunteara, and Mey Kamphot, I learned things about their relative, but it was from watching and listening to Vitou when he came for visits with Keang and my mother that I began to appreciate his enthusiasm for life, his bold spirit and integrity, and to question his rashness.

While we waited for the district's wedding date to be announced, I was allowed to stay in Tra Pang Sral, and work with the married women's crew again. There seemed to be an unusual push to harvest the crops as quickly as possible. Vitou was busy with the sugar harvest in his own village, but he sought opportunities to see my family whenever possible.

He visited my family five or six times during the next six weeks, and talked with my mother and Keang. I seldom spoke directly to him, but I paid close attention to what he said to the others. Naturally, we were never alone together. That would have terrified me, and it would not have been proper.

Vitou had turned twenty-one in August, the same month I had turned nineteen. In some ways, he seemed much older. He had lived pretty much on his own since he was thirteen.

It quickly became apparent that Tu, as his relatives called him, was self-assured and hard-working. He was intelligent, and had a sense of humor. I liked to watch his pleasant, expressive face when he recounted hunting exploits. His enthusiasm was catching.

Each day, while I worked silently in the fields, I caught myself thinking of the interesting stories he told about himself. It helped the time to pass, and the work seemed less arduous. I found myself looking forward to his visits.

My family's insistence that we live in Tra Pang Sral was the main reason my village leaders had fought so hard to allow our marriage. My leaders wanted Vitou to hunt for them. Vitou's leaders had tried with the same energy to prevent his moving, as they had grown to depend on his prowess. When he recounted his hunting experiences, I understood why they valued him so highly.

One evening, he told us about the biggest python he had ever seen, claiming it was as big around as a dinner plate. He and his hunting partners had lowered a cable noose over its head, then clubbed it with the back of an ax. It had required all four hunters to carry the snake to their village. My mouth watered when he described how the snake had flavored the villagers' rice for several days.

Vitou and his companions had evolved a method for catching medium-sized snakes. When they located a snake, they armed themselves with forked branches. On signal, one hunter pinned the snake to the ground just behind its head and straddled it. Simultaneously, another pinned the snake's middle, while the third secured its tail to the earth. The fourth hunter administered a quick blow to the head, which usually killed it. However, the animal's violent muscular contractions might continue for ten to twenty minutes, during which time the hunters had to struggle to hold their forked branches in place.

Vitou's stories about snakes emboldened me to mention the time I had helped my crew catch a python for our central kitchen. Vitou then told us that forked stakes were useless for a larger python. The creature was much too powerful to hold down. Instead, he usually approached the slow-moving animal from the side and would hit the head repeatedly until he felt he had killed it. Then he stood well back and waited for the snake to cease its wild thrashing.

Even in death, a huge python's contracting muscles could crush a man, he said. In its death throes, it sometimes coiled around a tree so tightly that it had to be unwound once it stopped moving.

I admired the ingenuity and resourcefulness Vitou and his companions showed, and I was beginning to appreciate other attributes of this handsome, muscular young man who would soon be my husband. It was apparent why village girls, new and old, were jealous of me.

His strength and fearlessness were qualities I admired, but I continued to be concerned at what appeared to be his willingness, almost eagerness, to take unneeded chances. Vitou's motto was not "Never do anything first."

The risks he took to feed the woman in the forest had surprised me. Chancing death for his brother's stolen rice and the dangers he faced as a hunter were risks few others would take.

Vitou told us of the time he had encountered a small enclave of Khmer Seri freedom fighters in the jungle. He felt sorry for these gaunt, hungry men, several of whom were survivors of the death trucks. Actually, they had done little fighting. They were merely trying to remain undetected. The men had been very polite, so Vitou gave them some meat and promised not to tell the soldiers that he had seen them. In Angka's eyes, that compassion would mark him as a traitor if it were known.

Though few men lived in the forests, and even fewer were Khmer Seri guerrillas, the Khmer Rouge soldiers were suspicious of everyone, and constantly tried to flush out any pockets of resistance. Occasionally, the soldiers had come across Vitou. Startled to find a man roaming freely, they treated him rudely, even threatening visits to Angka, until he produced his pass from the *srok* headquarters.

Before he learned of the mass murders, Vitou had wondered what the soldiers did with people they caught, so one day he foolishly allowed them to search him. Discovering his knife and other sharp tools not normally allowed villagers, they became extremely agitated. Out came a red parachute cord. At that point, Vitou decided to produce his pass. Fortunately for him, one of the soldiers had been able to read.

Vitou had an unnerving ability to get himself into, and talk himself out of, such situations time after time. He seemed to court danger.

As a child, Vitou had been shunted from relative to relative, feeling more like a servant than a family member in their homes. This had galled him to the point that, when he was thirteen, he had lied about his age and enlisted in the army. His justification for his rash act had been that his studies were often disrupted, because teachers and students at his school were endlessly on strike against unpopular government actions. Also, he lived with an uncle who could ill afford an extra mouth to feed. Without the backing of his family, a private school was out of the question. Impulsively, he had opted for the army.

Vitou had been in training only a few weeks, however, when he realized his mistake. By law, he should have been at least fifteen to enlist, eighteen was the age to be drafted. As a soldier in 1971, he had earned only 1,742 riels per month—$8.50 —hardly enough to risk death for. Since he was too young to be in the army legally, his uncle tried, unsuccessfully, to get his release. Vitou was stuck.

Many young boys had been conscripted from the streets by commanders who merely wanted to fill quotas. Most units were understaffed and poorly trained. Routinely, a commander had claimed more soldiers by padding the rolls, so he could glean the profits—money earmarked for uniforms, weapons, food, ammunition, and wages. Half the reported number of men in a given battalion were often phantom soldiers. It is hard to win a war or be rescued by "paper soldiers," but to some officers the personal accumulation of wealth had been more important than lives of men or victory in battle.

The soldiers' effectiveness was also hampered by their families. Relatives, uprooted from their own villages, had simply followed their soldiers, who often deserted in the heat of battle to protect and be with their loved ones.

As a lowly foot soldier, in this naïve, corrupt army, Vitou had fought the Khmer Rouge in the mountains near the borders. There, he encountered the hill tribesmen. He and his companions had tried to convince these backward people (with whom they had only a few words in common) that men had flown to the moon and back, that the earth was round and turned daily on its axis, as well as many other such novel ideas.

The tribesmen knew they lived at the center of the universe. Anyone with eyes could see the moon was much too small for a person to stand on. The earth was not a spinning ball because no one fell off. Obviously it was the sun that moved, not the earth. Fearing local spirits would be offended by such lies, the tribesmen were willing to do battle with those who promoted these heretical notions. Fortunately, Vitou was able to appease the local shaman and village elders, and he and his companions continued to be welcomed in their villages.

Vitou and his undersized partner had been assigned a shoulder-mounted rocket launcher, which weighed almost as much as they did. Vitou carried the weapon, and the other fellow carried the ammunition and loaded the launcher. To hit an enemy target, they had to fire from within thirty yards, which left them hopelessly exposed every time they fired on the Khmer Rouge.

Like most soldiers, he and his young companions had done more walking and waiting than actual fighting, but Vitou had been involved in four major battles and several skirmishes during his two-year army stint. In one encounter, he nearly lost his life when, for three days, his company had been surrounded by an ever-tightening circle of Khmer Rouge. The fighting was fierce, and they had run out of food and water. Ammunition ran low. Though scared, the young men, ready to fight to the death, had stood their ground and survived.

One evening when Vitou came to visit, Keang asked him about his involvement in a student riot in Phnom Penh in 1974. Vitou's face had been splashed across the front page of every newspaper in the country, he had been accused of murdering the minister of education.

A few days before the riot, the minister had been kidnapped by an angry mob in retaliation for the jailing of rioting students. A meeting had been arranged to exchange "prisoners." Along with other student representatives and administration leaders, Vitou and the minister sat at a table on a platform at the front of the room. Vitou's intention, though he was only sixteen, was to help cool his fellow students' tempers, so the explosive issue could be resolved peacefully.

Negotiations had been proceeding smoothly when, suddenly, angry students rushed to the front of the room. Vitou was jostled and a gun barrel thrust past his head, aimed at the minister. Five shots erupted. Blood from the dying man splattered Vitou's back and side.

"Murderer! Murderer!" Vitou had cried. He ducked under the table, and tried to aid the dying man. He had seen clearly the face of the retreating assassin. The crowd pressed in, and the man was gone. People screamed and ran in all directions. Security guards tried to barricade the doors.

A reporter, standing nearby, had urged Vitou to leave. "Since you were near the minister, you might even be accused of the murder."

Without stopping to think, Vitou had panicked. He ran. His picture, next to the stricken minister, showed him covered with blood, mouth open, turning as if to flee. The police arrested him a few hours later.

The interrogation lasted seven days, during which he had been questioned for hours at a time. He kept protesting his innocence, but the public clamored for speedy retribution. He feared he would be killed to meet their need for "justice."

The reporter who had advised Vitou to run finally came forward. The man had flown to France immediately after the shooting, and had not learned of Vitou's plight until he returned. Suddenly, Vitou was no longer a villain, he had become a hero.

Being cleared of the murder, however, only changed one set of fears for another. Vitou was one of the few who could identify the assassin, and the police felt his life might be in jeopardy. For three months, he had been kept in protective custody, housed in a special facility and followed by two armed bodyguards whenever he left his quarters.

For the year before his arrest, he had lived in a beautiful villa with the family of a wealthy widow. Despite student riots and boycotts of classes, he had tried to pursue his education. He had become part of this kind woman's household after he had helped rescue her son from three attackers. Vitou had waded into the fight to fend them off, though he hardly knew the boy. Learning that Vitou had no home of his own, the young widow had invited him to be part of her family.

One evening, Vitou showed us a picture of his substitute family. He obviously treasured the photo, the only souvenir of his former life. Because the widow's husband had been a high-ranking military officer, she and her children would have been high on Angka's list of people to be murdered. Vitou thought it likely they had committed suicide shortly after the takeover, as so many others of their class had done.

On the forced march from Phnom Penh with his Aunt Satah's family, Vitou had broken into a roadside villa on the outskirts of the city looking for rice. Entering the sitting room, he saw a roomful of beautifully dressed people lounging comfortably on elegant sofas and chairs, as though the hell outside their door did not exist. They were smiling, but no one moved. Vitou realized they had died perhaps an hour or so before. The smiles were the grimace of death by poisoning. Forgetting that he had come for rice, he stumbled over furniture in his panic to leave.

After a few of Vitou's visits, I decided I liked him very much. Apparently, Vitou also liked what he saw in me, though he knew much less about my personality than I did about his.

On his fourth visit, he told us about his initiation into village lore. Much of it harked back to the animistic beliefs of the hill tribesmen coupled with Buddhist teachings. These beliefs were a complex blend of superstition, practical advice, magic, legend, useful medicines and cures. Like our family, the longer Vitou lived in the villages, the less he scoffed at the ancient religion.

To a self-sufficient boy from the city, unaccustomed to boring routine and close supervision, life in the backward village of Bun Tear Chey had been stifling. So, shortly after his arrival from Phnom Penh, Vitou's high spirits and curiosity had led him to seek out the old men of the village. He had been drawn particularly to two of them: a wise *krou* Khmer and a crippled hunter. The *krou*, or folk doctor, had been pleased that someone showed interest in his ancient craft.

The disabled hunter also had enjoyed an audience and filled Vitou with visions of hunting in the days before guns were

178

commonly used, when hunting had required cunning and skill, and a great deal of daring. The longer Vitou listened to the hunter's tales, the more he had wanted to try his hand at catching wild game. He was ripe for a new adventure.

As food grew critically short during the first summer of our captivity, Vitou and three companions had been able to convince their village leader they could be more useful to the community by bringing back meat than by digging ditches. Few Cambodians willingly entered forested areas. Jungles were infested with life-threatening creatures, both real and supernatural. Hunting was dangerous work, and no one else had been willing to hunt on a regular basis. So for three months the young men had been allowed the unprecedented privilege of roaming the forests for game, only returning to full-time village life each fall to help with the harvests.

The four novice hunters were never allowed to use guns, and at first they had not even been given pointed weapons. Though all of us needed to use knives and machetes for routine village work and for clearing the jungle, we weren't trusted with objects that could readily be used as weapons, so the sharp ends had been cut off all our tools.

Until Vitou and his companions proved themselves, they had been accompanied on their forays by soldiers, to insure that they really hunted. Despite inexperience and poor equipment, the hunters soon perfected their skills.

In the fall of 1978, after Vitou had been released from the labor camp, the old hunter loaned him a beautiful, handcrafted, black wood crossbow. No one in the delta villages made them anymore, and crossbow hunting had died out after people turned to guns. The antique weapon required great strength to even pull the bow, but its poison-tipped arrows, and its accuracy, had been a boon to hunting, once Vitou learned to use it.

By sharing the hunters' bounty with the *srok* leaders, Vitou's village chief had been able to obtain a general pass for the young men. This unique pass had allowed them to roam throughout Kompong Cham and Kompong Thom provinces without a stated destination.

They were away from the village for weeks at a time. Every few days, they gave their game to men from their village sent out to meet them at rendezvous points. They were monitored too closely to escape, but their work did allow them to miss the evening *kosang*s, the dull lectures, and the tedious field work. Though I would never have volunteered to enter the jungles for months on end, I did envy Vitou's freedom.

Village life was less threatening and repressive for Vitou than it was for most people from the cities, and he ran minimal risk of being killed unless he did something specific to displease the leaders. As far as the Communists knew, he had no ties to prominent figures. Young and unattached, he blended into rural Cambodia as though he had been raised there.

Unlike most newcomers, Vitou wanted to learn from old villagers. Because he had respect for their knowledge, they took him into their confidence. The *krou* Khmer actually considered him a son.

One of the most useful things Vitou learned from the folk doctor was a formula for making poison for spearpoints. A vital ingredient was cobra heads, and Vitou's friend, the crippled hunter, taught him how to catch them safely.

"When cornered, the cobra will make a frightening noise halfway between the hiss and meow of an angry cat. That is when he will strike," the old man had said. In measured words he had encouraged Vitou: "You can fight him. You can win. You must not use a long stick, just one the length of a man's arm, but slender—the thickness of your little finger and very supple. You need a short stick, because you must strike fast. You must hit the snake very fast and very fast again. Do not get behind his head. The snake is nervous when it cannot see, and will strike without warning. The cobra can strike farther backward then forward. You must always stay in front of the snake's head. Hit it often and fast. You are a good hunter. You can fight the cobra and win."

Several old hunters had agreed to accompany Vitou and his friends on the first search for cobra, although their own hunting days were over, and they spent no more time in the jungle than necessary. The old hunters had no fear of wild animals, but they feared the unpredictable spirits that dwelled in the treetops in deep woods. Appropriate offerings had to be made to these spirits, and a person had to be careful not to offend them.

In the city, Vitou had never concerned himself with the intricacies of our Buddhist religion, let alone the spirits of the jungle. Eager to get on with the cobra hunt, Vitou had willingly learned the appropriate rituals. All that was required, after all, was to leave a simple offering to the tree spirits when an animal was killed: the end of the nose, a piece of the lip, one ear, a toenail. Fortunately, the spirits did not require the parts humans wanted to eat.

Vitou was instructed never to say anything bad about the spirits while in their domain, and to share his meals with them by making a small offering of a few grains of rice placed on a leaf and set at the base of a tall tree.

Vitou had returned from that cobra hunt with several snake heads in his possession. Guided by the shaman, he set about learning the secret of making poison for the spearpoints.

We thought it sounded like making a witch's brew when he explained the process to us. But it worked very well, he said. As instructed, he first boiled the cobra heads with tobacco leaves and the bark of a poisonous tree. After allowing the mixture to simmer until it thickened, he dipped his spear in it and let the blade dry. Then he coated the point with the white sap of a papaya tree, which prevented the coagulation of blood.

If an animal didn't die from a spear wound immediately,

then the poison entered the bloodstream and brought a slower death. If the wounded animal escaped, the papaya sap kept the blood flowing so the animal could be tracked more easily.

Vitou and his colleagues became far more successful in their hunts after they began using the cobra poison, the papaya sap, and the prescribed ritual. Perhaps the forest spirits had actually been appeased. Nearly three-quarters of those sent to the jungles to clear land contracted malaria. Many died. Vitou had never been afflicted.

Vitou also developed his own methods of hunting. A long-shafted spear was the most common weapon, but in the closeness of the jungle, Vitou found spears unwieldy. He preferred an ax. He liked to get close to his prey, and trusted to his sure aim and quick reflexes. Whenever possible, he clubbed animals on the top of the head because he hated the sight of blood. He began setting snares, made of brake cables from cars, for the larger animals, and bicycle cables for the smaller. When this supply had been exhausted, he persuaded his chief to trade for some thin cable used on fishing boats. Vitou had seen coils of it in an old warehouse in a village of Chinese-Cambodians. One hundred and twenty-five pounds of boned, skinned meat was secretly exchanged for six hundred feet of cable.

Such large-scale illicit trade, in which several people had been involved, including his leader, was very dangerous. It could have brought death if one of the participants had been an informer.

Officially, all transactions in and between villages went through proper channels. However, this was not practical and was routinely circumvented. Whenever Vitou spotted a weapon or piece of equipment the hunters desired, he simply dropped hints to his village chief and before long the weapon was theirs.

With each new piece of hunting equipment, the success rate increased. But the local animal population diminished, so the hunters set snares over ever-widening areas.

One day, Vitou and his companions snared a huge boar. Hearing a startled squeal, they had rushed to the site and found the boar twisting to get free of the cable around its hind leg. Lashing its tusks from side to side, the enraged beast tried to attack. Vitou and the others rushed the wildly gyrating animal, thrusting their weapons repeatedly. Finally, Vitou slit the jugular vein. A stream of hot blood sprayed everywhere. It had taken six men to haul the four-hundred-pound pig, suspended from a bamboo pole, into Bun Tear Chey.

We had even heard about this exploit in our own village, though, at the time, we had not known who the heroes were. How we had envied not only the villagers' meat, but also the thirty-six quarts of highly prized cooking fat that had been rendered from the animal.

Though the hunters occasionally snared wild pigs, enormous deer, and other large game, and once even trapped a tiger, most of their hunting exploits had been less challenging. The bulk of the meat they provided the village came from monkeys, snakes, birds, little deer, and other small animals.

For trapping monkeys, the old hunter had helped Vitou weave basketlike traps of split bamboo with a large interior and a narrow opening that slanted inward. He put food in the rear of the basket, then placed it near the foot of a monkey-infested tree. Before long, several monkeys would enter the trap. Because monkeys were easy to catch, few remained near the villages. The hunters had been able to find them in quantity only in areas away from civilization.

After Vitou proved his abilities to his crippled friend's satisfaction, the old man had loaned him his prized *pwompring* hunting dog. This hound, though old, was still sleek and strong. The disabled huntsman claimed that his unusual dog came from a special breed that was not easily killed by the bite of a cobra. Before he took the dog hunting, Vitou had been told by the *krou* Khmer what he should do if the dog was ever bitten by a cobra

183

—locate flowers from a special tree, chew them as he had been instructed, and spit the juice on the wound three or four times a day.

To supply themselves with food while hunting, Vitou and his band caught four-foot-long tree lizards. They were hard to catch, and the hunters seldom snared more than they needed for food. The fat-bodied reptile comes to the ground to dig for grubs only between midnight and 5:00 A.M. on bright moonlit nights. It spends the rest of its life in the tops of large trees. The old dog was expert at grabbing this quick-moving creature by the neck. Awakened by barking, the hunters would claim their next meal. Meat of this lizard was supposed to cure sore throats and chest ailments. Vitou didn't know about that, but claimed it tasted like chicken. To my embarrassment, my stomach growled hungrily whenever Vitou talked about the meals he provided for his village or himself. How I would have liked to sink my teeth into a succulent lizard!

Despite the success they enjoyed, the hunters and their villagers had often gone hungry. It had not been easy to find enough wild game to feed one hundred people with any regularity, especially using such primitive weapons and methods. But during the summer rationing, their efforts had often spelled the difference between hunger and starvation for their village.

Coming into the village at the end of each rainy season, with shaggy, black hair hanging almost to his shoulders, Vitou was happy to have survived the dangers of another wet season in the jungle. Until he returned to hunt, nine months later, he had to keep his hair short, attend indoctrination sessions, and work like the rest of us in the routine drudgery of village life.

One of the most dangerous, yet prestigious jobs in the village was climbing the sugar palms to collect sap. Vitou volunteered to do it. Even in the village, he had found work that brought admiration. It was no wonder then that old villagers pressed him to wed one of their daughters, or why his leaders had been reluctant to let him marry someone from another village.

Caught up in Vitou's visits and my personal affairs, I was slow to notice that more and more villagers were being removed. Only when Leng was taken in for questioning in December did the reality impinge itself upon me once again. How quick I had been to forget the cruelties while I spun daydreams.

They came for Leng on three different nights after he had already gone to bed. Each time he left, Rasmei feared she would never again see him. At each session, they pressed him further about his former work. Finally, Leng could no longer deny what they obviously already knew. Yes, he had been the supervisor of the airport.

They let him go home, but he knew it would not be for long. Each day, he anticipated that he and his family would be killed. Keang felt that he, too, would be called in for another series of questions. If they knew the identity of his brother-in-law, they must also know his. He was one of the few Phnom Penh men left in Tra Pang Sral. If the killings were to continue, he was sure to be on the lists. He could not be so lucky as the last time.

Mum and Satah were among the few widows of important men from the former regime who were still alive. One by one, the city girls in my crew had disappeared. Village by village, new residents were being exterminated. Our turns would surely come. Would my marriage simply serve to drag Vitou down with us?

On January 1, 1979, in the midst of my fear and despair, Vitou Mam and I were informed that we would marry in two days.

185

Chapter Thirteen

A soft orange glow colored the eastern sky. I slipped out of bed and bathed at the well. I had wanted this time alone with my thoughts before the village began to stir. Had Si Ton lived, this day would have been our wedding day—the same location, the same words. Instead, in a few hours I would stand next to a man I barely knew and promise my life to him—the only girl in my family not to marry a relative.

There was a sweet tenderness in my thoughts for my dead cousin, but no regrets at marrying Vitou. I could not change the past. I could only look to the future, and Vitou Mam was my future. I hesitated calling him "Tu," even to myself. It seemed too personal.

I had studiously avoided listening to any advice about sex. I did not want anyone to talk about *that*. As a Phnom Penh schoolgirl, I had read in textbooks about reproduction. What I didn't know, I would learn for myself.

By the time Vitou's Aunt Satah arrived, I was dressed in my best black blouse and least worn *sampot*. I had washed my hair with the shampoo from America that this kind woman had hoarded for years. It was important to look like a loyal comrade on my wedding day, so I had had my short hair cropped even shorter. I hated it and felt ugly, but at least it smelled nice. I let

Satah apply a facial cleanser, but I protested when she brought out rouge. I didn't want to stand out.

Old village girls felt secure enough to wear lots of makeup, gold bracelets, and other jewelry for their weddings. Not I. I had no intention of letting the Khmer Rouge know we still owned jewelry. I did agree to wear a sapphire bracelet and my old gold watch, but if I couldn't marry as Rasmei and Mearadey had done, in a traditional Buddhist ceremony, I was not interested in doing something halfway. I hated the thought of marrying in black. I just wanted to get it over with.

My old watch still ran. My father had given it to me several years before the takeover, and I'd kept it hidden for almost four years. But on my wedding day, I wanted something to remind me of Papa. How I wished he could be with us.

By 7:00 A.M., Leng, Rota, Chenda Poong, and a very pregnant Rasmei arrived. We were astonished to see them. They had left their district without permission, having made up their minds to see us at least once more before they were called for further interrogations or execution.

While we waited for the arrival of Vitou and his uncle, my sisters and mother put finishing touches on the rice cakes they had cooked in secret the night before. Only two other people from Tra Pang Sral were marrying this day, and by the time they and their families started for East Khum Speu, we were ready. My nieces and nephew stayed in the village. The rest of us walked with the other couples across the sandy field.

During the half-hour walk, neither Vitou nor I had much to say to anyone, certainly not to each other. I stayed near Mum and my sisters. Vitou walked further back in the group with his relatives. His uncle, Mey Kamphot, had recently married, and his new bride walked with us.

In my bashfulness, I paid little open attention to Vitou, but I had noted the untanned skin near his hairline and knew that he, too, had recently cut his hair extra short for the occasion. He appeared nervous and well scrubbed. His scarf, wrapped loosely around his neck several times, suited him well.

I heard Vitou chuckle over the way I walked in my tightly wrapped skirt, as I tried to avoid the prickly weeds in the trail. I couldn't blame him. It had been so long since I'd worn one, that I had forgotten how to walk like a lady. With every step forward, I seemed to slip backward in the loose sand of the rutted trail. I was unable to avoid all the weeds, and my bare feet felt like pin cushions. Not even on my wedding day did I have shoes. Almost no one did any longer. Vitou and Leng were lucky, they still had homemade, rubber-tire sandals, and could afford to laugh at the rest of us as we dodged the weeds.

Thirteen couples and their families arrived in East Speu about 8:00 A.M. Vitou and I and the other couples sat on benches at a red-cloth-covered table, which filled the room from the back wall to the front door of the largest hut. Standing at the far end of the long table, his back against the wall, the speaker faced the open door. Guests crowded against the thatched walls or craned to see into the room from the door and window openings.

The assistant district leader was in charge, and began with a welcoming speech. Then everyone stood, turned toward the flag, and observed a moment of silence in remembrance of the nation's slain heroes. During this moment of silence, each person saluted by placing the thumb of his right hand against his temple with fingers curled tightly, arm held out rigidly at a right angle from the body. It reminded me of shooting someone in the head, and the red-flag-draped room reminded me of blood.

After the moment of silence, each person's right arm shot forward, angled toward the flag, fingers close together. The leader made a short, impassioned speech about the flag and the need for allegiance to the country. Then, those of us who could sat down. The rest shifted from foot to foot as the speaker launched into a two-hour harangue.

I had to keep reminding myself that this was my wedding

ceremony. It sounded just like hundreds of other speeches, filled with slogans and dogma, that we were forced to endure nightly.

Out of the corner of my eye, I could see Vitou sitting next to me, and was sure everyone would agree that he was by far the best-looking groom at the table. At nineteen and a half, I was expected to be a woman, yet I felt like an awkward little girl. Vitou, only two years older, seemed so assured. I longed to know him better, but felt so reticent in his presence.

The speaker droned on about how the government liked young people, how much better it was now for young couples to marry than it had been in the old days. No money was required, no gold, no extra food, no expenses that often indebted poor peasants for years.

I nervously fingered the beautiful *kroma* on the table in front of me. Mum had loaned this same scarf to Soorsdey for her wedding almost three years before. There were similar *kroma*s on the red tablecloth in front of each bride and groom. They had been removed from around our necks as a mark of respect, just as in the West one removes a hat.

I wished I could offer my chair to my mother. It was nothing for me to stand for a few hours, but for Mum, even the walk had been exhausting and painful.

Weddings should be fun, and this was anything but fun. It seemed more like a funeral, with everyone dressed somberly and looking glum. The slivers in my feet hurt, and I didn't want to hear about the need to build the country, the need to devote extra effort to bring in rice.

I was startled from my own thoughts when I realized the speaker had finished. Flustered, I listened closely as a bride and groom rose in turn and made short speeches, pledging loyalty to Angka and then "marrying themselves," being sure to add the required "I will never divorce my partner."

One by one, each person at the table stood and made a similar pledge. Most couples worried about speaking too briefly.

It might appear disloyal. My great concern was saying more than was absolutely necessary, since every word had to be weighed to be sure nothing incriminating was uttered. I did not mind appearing dull-witted, but I wanted to guard against being trapped by my own words.

I had learned from past experience that it was safest to parrot back whatever the leaders had just emphasized. That way I was sure to stress the things currently considered important. I made a mental note to include something about the harvest when my turn came, and chided myself for not paying better attention. My stomach knotted as each person sat and one closer to me rose. Soon all eyes were on me.

Tensely, I pulled myself upright. "I love the Angka. I will work hard for Angka. I will obey whatever the Angka says. I will work extra hard during the harvest." I rushed to a conclusion with "I am very happy to marry with Vitou and will not divorce my husband." It was over; I could relax.

Vitou stood next. He seemed so calm. I studiously kept my eyes averted from his face as he spoke. He said he would obey Angka and work hard. He promised to help finish the dam project, and help Angka keep to the projected schedule for the harvest. He seemed to know all the right Communist slogans and phrases that pleased the leaders. They nodded their approval as he spoke. His was one of the longer speeches. Then he turned toward me as he finished: "I am happy to be married to Teeda."

I blushed. We were now man and wife.

After the couples had given their stilted speeches, one groom's father and one bride's mother were selected to make extemporaneous speeches of advice. These two talks were short, but in them the parents gave heartfelt traditional advice carefully couched in acceptable Communist phrases. I noted quiet nods of agreement from the older people in attendance.

It was almost 11:00 A.M. when the leader stood again, gave a few closing remarks, and adjourned the meeting until two. At that time, only the brides and grooms and their parents were to meet in Po Preng with other couples from the district who had married in the morning ceremonies.

Keang had missed my wedding because he had an assignment to gather palm sap, but he had gone to work extra early in order to join us for the afternoon activities. Mum could not walk to Po Preng. She would remain in Tra Pang Sral with the others, while Mearadey represented her at the afternoon ceremonies, and Keang filled in for my father.

At least I had a family to represent me. Many people had disappeared in recent weeks, and several young couples had no one to accompany them to the ceremonies. I felt sorry for Vitou also. As far as he knew, Sarakun was the only other member of his immediate family left alive.

In fact, Vitou had learned from Keang that his father had been one of the volunteers who passed our camp on his way back to Phnom Penh. Vitou knew that meant death. One of his hunting companions, a plumber, had also returned to help rebuild. He was one of the few to survive. Before he was sent back to the country, he had seen hundreds of bodies stacked in the public buildings throughout the city. Some rooms held only heads, he said.

Vitou's father was from a prominent family, but had been ostracized by family and friends in 1960, when he displeased Prince Sihanouk's court. As a conscientious young customs agent, Mr. Mam had arrested one of Sihanouk's relatives after discovering large quantities of opium in the man's luggage. Mr. Mam's fall had been swift and cruel. He could find no employment. His family disowned him.

"Mam" had long been an important Cambodian name. Vitou's grandfathers for generations had ruled their own fiefdoms. Grandfather Mam, a polygamist, had placed many of his children in high government posts under Prince Sihanouk. Vitou's father, he felt, had disgraced him. There had been friction in the past between them. Grandfather Mam operated expertly within the traditional system of power brokering, while Vitou's father backed leaders who fought for equality under the law. Learning of Mr. Mam's resolute stand for a principle, even under adversity, gave me insight into Vitou's own apparent stubbornness when he felt he was in the right.

Mr. Mam's in-laws, as well as his own family, turned against him to protect their personal interests. Problems developed in his marriage, and Vitou's parents divorced. Vitou, Sarakun, and their two older brothers, all just children at the time, were sent to live with relatives.

Mr. Mam had been grateful, after his "disgrace," to find any work at all—even as a lowly office boy for the U.S. embassy. It was not until the Republic came into being that his fortunes improved. By then, both Mr. Mam and his former wife had remarried and were raising new families. Their sons had been left to fend for themselves as poor relations in the homes of rich relatives.

Returning down the dusty road to Tra Pang Sral after our wedding, Vitou again walked with his uncle. I joined my mother. Villagers, curious to meet my husband, offered noisy congratulations. Our wedding party was given a separate table in the dining hall as a special honor.

I crossed the room to comfort a distraught-looking girl who had just arrived from a village on the east side of the Mekong River. Her crew had almost finished harvesting a field when they were ordered to board a waiting truck. They had been driven to the Mekong, put on a boat, then onto another truck. The vehicle hadn't stopped until it reached Tra Pang Sral, where everyone was ordered out and told to settle.

The girl had no idea where her parents had been sent, or

if other members of her family were even together. She and her co-workers had only the clothes on their backs, and nowhere to call home.

To Keang and Leng, these new arrivals were another indication that the Vietnamese were continuing to offer a real challenge to the Khmer Rouge, despite what we heard over the loudspeakers every day. We prayed that this was so. The Vietnamese Communists had one of the largest and most battle-hardened armies in the world. They could certainly become a formidable foe.

We sensed change all about us.

Twelve days had passed since Leng had last been called in for questioning. Was this lapse of time intended to inflict pain and uncertainty, or were the leaders too involved with the war effort to pursue his case?

There was an unusual air of urgency about the harvest. Surrounding districts as well as our own bustled with activity. As each crop was gathered, it was quickly processed and moved to hidden forest retreats rather than the village granaries. Even as new residents descended on us, many others were leaving for the war zone. To encourage enlistment, leaders had volunteered themselves. In a wave of patriotism, five of the eight village leaders in Khum Speu District had volunteered, as had the district leader himself.

So not only was January 3 my wedding day, it was the day set aside to honor the leaders and their men who were leaving for the front that evening.

Concern for the displaced people, and talk of war, had taken our attention from my wedding until we realized it was time to leave for the afternoon ceremony.

The meeting in Po Preng was devoted primarily to honoring the district leader and the five village chiefs. Secondarily, it celebrated the weddings of seventy couples who had married in

193

the morning ceremonies in district villages. Five hundred people had been invited.

Again, for three hours, I sat in a stupor, listening to speeches. The district leader gave a lengthy introductory speech that was also his farewell address. This was followed by the routine moment of silence and pledge of allegiance. Then one bride and one groom were asked to volunteer to address the crowd. My crew leader, a respected old village girl, stood and spoke, then there was an awkward silence. No groom had volunteered.

Suddenly, Vitou jumped to his feet. I was appalled. Why had he put himself forward like that? Had we misjudged him? Was he one of them? I looked at Keang and Mearadey. Their faces revealed they were not pleased with Vitou's action either.

By Communist standards, Vitou's fifteen-minute address was ideal, filled with promises that all the young couples would be willing, eager, loyal. He said just what the leaders wanted to hear. The speech was almost too good. Did he really believe all he was saying? I was deeply troubled. What had I gotten into?

Next, a father and a mother were asked to represent all parents and give advice to the young people. Following their talks, the district leader spoke yet again, encouraging more of us to join the fight against the Vietnamese. He asked the couples to carry on in the tradition he had set, to be diligent, unselfish workers. He and the five leaders, he said, had assumed the initiative. They would be the ones to die first, so others could march over their dead bodies to continue the glorious fight against the enemy. What a wonderful thought. Perhaps the Communists would just consume one another. The village chiefs issued similar impassioned pleas for volunteers, and bid us similarly melodramatic farewells.

It was over. We were invited to a special banquet in honor of the occasion. While tables were being set up in the dining hall, people had time to visit. Conversation in our group was strained.

A leader who supervised the labor camp where Vitou had been a prisoner elbowed his way through the crowd. He clapped Vitou on the back and announced how proud he was that Vitou stood when he had motioned to him. He had thought this was a good opportunity to bring Vitou to the attention of important men in the district. He told us it had been a singular honor, especially since Vitou was a new villager.

As soon as the officer left, an embarrassed Vitou explained how he had hated to stand and make that speech, but the man had insistently beckoned him to rise, and he dared not ignore the mandate. His explanation allowed everyone to relax.

For the five hundred diners, three pigs and a cow had been slaughtered. The pieces ladled into our bowls were actually large enough to be identified as meat. We could not believe our good luck. In addition, there were fish, and even white rice was served, instead of poorly polished local rice. Tea, not water, was offered, and there were ripe bananas for dessert—a real feast.

It almost compensated for the six hours I'd spent warming hard benches. Of course, the food was not really in our honor —it was for those leaders leaving for the front. By the time we finished, envious villagers, drawn by the good smells, had lined up for their turn in the dining hall. As usual, they were served rice gruel.

Dusk enveloped us as we walked to Samol and Soorsdey's hut with full stomachs and good feelings toward each other. We planned to hold the real wedding ceremony there. The hut would also be our honeymoon cottage, thanks to Soorsdey and Samol, who had graciously offered to stay with my aunt in West Speu for a few days. In a few weeks, Vitou and I could request a plot of land, and build a hut of our own.

Since it was essential to keep our family ceremony secret, guests wandered in and out of the hut, so informers would think neighbors were just visiting with Vitou and me.

On the floor in the center of the hut, Mum had arranged

two candles, several sticks of burning incense, a picture of my father, a Buddha statue, and the food. Sitting cross-legged on the floor, we performed a makeshift Buddhist wedding ceremony, making a real effort to explain to the listening dead the need for deviation. It was important to us that our dead loved ones recognize we had done the best we could under difficult circumstances. Prayers were offered to explain that Vitou and I were married. We hoped our departed relatives would understand, and not accuse us of living in sin. We prayed for peace, health, and some measure of happiness for the two of us.

After the rice cakes and tea, guests slipped away one by one, back to their own darkened huts.

Vitou and I did not have to experience the humiliation of a communal honeymoon cottage, nor did the other couples at the group ceremony. The leaders were much too busy this year to concern themselves with nonproductive brides and grooms. War, and the ongoing harvests, had turned their attention in other directions.

Some years, newly married couples had been allowed one or two days to visit relatives and introduce their spouses to the extended families—a modified version of traditional Buddhist custom. This year, however, brides and grooms were obliged to forgo this frivolous practice. We had been pressured into pledging ourselves to the harvest.

Shortly after our guests departed, the village leader appeared on the front porch. He got right to the point.

"I've come to remind you that tomorrow you are expected to work. Comrade Vitou, you will help with the sugar harvest. Comrade Da, you will go with the women."

That was all. No acknowledgment that Vitou was new to the village. No wishes for our happiness. No indication that this was our wedding day. Nothing.

We watched in awkward silence as the pompous leader turned on his heel and swaggered into the night. Then it struck each of us just how absurdly comical this warped, artificial society was, and how ludicrous were the men it produced. Vitou started to chuckle. I joined him. The strangeness each of us felt in the other's presence began to melt. We turned back to our honeymoon cottage laughing. We were one.

Four days later, Phnom Penh fell.

Rumors flew throughout the villages: the Vietnamese had overrun the country. Pol Pot, Khieu Samphan, and their Angka cohorts had fled the capital and taken refuge in the jungles.

Confusion gripped leaders and villagers alike. Soldiers departed in haste. Before leaving, they threatened us with death if anyone looted or caused trouble. We were to keep working. Many villagers, however, refused to go to the fields after the leaders and soldiers fled. They felt free—cautiously free.

Keang was not so optimistic. This might be just another of the endless Khmer Rouge tricks, to see which villagers would rejoice at the overthrow of Pol Pot. Soldiers might be lurking in the jungles to pounce on those disloyal to the current regime. Which villagers were spies? Once again, we decided not to be first, not to stop work, not to show pleasure. If the overthrow of Angka Loeu was true, we would soon find out. All we would lose would be a few days of expended effort. If we were deceived into quitting, we could lose our lives.

On December 25, just four days after Leng's last interrogation, Vietnam had launched its full offensive. This was why there had been no continued investigation of Leng's case, why there had been the urgent plea for army volunteers at my wedding.

The Vietnamese crossed into Cambodia on January 6, 1979, and were in Phnom Penh a day later. Instead of launching a direct assault on the three well-manned defensive lines of the Khmer Rouge that ran the length of the border, the Vietnamese

197

simply went around the ends. They met almost no resistance and cut into the heart of Cambodia.

Deployed behind the Khmer Rouge, the Vietnamese effectively blocked retreat, leaving Pol Pot's soldiers without supplies and isolating them from their countrymen. They were trapped in a barren no-man's-land that Angka had created by evacuating border residents and destroying villages as soon as their crops were harvested. Confused and leaderless, Khmer Rouge soldiers fled into the jungles.

By January 10, while we continued to toil in our village, the Vietnamese gained control of the country. Isolated pockets of Khmer Rouge still lurked in the forests, but without central organization, savage hit-and-run attacks against the Vietnamese were sporadic. Many soldiers did not know their government had fallen.

Old villagers tried to convince us we were foolish to keep working. On January 11, Leng's family brought their possessions to Tra Pang Sral. The next day, Vietnamese soldiers moved through our village. At last, we had the confirmation we needed. We laid down our hoes.

Everywhere the Vietnamese went they were hailed as liberators. Their lightning invasion was totally unexpected by the populace, yet so welcome. The outside world, however, still not believing how horrendous conditions had been, was vehement in its censure of the "invaders."

The Vietnamese correctly called Cambodia "hell on earth," and stated that they planned to free us from the oppression under which we labored. My family did not credit Vietnam with such humanitarian motives, but we, and the rest of our countrymen, were deeply grateful that the secondary effect of Vietnam's drive for expansion had been liberation from our bondage.

At a time when Angka seemed to be closing in relentlessly on any remaining new residents, we had miraculously been given a reprieve by our country's perennial enemy. If Pol Pot had retained power even a few days longer, we felt that our entire family would have been decimated. We had cheated death once more.

As villagers grew confident, the storehouses and granaries and central supply sheds were broken open and people helped themselves to all the rice they could carry away. Everyone was happy, helpful.

Most people did not stop to ask what life would be like under the new leaders. They enjoyed the moment. The Khmer Rouge were routed; they could obtain food. They were free to find long-missing loved ones. Hopes soared. Life under Pol Pot had been so repressive that people willingly switched allegiance to the invaders.

For the time being, the Vietnamese did not care where we went or what we did. They were most indulgent, accepting the adulation heaped upon them, and making no effort to control anyone. They were too busy pressing their advantage against the disintegrating forces of Angka to care if we helped ourselves to supplies.

Vitou used his ax to break down a granary door and grabbed a hundred-pound sack of rice. Leng joined a group who broke into a storage area hidden in the forest, carrying back sugar and rice as his prizes. Everyone took what they could.

In a family conference, we discussed leaving Cambodia. If we remained, the best we could hope for was a less-repressive Communist government likely to treat Cambodia as a colony, taking more than it gave. Because Keang and Leng had once worked in the American-backed Lon Nol government, they could always be accused by any Communist regime of being agents for the West. It was not safe for them to remain.

Food supplies would likely remain inadequate for years to come, and the very real possibility existed that life might revert to what we had known during the past four years. We had given up all hope that Papa was alive, and concluded that other loved ones had perished also. There seemed to be nothing holding us back, no one to wait for. If we were ever to leave, it would have to be before the new government had time to restrict movement, as we felt sure they would.

Satah, Vitou's uncle, and several of their relatives wanted to go with us. I wondered what Vitou would choose to do. This was a time when many who had married for convenience went their separate ways. I was relieved, though I didn't dare show it, when he said he would leave with us.

Vitou told me that ever since he was young, and had seen how his father was treated, he had resolved that someday he would leave Cambodia. His only chance had been to do well enough in school to be granted a scholarship for study abroad. He had hoped to earn an engineering degree like Satah's husband had, then never return. He thought his dream had died when the Khmer Rouge came to power. He was ready to revive it again.

Vietnam, though less than one hundred miles to the east, was no longer a viable escape route. Laos, the next closest country, was also Communist-held. To the southwest was the Gulf of Thailand, but we could not depend on finding boats. That left Thailand, which wrapped around Cambodia to the north and west like a giant paw. North was the shortest distance to the border, but there were few roads, and the wild mountain jungles were becoming a Khmer Rouge stronghold. We chose the longest but most logical route to the Thai border—west.

Forty of us constituted the entire group, but each subgroup was responsible for its own members and its own needs. Fourteen people made up the group under Keang: Keang's family of five, Leng's family of four, my mother, Samol and Soorsdey, Vitou and me. Sarakun and Naly, plus Vitou's Aunt Kunteara, who had married a few days before we did, were part of Aunt Satah's group. Uncle Mey Kamphot headed another.

The fourth leader was a distant uncle of mine. These four individuals were empowered to direct our affairs and make final decisions.

It was over two hundred miles to the border. We could make the trip in twenty days if there were no delays and we averaged ten miles per day. Could we reach the border before Rasmei gave birth? That was still two months away. With luck, the child would be born in Thailand—it seemed symbolic, since Thailand means "Free land." We prepared enough food to last sixty days.

Using crude devices, my sisters and I polished four hundred pounds of rice. Stepping on a log lever, we raised and lowered a pestle, teeter-totter fashion. For each twenty-pound batch, the pestle had to be raised and lowered into the rice three hundred times. We tossed the rice into the air with winnowing baskets, and let the wind blow the remaining chaff away. Despite all our efforts, the rice was barely edible. It remained full of grit that would wear our teeth down rapidly.

The men confiscated a pig from the central pen, and we cooked and pickled it in brine, and rendered lard. We ground cornmeal, packed sugar, cooked beans. We tied our possessions in bundles. In three days, my sisters and I had everything in readiness.

Meanwhile, the four brothers-in-law commandeered an ox cart from the communal supplies, and replaced its broken axle with a huge, cogged wheel attached to a metal shaft—the remains of a machine they found in an abandoned factory. The cogged left wheel promised a bumpy ride, but it worked. Though unconventional, the cart was big and sturdy.

Late one night, Vitou and Samol hitched themselves to a lightweight cart they had found in another village, and stealthily pulled it back to Tra Pang Sral to hold our pots, pans, extra food, and firewood.

Most of our food would be loaded on the cart with the

cogged wheel. We wove a bamboo sunscreen for it to shade my mother and the smallest children. Rasmei could also ride if she became weary. The rest of us would walk. To pull this cart, the men rounded up two oxen from the scattered community herd. We constructed two makeshift handcarts to hold the rest of our belongings.

Having confiscated more food than we could carry, we gave some to Samol's parents, who planned to take up life again as independent rice farmers. One of their sons had been drafted just before the Vietnamese invasion. They did not want to leave Cambodia in case he returned. (He never did.)

Valuables, mostly our remaining gold and diamonds, had been sewn in jacket linings, or secreted among the supplies. Good clothing was well hidden in the bags of food and household objects. We left our stacks of Cambodian riels moldering in Soorsdey and Samol's thatched roof, at last conceding that our carefully hoarded money was worthless.

It had been eighteen days since I married, ten days since we ceased toiling for the Khmer Rouge. All was in readiness.

Skirmishes between the opposing forces still blocked the roads west. But in anticipation that they would soon open, we began questioning travelers. As soon as it seemed safe, we would make a dash for freedom. We did not know if we would be allowed to reach the border, let alone cross it, but we were determined to try. We would attempt escape, whatever the cost. If death found us, it would at least be in the act of doing something positive for ourselves. To be our own agents, to think, to dream and plan, was exhilarating.

On January 21, 1979, at 3:00 A.M., the four leaders quietly marshaled their families, and we turned our backs on Tra Pang Sral.

There was no need to hide our movements; the roads were filled with people. We headed for Highway 6, a main artery between Phnom Penh and Bangkok. We told anyone curious enough to ask that we were returning to our ancestral village.

Everyone was in high spirits as we began our long trek. Children ran from group to group until they tired, then hopped on a cart to ride. The temperatures were still relatively cool; the weather, dry; and we planned to be in Thailand well before the rains and heat descended in May.

By midmorning, Soorsdey and I were skipping along, singing at the top of our lungs. We had just begun "We all live in a yellow submarine," from an old Beatles song we had memorized in Phnom Penh. To our astonishment, from the tall grass by the side of the road, someone joined in.

Rising from his nap, a grinning young man said, "Your English could be better, but, otherwise, not bad."

Chapter Fourteen

The makeshift food wagon, tied behind the big cart, collapsed a few miles from Tra Pang Sral. Rather than attempt repairs, we transferred food to the other carts and abandoned the wagon. Samol pulled the clothing cart. Vitou pulled the heavier handcart loaded with pots and pans. Keang walked beside the main wagon, wielding a bamboo switch to urge the oxen forward, controlling them by ropes attached to rings in their noses. When Leng was able to drive the oxen, Keang relieved Samol or Vitou by pulling one of the other carts.

Leng's health had broken down during the harsh village years, especially under the strain of the recent interrogations. Most days, it required all the energy he could muster merely to keep pace. He gathered grass for the animals at rest stops, and did light work in camp.

Mum, in an effort to spare the oxen, wanted to walk, but we convinced her it was vital she stay well, or everyone would be slowed down. Her strength would be needed at the end of the journey, if we were actually able to cross the mountains into Thailand.

Perched atop the sacks of food, two-year-old Chenda Peach and her six-year-old cousin, Chenda Poong, rode with their grandmother. Rota, too impatient and restless to sit for long, scampered up and down the line of travelers like a young pup. Tevi and Moni joined him.

Rasmei seldom rode. During the past four years, she had grown accustomed to hard work, and the walk through the flatlands of central Cambodia was not difficult. Mearadey, Soorsdey, and I shepherded children and tried to anticipate the men's needs.

We required the children to stay near the carts when we approached the giant rubber plantations that lined the route, since they were ideal hiding places for an ambush. The Vietnamese controlled major highways and villages, but in some places this control stretched no more than two or three miles off the road. Isolated villages were still in Khmer Rouge hands.

Some days, the men explored the plantations to gather wood or look for food and abandoned items that might be useful. Occasionally, they discovered a granary the Khmer Rouge had hidden in the jungle in an effort to keep food from the Vietnamese. Sometimes, in their quests, the men stumbled upon decomposed bodies.

From travelers who overtook us, we learned that, following a bloody battle five days after our departure, our district of Khum Speu had again fallen to the Khmer Rouge. We prayed that Samol's family and our other relatives were safe, and that Vietnamese troops would drive the butchers out. Fear for loved ones, however, was balanced by relief that once more we had escaped.

The three groups traveling with us also had an assortment of carts, baggage, animals, and people. Most days, those using water buffalo started two hours before we did, to spare their animals during the heat of the day. They waited for us at a midday rest stop, then traveled two hours later in the evening to catch us again.

Vitou and Samol entered camp each day exhausted, but after a meal and rest, they were ready to pull again. In the evenings, Vitou roughhoused with the children, soon becoming a favorite of theirs. They enjoyed his hunting stories and other adventures as much as I did.

Whenever we met travelers approaching from the west, Keang and Leng questioned them about the safety of proceeding. We tried to keep close on the heels of the advancing Vietnamese, and to sleep in villages rather than along the side of the road. The Khmer Rouge considered all travelers traitors, and since Pol Pot's soldiers dressed like other villagers, we never knew whom to trust.

Many times, the need to camp in a village meant we had to stop sooner than we wanted, simply because we could not reach the next village before dark. No one wanted to be on the road during the hours the Khmer Rouge were most active. To avoid walking into fighting, we stayed in a village until we saw refugees coming from the west, and our four leaders had a chance to question them about conditions.

Vitou and Samol occasionally scouted ahead when we were stopped. Depending on their report, we advanced or stayed put. Vitou's previous jungle experience as a soldier and later as a hunter allowed him to move close to the enemy without being detected.

Vietnamese soldiers patrolled the highways every few days to keep them open, and freely discussed their progress with anyone who asked. We were grateful Keang had mastered enough Vietnamese to communicate effectively with these troops. Despite our precautions, danger was not always avoidable. Once we were caught on the road as a skirmish raged between the opposing forces. Just ahead, a Vietnamese fuel truck lay enveloped in flames. Behind, we heard automatic weapons. Not daring to retreat, we hurried forward, skirting the truck before it exploded, and taking shelter in the nearest village until the sounds of battle faded behind us.

The Vietnamese had not restricted travel within Cambodia as long as those traveling could provide justification for their presence on the roads. They did not, however, allow people to leave the country.

Keang repeatedly told the soldiers, "We need to see if any relatives survived the years of bondage, and if they are still in our home village, near Sisophon." They seemed satisfied with that explanation.

The roads became crowded by the time we reached the junction where Highway 21 meets Highway 6, but few people were traveling west. Most were city people going home. Some hoped to resume living as they had before the takeover. Many from Phnom Penh and other cities no doubt planned to leave Cambodia later, but were making a detour to reclaim valuables they had hidden in their homes. Others were heading for the cities in search of treasures hidden by those who were now dead.

My family had little desire to see what had happened to our Phnom Penh home in the intervening years. We had left no hidden valuables. Vitou and Sarakun had helped Satah bury a fortune in her garden, but even they weren't tempted to return. A chance to gain freedom was far more precious. Satah's treasure was her children, and they were in California.

Most surviving city people were not trying to escape. Those with good educations had already been killed, and those who were left no longer felt in any special danger. Villagers wanted to take up their former pursuits. They had not been part of any leadership in former regimes and offered no threat to the Vietnamese. All they expected from these new leaders was freedom to work in peace. They were more trusting than we were.

Everyone we met along our route advised us to turn back. Why did we want to go where there was still fighting? Surely starvation awaited us to the west.

"We must look for relatives," we persisted. People thought we were crazy.

Occasionally, Vietnamese soldiers asked why we were headed against the general flow of traffic, but they never stopped us from proceeding. Because we traveled in such a large group with men, women, and children of all ages, our motives were not suspect, nor would they be until we got closer to the border.

Because we had married for practical reasons—many no longer valid—I knew Vitou might be reconsidering the step he had taken. Perhaps he wanted to annul the marriage. I no longer needed a husband to save me from an unwanted union with a Communist soldier, and Vitou no longer needed a wife to keep him out of the army or from a less desirable marriage.

It was an anxious, awkward time. Our reasons for marrying had evaporated four days after our wedding, when the Vietnamese overran Phnom Penh. I wanted to give Vitou the opportunity to back out if he desired, and because of that, I dared not show how deeply I would be hurt if this happened. To my relief, Vitou said he had these same concerns.

What had begun as a marriage of convenience had become something more. We loved each other. Once this was established to each other's satisfaction, we were joyfully free to build the relationship. Though we had had little to do with the original choice, we now freely chose each other.

I enjoyed walking beside Tu, and visiting with him. Though still unable to address him by this diminutive, I was trying it out often in my thoughts, and looked forward to the day "Tu" would slip naturally from my tongue.

This trip was the equivalent of our honeymoon, although a very public one. We had many hours together to become better acquainted as we walked. Because I could rely on Keang to worry about our safety and other details, I focused my attention on Vitou, the beautiful countryside, the people we passed.

Like the aftermath of all war, this was a time in which life for many was reduced largely to personal survival. Fortunately,

208

there were four men in our family to provide for us and protect us, and four grown daughters to look out for my mother and her five young grandchildren. Without us, Mum and the children would never have been able to make this trek. Without the men, there was little chance of escape for the rest of us.

Two-thirds of Cambodia's adult population was now female. Most males in the prime of life had been killed by the Khmer Rouge during the takeover, or had died in village reprisals. Miraculously, we had four strong men in our family. The army of widows we passed looked on us with envy.

Sometimes there were not many people on the road, but when the road was safest for travel, thousands headed for the interior. Occasionally, we had to fight our way forward, just as we had done during the exodus from Phnom Penh, only this time we were moving against the tide. At such times, we required the children to ride or hold an adult's hand. Once again, as the crowds pressed in, people became separated from their families if they weren't careful.*

To our surprise and relief, the Vietnamese denied having any need for Cambodian men to help fight the Khmer Rouge. They did, however, announce in each village and among refugees on the roads that men with leadership ability and technical know-how were needed to reconstruct the nation. There was urgent need for teachers, engineers, technicians, and other trained personnel. Keang and Leng were not even tempted to answer the call.

Soldiers sometimes asked if the men in our party had

---

*Uncle Ban's missing daughters, who'd buried their mother, sister, and husbands in western Cambodia, moved east with the crowds to look for Si Ton and the rest of their family. As we moved west, we passed them, though we did not know it. One of their children became separated from them on this trek and was never seen again.

skills they could offer the new government, and Keang nervously explained that perhaps they could volunteer later. Then, pointing to Rasmei, he said we had to get her settled before she gave birth. Fortunately, the Vietnamese did not press the issue, and we continued our trek.

Progress toward Sisophon became slower and slower as we waited for the Vietnamese to clear the way. From Voice of America and BBC broadcasts, Keang learned the Vietnamese invasion had caused an upwelling of condemnation throughout the rest of the world, which charged them with expansionist aggression. In rebuttal, Vietnam claimed its soldiers were only in Cambodia as a humanitarian gesture to help free the people from oppressive rule.

Leng and Keang felt the Vietnamese had deliberately slowed their attempts to rout the Khmer Rouge. Otherwise, they would have no excuse to offer for their continued presence in Cambodia. Before wiping out the opposition, they needed time to become firmly entrenched, and to set up a puppet government, using sympathetic Cambodians in leadership positions.

Keang and Leng had good reason to suspect the motives of our liberators. According to reports, at the time we were trying to escape, there were fewer than 50,000 disorganized, poorly equipped Khmer Rouge, compared to more than 200,000 well-supplied Vietnamese. With world attention focused on Cambodia, we felt the Vietnamese were more lenient than they might be in the future. We didn't intend to remain in the country long enough to test our hypothesis.

Khmer Rouge guerrillas had dug up sections of the road to block passage of Vietnamese trucks and tanks. Highway 6, still littered with rusting appliances and cars that had been jettisoned four years before, was now pocked with hastily filled potholes as well. Though unable to overpower the Vietnamese, Pol Pot's forces were able to hamper progress and harass movement along their enemy's flanks. We had to wait days at a time for the road to be repaired. The farther west we went, the longer the delays became.

We were definitely behind schedule. At night, when the rest of us slept, our leaders discussed the situation. As we followed Vietnamese soldiers into villages, we participated in the "liberation" of storehouses to replenish our dwindling food supply.

At the city of Kompong Thom, we took supplies of rice from the central storehouse and traded for additional foodstuffs with peasants along our route. Clothing was especially prized by them. Leng, our best bargainer, traded rice and clothing for gold whenever he could. He knew we would need it later.

The need to cross the border before Rasmei's baby was born, and before the rains began, weighed heavily on the men. In the meantime, during the enforced stops they tried to keep our morale high.

When we camped near Lake Tonle Sap, waiting for the road to be passable, the men suggested fishing, as a diversion and an excellent source of needed protein. There was an abundance of fish in this shallow lake. They could be caught by hand at this time of year, when the lake shrank to one-seventh its largest size. In years past, Phnom Penh residents had taken the one-hundred-mile excursion to the lake to join villagers for the annual fish harvest, which took place at the end of the dry season, when the lake was only five feet deep.

It was easy to catch the fish. We scooped them up with nets or simply grabbed them bare-handed. After four years of doing without, we gorged on fresh fish.

In mid-February, we arrived at the little city of Siem Reap, near the ruins of ancient Angkor Wat, at the upper reaches of Lake Tonle Sap. The fighting ahead had increased, so we were forced to make a month-long stop. To help the time pass, the four leaders organized an excursion to the ruins and the famous temple compound. We felt the children should see this site of Cambodia's former glory. They should remember something of the homeland they might never see again, something besides hardship and deprivation.

Like other Phnom Penh residents, most of us had been to Angkor Wat and the nearby, newer Angkor Thom several times, and we looked forward to seeing the ancient buildings again.

What we saw appalled us. The magnificent structures, painstakingly freed from four centuries of jungle growth by French and Cambodian archaeologists, and lovingly restored as an area of worship, had been desecrated by the Khmer Rouge.

Where men once removed their shoes and walked with bowed heads, tanks had irreverently been driven. Statues of Buddha had been used for target practice. Black paint defiled others. Walls of the wat were pockmarked with bullet holes, small antique statues stolen, gold leaf stripped from sacred objects, statue heads toppled. Soot from recent fires had blackened the rooms.

Incensed by this blatant disregard for the cultural as well as the religious heritage of Cambodia, we wandered around the overgrown, neglected ruins of the once brilliant capital that filled an area twice the size of Manhattan. This hallowed place belonged to the ages. The Khmer Rouge had deliberately looted and defaced it.

From Angkor, the ancient Khmer god-kings had ruled a vast Hindu kingdom that stretched from Burma to Malaya in the southwest, including half of Thailand to the west, and most of Loas and Vietnam to the north and east.

Ironically, the ancient Khmer kingdom had also been built on slave labor. Millions toiled to support its opulence. Rice paid for everything. Like ours, the old kingdom had depended on extensive dike and dam building so multiple rice crops could be grown each year.

To Angka Loeu, rice was synonymous with wealth. Each day, we'd slaved to build more dams and grow more rice. Each night, we'd been bombarded with slogans: "Rice means steel." "Rice means industrialization." "Rice means fuel, factories, and equipment." "You have rice; you can have everything." For four years, we'd slaved and starved, yet Cambodians had nothing.

Ironically also, invasion had easily toppled both the ancient god-kings and their mirror image, Angka Loeu, because neither had support from within. Sacked and burned, ancient Angkor had quickly slipped into oblivion, the people dispersed, their records destroyed. Jungle claimed the monuments, and all knowledge of our fabled past had been lost to us for hundreds of years.

As we wandered among these toppled stones of Angkor, we mourned for our nation. Cambodia had once again been willfully plunged into ignorance. Our records burned, intellectuals killed, temples desecrated, traditions destroyed, cities emptied, our language stripped. How often must our history be repeated? How often would the "wheel of history" grind Cambodians into the mud?

In the ancient kingdom capital offenses had been punished by barbaric practices: people had been buried alive, their fingers, hands, noses chopped off. The dead were left in the street or tossed into fields to be devoured by wild beasts. What had changed? Had the hundreds of intervening years failed to civilize our nation?

In a way we never had understood before, we empathized with the millions who had toiled to build this ancient city for harsh masters. We could never again look on Angkor with the same pride and awe we had felt on former trips. We now knew the price paid for the temple mountain. We turned in anguish from Angkor Wat as we turned from the country we dearly loved. Both were places of ghosts.

Chapter Fifteen

We reached Kralanh in mid-March. We were still seventy-five miles from the border, and it was evident we would have another lengthy stop. The road west was controlled by the Khmer Rouge, and Rasmei's baby was due any day. For two months, we had camped under the stars or in makeshift shelters, but in Kralanh, we were lucky to find a brick schoolhouse at the edge of town with a stream of cool, clear water running past. Each family set up housekeeping in a different classroom. Here we would stay until the baby was born, and the Vietnamese gained control of the highway.

Though small, Kralanh was the largest community between Siem Reap and Sisophon, and offered the safest haven for weary travelers. As the refugee population in the village mushroomed, others joined us in the school.

We had suffered innumerable hardships during the past four years, but we knew we had been lucky as well. A way had always opened whenever we had done all we could on our own. Kralanh, with its sheltered living quarters, was one more unexpected bit of luck. In addition, a nurse had taken refuge in the school, and was able to help with Rasmei's delivery.

With nothing but folk medicines to rely on, the nurse used a powdered-tree-root anesthetic to ease my sister's pain. Though the weather was hot, she lit a small fire under Rasmei's bed to keep her extra warm. The villagers believed such a fire was essential. Just as Mearadey had done two years earlier, Rasmei willingly agreed to any practices the nurse or others suggested.

On March 19, a little girl was born. Though tiny, she was quite healthy, and Rasmei's improved diet during the previous two months of pregnancy enabled her to breast-feed the baby.

We had lived on a substandard diet, without proper medical or dental attention, for four years. Despite our recently improved conditions, we were all plagued with chronic illnesses. By this time, however, we hardly noticed our poor health and simply put up with aches and pains, internal parasites and chronic toothaches. Rasmei's rotten teeth marred her beautiful smile. Mum had to push her prolapsed uterus up with her hand in order to urinate. Walking with her "insides" hanging between her legs was painful, though Mum seldom complained. I suffered from a nagging cough and a constant burning sensation in my chest, the result of inhaling insecticide. Vitou's legs were bowed and his back slightly twisted from years of carrying heavy loads. Leng was still ill from the anxiety he'd suffered during his interrogation. Yet all these ailments seemed insignificant. The weeks spent in Kralanh seemed like a vacation, a time to relax and improve our physical strength for the effort that lay ahead. With enough to eat and extra protein, our bellies became less distended, our hair regained its shine, and our festering sores healed. We took walks, fished, strolled through the village, and played with Rasmei's baby. With clear, running water as near as the closest stream, bathing became a favorite pastime. What a treat it was to feel clean again.

Though we rested, it was not a time of inactivity. We washed and mended clothes, salted fish, and collected foods against the time we could move closer to the border. We cooked and repackaged, much as we had done when leaving Speu. The men mended the carts and reconnoitered, and Leng tried to fatten the oxen. Keang visited villages near the border to pick up gossip about road conditions and possible escape routes.

Rota, Tevi, Moni, and the two Chendas spent the month regaining their childhood. We delighted in watching them in normal, everyday childish pursuits. The girls spent hours piling leaves and grass in neat rows to represent walls of their make-believe rooms. They played hide-and-seek and tag, and their pinched little faces filled out. In shedding reserve and fear of strangers, their wary looks gave way to smiles.

Tu entertained the children and set a few snares in the woods. We never knew when we would be leaving, so he never went far enough from the village to trap anything but small game. Somewhere between Khum Speu and the village of Kra-lanh, I learned to call him "Tu." I don't remember just how or when it occurred, but sometime during the previous two months it had surfaced naturally.

A few days before the Cambodian New Year, in mid-April, Keang returned from his latest reconnoitering trip, to report that the road would soon be safe for passage. People were escaping into Thailand, slipping from the border villages into the jungle every few days. On New Year's Day, Voice of America and BBC broadcasts talked of Cambodians making successful crossings into Thailand.

The Thai government did not encourage refugees, but it made no serious efforts to stop them, and refugee camps were being expanded to house the recent influx.

The new year seemed full of promise, but it was another *Tchap Pdum Pee Saun*—"Year Zero." Again we were starting with nothing. But this year, we had hope, which made starting again seem possible, even exciting. We celebrated by indulging in giddy, newfound thoughts: "When *I* go to the United States," or "When *I* finally reach France . . ." Plans expanded to impossible proportions.

The desire to be free was so overpowering on New Year's

night, I found it hard to sleep. Like the bamboo, we really had outlasted the storm. A little longer and we could try to right ourselves in a free land.

From what news he picked up in the villages, Keang learned we could go as far as Sisophon, forty miles away, then on to Poipet. Beyond Poipet, the road was tightly controlled by Khmer Rouge, but generations of villagers had smuggled goods back and forth along unmarked trails through rugged mountain passes and for a price they would even smuggle refugees. The going rate was an ounce of gold per refugee, so Keang and Leng began trading our good clothing, and any food we would not need, for gold, diamonds, or other small valuables. Whatever wealth was left after paying the guides would be needed to begin life in a new country.

In Cambodia, jewelry was a common asset, especially in times of political upheaval. Even poor peasants kept gold jewelry in lieu of bank accounts. We had traded most of our gold while in the villages. It had been readily accepted and was easy to cut into small pieces, or to trade a link at a time. Diamonds, however, were more difficult to barter. They were too valuable for most purchases, and it was harder to determine quality. Because of this, people had little gold left, but quite a few jewels, which they willingly traded far below their real worth. We traded our extra rice for gold and, when people didn't have gold, we accepted jewels.

We planned to settle in Thailand. We had relatives in France, and several family members spoke French, but we did not expect a Western nation to be open to us. However, if we were free to choose any country, we decided it would be America, because it had the most freedom and the best opportunity to build a new life. Though we would arrive with few marketable skills and a limited ability with the language, we wanted America.

As the chance of escape became more real, I also began

considering skills I would need to develop. Both Tu and I had little formal schooling to fall back on to start a new life. I didn't know how to cook, sew, or clean a house. I had no job training except as a manual laborer. If we actually reached Thailand, we would have to do a lot of growing, a lot of changing, and it would take great effort to gain the needed skills and education. It was frightening to think of all the work it would take to turn our dreams into reality.

The influx of refugees into Kralanh and nearby villages had created an ideal opportunity to trade food for the gold we needed, but we were running short of the most desired food-stuffs. People were hungry for protein and were paying a good price for it. Keang decided to hurry back to Tonle Sap Lake, buy fresh fish, and return to sell them at a profit. Mearadey saw the need to acquire more gold, but she did not want him to go back to the lake. The highway to Sisophon could be opened any day, and it was impossible to know how long the Vietnamese could control it.

Mearadey urged her husband to stay. It had been three weeks since Rasmei gave birth, and she and the baby were strong enough to travel. We were packed, ready to go on a moment's notice. Keang sympathized with Mearaday's concern but was confident he would be back before the road ahead opened. The other men encouraged him in his plan. No sooner had he gone, however, than word raced through the village that Highway 6 was passable as far as Sisophon.

Refugees streamed out of Kralanh. The three families with us decided to go while they had the chance. We had already waited a month and it was impossible to know when the next opportunity to leave might come if the road closed again.

My family was torn between leaving and waiting. Mear-adey was angry with Keang for jeopardizing our chance of escape, but she feared permanent separation if she left. We would not leave without her. Blinking back tears of disappointment, we watched the other families disappear from view. They and the refugees Keang planned to sell fish to were gone.

It was only a few days, but seemed an eternity before Keang returned. With no time to bargain, he traded the fish in Kralanh for little more than he'd paid for them. Then we took to the road, pushing to rejoin the others.

The nearer we got to Thailand, the steeper the road became, and Vitou and Samol found pulling the handcarts increasingly difficult.

There was dense forest on each side of us, beyond the rice fields that lined our route. These were not the friendly, lush jungles of Tarzan movies or fairy tales, where tropical fruits hang ready for the plucking. The area was formidable once a person left the protection of villages and roads. It was rugged country and difficult to penetrate—a wilderness.

Wild animals roamed this untamed region. Thorn bushes and tangled vines, poisonous plants, snakes, mosquitoes, leeches, and huge, impassable bamboo groves discouraged entrance. Fresh water was scarce. Still, it was not these dangers that brought fear to travelers.

Severed heads had been placed here and there at the side of the road. Pol Pot's soldiers intended these grisly sights as a warning of the fate awaiting anyone caught while attempting to exit the country. Travelers heading west this close to the border were considered the worst of traitors. We were either cowards trying to escape, or lackeys of the Vietnamese.

Fearing ambush by roving bands of Khmer Rouge at every bend in the road, we were relieved a few days later to reach the security of Sisophon, and doubly gratified to find our friends in the milling crowds. We talked to refugees from all over the country and learned that under the Khmer Rouge families had been separated in some districts, with women segregated from the men, and children housed in yet another place.

In those villages, husbands and wives had had to seek special permission for conjugal visits.

Western Cambodia, though only two hundred miles from Phnom Penh, was vastly different from central Cambodia, not only in geography, but also in makeup of the population. Many residents in these western mountains spoke both Thai and Cambodian, and had relatives in villages on both sides of the border. Rice did not grow well. As a consequence of the Communist fixation on rice as the crop to be grown by everyone, villagers from this area had suffered chronic hunger under Pol Pot, even more than the rest of us, and often actual starvation.

In general, leaders in the western districts had not pried as deeply into the lives of their charges as the leaders in Kompong Cham Province had. More government officials and former army officers who disguised their backgrounds had survived. Perhaps physical hardships imposed by the land itself were so great that the Khmer Rouge had been less concerned with controlling every facet of the peasant's daily routine. Perhaps the greater distance from Angka's Phnom Penh headquarters had made leaders less diligent.

In the west the communal system was not so pervasive. Some leaders had allowed the villagers to cook allotted portions of rice for themselves, rather than eating in common dining halls. In sharp contrast to these benefits, however, had been the openly bragged-about mass murders and torture. People had even been publicly executed in village squares. From those living in the west came reports of the worst atrocities.

In Sisophon, we found it much easier to build a hut than it had been four years ago in Speu. We commandeered nails and lumber from a Pol Pot lumberyard and quickly lashed palm branches and dried grass over the framework. Plastic tarps were in short supply, but we traded for enough to provide a dry corner for Rasmei and the baby. We did not want to waste time constructing a more permanent home, as we hoped to leave before heavy summer rains set in. Fifteen of us lived in an eight-by-ten-foot area. Often we ate and slept in shifts.

Among the throngs of refugees in temporary shanty-towns on the fringes of the village we came upon a woman who told us Uncle Ban's daughters had headed for Khum Speu, in search of their father, Si Ton, and the others. We were happy to learn they were alive, but feared they might never reach Speu. If they made it, we knew what disappointment awaited them.

Mearadey began writing letters to relatives in France. She paid smugglers to give the letters to a friend in the Thai border town of Aranyaprathet. To help insure that the messengers would actually deliver her letters, she asked her friend to pay them again on delivery.

The whole venture was a gamble. Mearadey did not even know if her friend still lived in Aranyaprathet. She did not know if the messengers could be trusted, or if they might be captured in crossing the border. Perhaps they worked for the Vietnamese or the Khmer Rouge. We remembered so few relatives' addresses after four years under the Communists, and had no way of knowing if they had moved. Perhaps no response from the relatives would reach Mearadey's friend even if the woman actually got Mearadey's letters and sent them on. Still, my sister felt she had to try every avenue. We would need help if we ever made the crossing, and certainly our relatives would be relieved to know some of us had survived the slaughter.

Tu and my brothers-in-law spent most of their time gathering information in the nearby villages, or listening to the radio for snatches of news about the war between the Pol Pot forces and the Vietnamese.

At the end of the second week, word suddenly spread that the road to Poipet was passable. Quickly we broke camp and trekked the thirty miles to the border village. There was an air of excitement in Poipet; the border was only five miles away. I could almost smell freedom.

Once again, we constructed a rude shelter, preparing to stay only long enough to hire a reliable guide.

Up to now, we had relied on Vietnamese protection. Our days had been filled with the sheer physical effort of transporting forty men, women, and children and their possessions from Khum Speu to Poipet. The truly dangerous part was about to begin. From Poipet onward we could no longer travel by ox cart or carry the extra food and equipment we had depended on up to this point. The final miles across the border would be made on foot, in secret, over unmarked jungle trails, through minefields.

Vietnamese soldiers allowed refugees to reach mountain villages near the border, but if people attempted to cross, the soldiers had been ordered to stop them. Bands of Khmer Rouge dedicated to killing "traitors" and keeping Cambodians in Cambodia were lurking in the jungles. In addition, Thai soldiers lined the border to block passage into their country.

Vietnam and Angka Loeu wanted no defectors. Thailand wanted no infiltrators or refugees, though Thailand usually allowed people to stay if they escaped successfully. The three armies patrolled the border in strength. Each was pitted against the other and the defenseless escapees.

Though many smugglers were familiar with the hostile mountains, we realized anyone who could be bought to take us out might also be bought by the opposing forces to turn us in. We were often dealing with bandits and outlaws. There were shocking stories of groups who had unwittingly been led to the very people they most wanted to escape. Others had been taken into the jungles, robbed, then abandoned. To be lost in the jungle was a death sentence. With no water or food, if patrols did not shoot us or wild animals devour us, we would die of thirst. Even native smugglers who agreed to take refugees and intended to honor that commitment sometimes lost their way in the steep mountain passes or were killed by land mines and booby traps, stranding their parties in the wilds.

With knowledge of these unfavorable odds brought sharply to our attention, the time had come to choose. It was not too late to turn back, or to settle in villages near Poipet. Did anyone want to drop out of the escape attempt? *No* was the resounding answer.

Some guides refused to take women and children, because they slowed progress and increased the danger of detection. Smuggling was their occupation; guiding refugees, a sideline. No guide liked to take along babies. An infant's cry could give the entire group away. We heard rumors of fathers and mothers who had strangled their own child in order to save the group, if the baby threatened to cry when soldiers approached. Babies with rags stuffed in their mouths sometimes suffocated.

Rasmei and Mearadey trembled at the price they might be required to pay, yet after weighing the alternatives, they remained as determined as ever. The chance of freedom was worth the deaths of any or all of us.

Most recent escapees had crossed south of Poipet, until that route was discovered by either the Vietnamese or the Khmer Rouge. Until a new way was found, everyone had to wait. One morning, Keang noticed some makeshift huts standing empty, the contents and occupants gone. He decided a viable route, not yet discovered by patrols, must have been forged. He and our other leaders stepped up their search for a guide they could trust. They arranged with representatives of sixty other refugees to form a group of about one hundred. By pooling everyone's gold, they hoped to hire two or three guides.

A week passed. If the border was again being breached, it was time to dispose of everything we could not carry. Anything of value not essential for the actual crossing was collected, and Vitou, Leng, and Sarakun were chosen to make a return trip to Sisophon to sell the oxen and the carts, as well as our extra food and clothing.

It was painful to part with so many things. It left us vulnerable in case something foiled our escape plans. What would we do for food if the route closed before we crossed? It might be weeks before another safe passage was found.

After the bad experience we'd had when Keang went back to Tonle Sap, we had decided the group's opportunity to escape must never be jeopardized again. If the chance came to move forward, we would go. It would be the responsibility of anyone left behind to try to rejoin us. A man had a better chance of getting through a tight spot alone than did a family.

Just before he left for Sisophon, Vitou made me promise once more that I would go if the opportunity came to escape while he was gone. He could not bear the thought that I might lose my chance by waiting for him. Since he would only be gone three days, and we had not even settled on a guide, I agreed.

Mum gave Leng her diamond ring in case the three men missed us and had to pay another guide. At dawn, they started down the road. It would take most of the day to travel the thirty miles back to Sisophon, a second day to sell the goods, and a long third day's hike to make the return trip—two and a half days if they sold everything quickly and started back immediately.

Incredibly, within hours after Leng, Vitou, and Sarakun left for Sisophon, Keang located a guide. He was a relative of one of the men planning to escape with us, so the leaders had some confidence in the man's concern for the safety of the group. Also, Keang learned of a letter received by a person in Poipet from someone the guide had recently taken to Thailand. A coded message had informed the friend of the safe crossing. Keang went to examine the letter. After a few questions, he was satisfied. The guide could not have known which words had been agreed upon. It looked as if we had found the right man.

The guide said he would take us across the border on his next trip, but once we were on Thai soil, he and his companions would leave if soldiers approached. Thai soldiers often robbed the guide-smugglers, knowing they carried gold from the refugees as well as contraband goods. Payment was required in advance because he often had to leave in haste at the end of the trip.

We gave the guide and his two tough-looking companions partial payment, with the rest to be paid once the crossing actually began. The guides stated they would return in a day or two, after checking on the best route, and advised everyone to be prepared to leave on a moment's notice.

Three days passed. I could not believe how quickly everything had fallen into place, and I began to worry. Why hadn't Tu and Leng and Sarakun returned? All evening I waited anxiously at the edge of town and watched down the road toward Sisophon for some sign of them.

I refused to believe something had happened to Tu, yet memories of severed heads posted on the side of the road came unbidden into my thoughts. I watched the road until it was too dark to see.

Dejectedly, I made my way back through the congested village, passing the open doors of makeshift huts where families sat eating around evening fires. It had rained earlier, and mud oozed between my toes. The road was so rutted it was hard to avoid puddles.

As I approached our shelter, I was shocked to see the guide talking to Keang. The look of relief on Keang's face was apparent. He had been worried the fellow had taken our gold and decided not to return, or had been killed while scouting for a trail through the minefields.

A route was found that did not appear to be too heavily patrolled, and there were relatively few minefields in that direction. We would leave at 2:00 A.M. The trip was expected to take one long day and one night. Though Thailand was only five miles away via the road, we would have to go a considerable distance through the jungle to avoid hazards. There would be few stops and no sleeping. The guide was not certain the women and children could make it. Keang and Samol assured him we could. Each family was told where to rendezvous, and we were advised to get as much sleep as possible in the few hours that remained. How could we leave without our husbands? Sarakun's wife, Naly, Rasmei, and I were aghast. As we hid valuables and helped pack, our ears were tuned to every footstep. It was time. Keang gently woke the children, and asked us what we planned to do. Since the gold had been paid as part of a group price, there would be no refunds. Keang, Samol, and their families were leaving with the others, and it was up to the three of us to stay or go. Everyone waited for our decision.

I decided to stay. Mum would not leave me behind. If I stayed, so would she. If I stayed, Rasmei and her three children would stay. Naly decided she, too, would stay if the rest of us did. It all seemed to hinge on my decision. I couldn't stand the pressure; it too seemed part of a nightmare. It wasn't fair to put this burden of deciding for the others on my shoulders. The moments ticked by.

If something really had happened to the men, if they never returned, I didn't know how I could get my ailing mother, my convalescing sister, a seven-week-old baby, and two young children across the border, even with Naly's help. For that, we needed our husbands. Gold had already been paid, and I had no way to get more.

The guides would wait no longer. Others in the Khum Speu group had already moved to the rendezvous points. It was imperative the group be well on its way before dawn lit the sky.

I wanted to stay, but I would have to leave. Tu had made me promise to go, and I knew he had a better chance of crossing without me than with me, and all the women and children. There really was no choice.

226

As the last family slipped silently from the sleeping village, Naly and Rasmei, her children, and I followed. Heartsick, I looked back as long as possible, then turned all my efforts toward escape.

Four years of hiding valuables had taught us a few tricks to outsmart those who tried to wrest possessions from us. Just before we left Poipet, I had pried a diamond from its mounting, wrapped it in beeswax, wedged it in a large cavity in my back tooth, winced, then bit down hard. The stone, seated firmly, looked like the rest of my brown-stained teeth.

Some members of the family had rolled jewels in beeswax and pushed them into their ears, where they looked like dirty ear wax. We had concealed gold in hollow sections of bamboo walking sticks. Rasmei had hidden a gold chain between Leng's pair of Ho Chi Minh sandals, then tied the shoes firmly together and put them in her pack.

Mum put her diamond-studded gold bracelet into an eyeglass case, then wrapped the case in her bundle of clothing, along with the silver bowl—the wedding present she had kept hidden since we left Phnom Penh. Keang hid the second silver bowl in his bundle. All the adults, and even some of the children, had valuables sewn in the linings and hems of their clothing, or hidden in some bundle or body orifice.

A few less important objects had been deliberately hidden poorly, so anyone coming across them in a search might think they were all we had and would look no further.

We would not be dealing with accomplished thieves or well-trained, disciplined soldiers. Most robbers were unschooled peasants whose intent was not to strip a person of all he had but to make a profit from anyone they caught—a toll for passage. In a party of one hundred refugees, it was not likely everyone would be searched thoroughly. We wanted freedom, with or without our possessions. Nothing else really mattered. Mum

227

quoted a Cambodian saying about priorities: material possessions can be replaced, a life cannot. And she had extracted a
promise from each of us to follow that advice if we were stopped.

For an hour, our family and the guides hiked a circuitous
route through the jungle in silence. In darkness and drizzle,
others in our party, hidden along the trail earlier, joined us as
we passed the spots where they had been told to wait. When
everyone was assembled, we plunged deep into the jungle with
not a word spoken.

Several times during the night, we were motioned off the
path by the guides, who were stationed at the front, middle, and
rear. Usually it was a false alarm, but occasionally from our
hiding places we saw an armed patrol pass in the dark, weighted
down with machine guns, hand grenades, mortars, and rockets.
Patrols roamed the jungles in groups of four or five, hunting for
escapees.

By the time dawn streaked the sky behind us, we were
well on our way through the mountains. Like the rain, the pace
was slow and steady. No talking was allowed; the wet jungle
floor muffled each foot tread.

When it was light enough to see well, the guides allowed
a stop. We rested and ate, while they collected the last half
payment from each group. We had been depending on gold from
Leng and Vitou's sale of the oxen and carts to make our final
payment. Instead, we had to offer my father's diamond ring.
Mum was sorry to part with it, but its use demonstrated to her
how Papa continued to help us, even though he was dead. It
comforted her to know his ring would buy our freedom.

The guides, however, were loath to accept Papa's ring, as
its value was too hard to determine. Pure gold was what they
wanted. They knew, though, that Leng and Vitou had not returned, and realized we probably had nothing else to offer. Reluctantly, they agreed to take the ring, not realizing it was worth
much more than our passage money.

The guides became angry when several others offered jewelry as well, but finally accepted it. The leader made threats, but did nothing. Before we left Poipet, Keang had assigned two or three men, armed with axes or knives, to each guide, with instructions not to let him out of sight once final payment was made. As soon as payment had been collected from everyone, we resumed our silent march.

Children old enough to walk bore up surprisingly well on the trek. Still, all but the oldest had to be carried occasionally. The youngest children and babies had been drugged, so they would sleep or be lethargic throughout the trip. It was essential that no child cry. Rasmei's baby slept most of the way, tied to her back with Mum's all-purpose *kroma*. All day we walked in silence. Most of the tedious trip was uneventful, just exhausting beyond anything we had imagined. We stopped only long enough for something to eat or drink. Rain continued to fall.

By night, we were still deep in the heavily forested mountain passes, out of food and almost out of water. Darkness increased our chances of avoiding detection by patrols or bandits but made walking much harder. We had hiked twenty or twenty-five miles—four or five times the distance needed had we been able to go in a straight line. I had no idea how much farther we would have to continue slipping in the mud, groping in the dark, stepping on sharp bamboo shoots, at the same time not daring to slow down or call out, or lose sight of the person ahead. The very thought of being left alone in the jungle in the dead of night was enough to quicken anyone's pace.

I supported Mum as best I could, wondering if I could last much longer myself. I had to force my legs to move, and my brain to function. The rest of the family struggled forward with the children. Without Vitou, Sarakun, and Leng, we were definitely handicapped.

I had completely lost my sense of direction in the blackness of the second night, and wondered how the guides could possibly know which way we were headed. It would be so easy to veer in one direction or another in the moonless night. Perhaps we had been walking in a great circle.

Finally, first light appeared—behind us. What relief! I didn't know if we were in Thailand, but at least we were still headed in the right direction, and the terrain had flattened as we had been told it would.

Startled by movement, I looked up in panic, just in time to see the guides bolt like frightened game. Soldiers were everywhere. Surrounded, the rest of us stood in weary confusion. I felt sick. Had the guides failed to notice the soldiers in time, or had we deliberately been betrayed?

The soldiers began speaking—in Thai. We were free!

We shed exhaustion like a worn-out garment as the tears flowed freely. Freedom revived us. Though we had been warned Thai soldiers would frisk us before turning us over to the officials, it was still traumatic to have it actually happen. We were shocked to find there was little difference between Cambodian robbers and Thai border guards. Bristling with indignation, I endured a body search of my underwear and private parts, a gun pointed at my head. I had only the jewel in my tooth, and they overlooked it.

Bold little Tevi deftly removed a gold chain from its place of concealment and casually held it safely in her partially closed fist. Mum was obviously nervous and shook violently from fear and fatigue as she was being searched. From her bundle, a soldier slipped the antique silver bowl into his jacket, then shook her glasses case. Eyeglasses and the diamond bracelet tumbled into the mud at her feet. Stooping to retrieve the bracelet, the border guard glanced into Mum's stricken face and pushed the bracelet toward her.

"It's all right, Grandmother," he said, then left her to search someone else. Other members of the family had some things taken, but the antique silver bowl in Keang's pack missed detection.

Well rewarded for their early-morning border duty and satisfied we were not Khmer Rouge infiltrators, the soldiers marched us the remaining mile to a nearby Buddhist temple complex. We arrived at five in the morning.

The wat had been hastily converted into a temporary refugee camp. Two hundred inmates were camped in the mud. Our group swelled the ranks to over three hundred. Despite its squalor, the compound looked like a fulfilled promise to us, and at first we didn't concern ourselves with its inadequacies. Nor did it matter to us just then that we were classified as "illegal aliens" rather than "refugees."

In a muddy rice field, adjacent to the temple complex, we found an unclaimed spot, fashioned a rude shelter with sheets of plastic, and flopped down to rest.

It had taken us 109 days rather than the estimated 20 to reach Thailand from Khum Speu, but at last our dream had been realized and we wanted to celebrate.

Enterprising village merchants eagerly approached the temple compound to sell their wares. We bought canned fish, fresh vegetables, and ice—ice—our first in four years. Some of the children had never tasted it. We couldn't resist steamed noodles, a treat that had vanished under Pol Pot. We wanted some of every food we saw.

We exchanged gold for the food, but it didn't matter. We were like irresponsible children, intoxicated with freedom, giddy with fatigue. We had been deprived too long and would need to live austerely for years to come, but this first day of freedom we wanted to splurge on a few delicacies we had not tasted in ages.

We bought five cans of sweetened condensed milk, and several loaves of crusty bread, then sat contentedly, dipping the bread in the milk, relishing every bite. A feast.

Contentment was bittersweet for Rasmei, Naly, and me. Though profoundly grateful to have escaped, we feared for our husbands. Had the men returned from Sisophon? Did they get the message we left with friends in Poipet, telling them the hour of our departure? Would we ever be reunited?

With luck, we reasoned, our husbands would have returned to the hut shortly after we left and were perhaps on their way across the vast green wasteland. Perhaps they had joined a group already formed. We'd been told it was unusual for a window along the border to remain open long. I prayed it would remain open at least a little longer.

A few hours after our arrival, another group of bedraggled Cambodians were escorted toward the wat by the border patrol. Beside myself with joy, I leaped to my feet, raced to the gate, and climbed on a rock to see better. Dancing from foot to foot, I scrutinized every passing face until the last man filed past. Tu was not there. The letdown was like a physical blow.

By this time, Rasmei and Naly had joined me. We hovered near the gate the rest of the day, inspecting every group of refugees. Though groups of escapees trailed into camp throughout the day, our men were not among them.

Chapter Sixteen

Vitou, Leng, and Sarakun had had no difficulty returning to Sisophon with the oxen and carts, but it took two days, not one, to sell their goods. Leng exchanged an eighteen-carat gold chain for a small solid-gold rod, got a good price for the highly prized oxen and carts, and sold our radio, knowing he could purchase another in Thailand. The radio was bought by the first villager who saw it. Leng sold many items cheaply, taking jewels in exchange when villagers had no gold. By the time the market closed, the three men had done well. But Sarakun still had several more things to sell for his group and elected to stay in Sisophon one more day.

They had already been gone three days and knew we would be worried. Leng and Vitou decided to start for Poipet immediately, rather than wait for morning. If they hurried, they could stop for the night in a small hamlet halfway back to Poipet and could be home easily by midmorning of the fourth day.

When they reached Poipet, Leng and Vitou were shocked to discover our hut vacant. A neighbor handed them our message. They had missed us by a mere seven hours. When Vitou found I was gone, he had felt betrayed, even though he had made me promise to go. His head told him it was the only logical course of action—he would have it no other way—but it hurt him to think I cared so little.

Leng, though ill, immediately busied himself among groups of refugees, discreetly inquiring about escape plans. Within hours, he had located a group of wealthy Chinese businessmen who planned to leave that evening. They had agreed to take Vitou and Leng, but would not wait for Sarakun. He would have to join a later group.

Now it was Vitou's turn to feel torn. He hated to leave his younger brother behind, but realized there was nothing he could do to make Sarakun's passage any easier. The longer he and Leng delayed, the less likely it was that they would ever find us. Each hour, the probability of the route remaining open diminished and each departing group increased the likelihood that those following would be intercepted. Besides, Leng was not well and needed Vitou's help more than Sarakun did. Reason told him he and Leng should go with the businessmen. All Vitou could do was pray his brother could make a later crossing.

They left food for Sarakun and a note. They found the packets of clothing, food, and water we had left for them, and hid their gold in the bundles, but Leng gave Vitou a solid-gold plug, about the size of a pencil stub, and two loose diamonds. Vitou shoved one in each ear after wrapping them in beeswax. He could barely hear.

Early in the afternoon, he and Leng had sauntered from the village, then stealthily doubled back through the jungle to the rendezvous point a few miles west of Poipet. They chafed at the long wait. They would be sixteen hours behind us by the time their guides were ready to leave. Gradually, everyone assembled, remaining hidden in small groups near the trail.

This group would not be slowed down by many women and children; they would move faster. In fact, Leng had been able to convince the merchants to take them along by volunteering himself and Vitou to help carry children. In order to be included, Leng had had to conceal the fact that he was in poor physical condition.

At dusk, the party moved rapidly and silently through the rain-soaked forest. As they walked, light faded quickly from the western sky. A heavy shower drenched them as they trudged. After several hours of hiding from patrols, stumbling over tree roots, scraping shins, and scrambling up hillsides in the dark, the guides finally signaled a halt. It was 2:00 A.M. Vitou and Leng dropped wearily to the side of the trail for a short respite.

Suddenly, Vitou stiffened. Though he could not see clearly in the dark, he sensed the party was surrounded by a half dozen men with guns. Slipping the gold bar from his pocket, he dug a hole with his finger and shoved the rod into the moist earth.

Armed men approached, holding lanterns aloft, and demanded everything of value. One robber shuffled down the line of refugees with an open sack while another threatened them with his gun. After each escapee put his valuables in the sack, he was searched. Those on whom the robbers found more valuables were shot.

As the robbers neared, Vitou whispered to Leng to give him some gold to hide before the thieves got close enough to see his motions in the dark. The only object Leng had time to pass was Mum's diamond ring. Not knowing what else to do, Vitou swallowed it. It caught in his throat. He swallowed hard. A burning sensation seared his chest. With diamonds in his ears and throat, he could barely hear or speak.

When the outlaws felt satisfied they had claimed everything worth taking, they slipped noiselessly back into the trees.

The group had been fortunate that the robbers surprised the party before the guides had time to bolt. It took some convincing on the part of the Chinese merchants before the guides agreed to continue the journey. Everyone pooled what little remained of their gold and jewels and tendered these to the guides. Leng and Vitou had only the two jewels hidden in Vitou's ears. In vain, Vitou dug in the mud trying to locate the spot where the gold bar had been buried. Finally, the guides had insisted everyone move on. Doubly cautious, the dispirited group had continued its flight.

Later that night, the party had come upon the bloated bodies of a group whose escape attempt had been foiled. Possessions lay scattered along the trail, the bundles rifled, then carelessly tossed aside to rot with the owners. Relief rushed over Vitou when he satisfied himself that none of the clothing had belonged to me or my family.

All night, they slogged through the steady downpour, through swamps and up slippery trails. The rains only ceased with daylight. Vitou's group skirted open scrubland, where they might be spotted at a distance, and their guides gave a wide berth to a deserted village.

The village had a well that looked inviting to the thirsty travelers, but a whispered message, passed down the trail from person to person, warned that the spot was excellent for an ambush. Later, the guides told them that trails to such villages were often booby-trapped. A particularly cruel trap consisted of bits of barbed metal anchored to boards buried along the trails. The sharp points pierced shoes and even thick tire-tread sandals. In trying to pull free, people only stepped on more. By the time they extricated themselves, their feet were lacerated. Many had had to give up escape. Vitou decided he would consider himself lucky if he got out of the jungle suffering only chest pains from the swallowed ring.

Leng and Vitou were nearly asleep on their feet, having hiked more than forty miles in the last thirty-six hours. They staggered as they kept pace.

The sun hung low in the sky. The guides had pointed ahead, declaring the group was in Thailand. A Buddhist temple could be reached by continuing across the plateau.

The businessmen were reluctant to be left at this point, but the guides were adamant. Most of their profit had been stolen by the bandits. This had not been a good trip for them. With only the valuables the refugees had scraped together in the forest, the guides planned to do some trading that evening and be back in the safety of the wild mountains, headed for Cambodia, before daylight. Vitou marveled at their stamina.

Apprehensively, the group trudged on alone. There were green hills and gently sloping plateaus stretching in every direction as far as they could see. Everything looked the same. Vitou knew they had traveled west all day, but was it far enough? They soon found out.

Soldiers intercepted them on the muddy trail. This was a disappointing group of refugees as far as the Thai border guards were concerned. No valuables. However, they had already augmented their army salary quite nicely by escorting several refugee groups into camp, joking, as they searched, about the side benefits of patrol. Everyone in the nearby village benefited. What the guards did not strip from the Cambodians before they entered camp, their relatives would, no doubt, glean in trade. Almost too weary to feel jubilant, Vitou and Leng brought up the rear of the little procession as it entered the compound. With a wild scream, I leaped at Vitou as he staggered through the gate.

When he realized who it was, he was as excited as I. We couldn't believe our good luck. We had both escaped, and had been taken to the same camp. We thought our joy was complete until we looked into the grief-stricken face of Naly, as she realized Sarakun was not with his brother. Poor Naly. That night, there was nothing for her to do except return to the rude shelter Aunt Satah and her relatives had erected.

Home. A sheet of plastic laid over the muddy rice stubble, with a second plastic tarp propped over it. Fifteen of us lived and slept there. Naly's group, sheltered nearby, was only slightly less crowded. On this first night of freedom, however, we hardly noticed the inadequacies. Totally spent, but jubilant, we slept soundly.

Fear of permanent separation from our husbands had made the wait seem like an eternity to Rasmei and me. It had actually been less than twelve hours from the time we stumbled into the temple compound—the first group of the day—and the time Leng and Tu arrived in the evening—the last. It was the tenth day of May, 1979. We were free. Free.

On our second night in camp, Tu confided he had swallowed my mother's ring.

I was horrified, especially when he confessed he had not felt well since, and hadn't eaten much since his arrival because it hurt to swallow. My worry for him erupted into anger. How could he have done such a thing? Didn't he know his life was more important than any ring? If he didn't feel better soon, we would have to request a doctor. And if he needed an operation, it would cost much more than the stupid ring could possibly be worth. The thought of losing Tu after we had reached safety was more than I could stand.

To reassure me, he told about the time one of his relatives had forced a rod of gold, about the size of the first joint of his little finger, up his rectum, in order to keep it from being detected by the Khmer Rouge. His cousin did not know if it had been expelled or if it was still floating around somewhere inside him. The point was, he had been fine, and Vitou felt sure he would be, too.

The next morning, I was so worried about Tu that I confided in Mum, only to learn Leng had already told the others. Everyone in the family fretted about him. Whenever he disappeared into the nearby woods to relieve himself, quizzical looks accompanied his return. Each time his answer was a negative shake of the head. On the fourth day, he emerged from the bushes beaming, triumphantly holding aloft his sparkling prize.

He had retrieved the ring, scrubbed and polished it. With a flourish, he presented it to my mother. The story became a cherished family joke.

All anyone wanted to do for the first few days was eat and sleep. International charitable organizations provided more rice each day than we could possibly consume, though we tried. They occasionally supplied fish as well. We supplemented this basic diet with purchases from Thai merchants, who brought goods to the compound gate each morning.

No camp routine or assignments had been given when we first arrived. In fact, there was absolutely nothing we were required to do with our time, so we freely indulged in sleep. More than physical relaxation, our nerves needed rest. The strain of the previous four years would not soon pass.

The youngest were the first to recover. Rota, Chenda Poong, and their cousins soon joined other children in games.

Vitou and I went from group to group to see if anyone we knew had arrived in the latest waves of refugees entering the camp. We were on the lookout for news of Sarakun. None came. It was difficult for Naly to watch Tu and me so happy together. We tried to comfort her, but her sadness diminished the joy we shared in our own reunion.

Once again, I began to miss my father. Until recently, it had seemed better that he was dead. Now that we were free, I wished he were with us, and I found myself reading and rereading his letter.

The Buddhist wat was not an official refugee camp and had none of the usual camp amenities, which became apparent to us the longer we stayed there. A hastily dug trench behind some bushes served as a temporary latrine. A nearby brook was available for bathing. Guards kept the swelling ranks of refugees within the square half-mile compound. Other than that, we were left alone to entertain ourselves as best we could. Monsoon rains had turned heavy traffic areas into a muddy bog. Latrines soon filled, and people were forced to find their own spot in the woods to relieve themselves. The unsanitary camp reeked, but Thailand had nothing better to offer at the time.

The country was overwhelmed with refugees. Even before 1975, people had left war-torn Cambodia and Laos, seeking refuge. Thailand had simply absorbed the first immigrants into the culture—one not too different from those the refugees had left behind. Many had sought only temporary asylum, and educated people soon relocated in other countries. During the Pol Pot years, more escapees arrived than could be absorbed. The Thais converted every possible site along the border into holding pens to contain the influx, where they fed and housed us and attended to the most serious medical needs, until something permanent could be arranged. The floodgates had burst when Vietnam invaded Cambodia. Our family was part of the tidal wave of escapees that inundated Thailand at that time.

In our small temple complex, the population swelled from three hundred at the time we moved in to over forty thousand within the month. Unless help was forthcoming soon, Thailand threatened, they would be forced to stop border crossings, and send back those of us already in the camps.

Mearadey started writing letters again. This time she wrote directly to relatives in France, still not knowing if the addresses were correct. Leng was recruited by Thai officials to act as an interpreter when English-speaking fact-finding delegations came to our camp. He also helped take down family histories and register refugees who sought relocation in English-speaking nations.

When we learned some countries might allow increased immigration quotas, we decided to register for the United States. Soorsdey and I began filling out forms for each family member so we could request sponsors in America.

We wanted to be classified as one family under Mum, but that was not allowed. Each of the men and Naly had to be listed as head of a separate household, with their wives and children, but Mum could be included on any son-in-law's form. It did not seem to matter which list she was put on, since we all planned to be together in America. Tu and I had always intended that Mum would eventually live with us, so we put her on our form. Thus, my mother officially became part of our household.

While filling in forms for Mum, a problem arose. She simply could not remember the conversion system from the Cambodian to the Western calendar. Between one form and the next, we noticed she had given conflicting dates for her birth. We were afraid that she would continue to forget the date from one telling to another, and feared that discrepancies would keep her papers from being processed. Not wanting to take any chances, we decided that she should select a Western calendar date she could always remember and simply call that her birthday. The date she chose was January 1, one of the few Western dates she knew.

There was one other problem. Rasmei's baby was two months old and still nameless. If she was going to grow up in the West, we wanted a name to fit her new identity. Keang suggested one. In a little family party, baby Hong was named Helena.

Incredibly, of the forty people who had left Khum Speu, thirty-nine were still together, only Sarakun was missing. Most of the group wanted to emigrate to the United States. Some chose Canada. A few selected France, since they had relatives there and knew the language. One couple, Mey Kamphot and his bride, divorced. She wanted to settle in France with her relatives; he was determined to try Canada.

Governments were more inclined to process forms if people listed relatives in the country they hoped to settle in, especially if those relatives volunteered to sponsor the new immigrants. Transition to a new culture was much easier with established relatives to help, thus requiring less government aid. We knew this, and had distant relatives in America, some of whom would, no doubt, be willing to serve as sponsors. However, we had no addresses for the U.S. embassy personnel to verify. We hated to turn in forms with that category left blank, but we couldn't wait forever for our relatives in France to send the American addresses to us. We feared being returned to Cambodia if we stayed in the filthy camp much longer.

Officials from different embassies assured us everyone in the camps would be processed to Western countries, as soon as places could be found. We relaxed a little. Apparently, it was not essential to have proof of relatives living in the country of immigration, though it did seem to speed up paperwork and give priority to those who provided precise addresses and names. When we turned in our forms, we had been in the compound just over a week.

Trying to live in a rain-soaked rice paddy on a square of plastic, with little to do, made time drag. I had not been well. Before we left Poipet, I had again begun suffering from the recurring illness I had developed in Khum Speu. Every hot, humid season, the chills and fever attacks had returned. Vitou bought ice to slacken my thirst, which helped, but it was too expensive to purchase often.

Sickness pervaded the temple compound. Many refugees arrived with serious diseases and infections. Everyone was malnourished, and some were near death from starvation. Sanitary conditions were hard to maintain with thousands of people camped in a confined area in puddle-pocked fields. Drinking water was not clean, medical help minimal, and medicines in short supply.

It was so crowded in our shelter that it was difficult for me to sleep, so Vitou and I often slept under the trees in the daytime when I wasn't helping people fill out forms. Sometimes, we stayed up all night visiting with other refugees, which left a little more room in the shelter for the thirteen others. Still, they slept head to toe like canned sardines.

The trees we slept under during the day were just outside the main temple complex. Refugees and Thai villagers had access to the area, but some Thais took unfair advantage of this arrangement. Upon finding refugees sleeping alone or visiting in small groups, Thai villagers accosted them and demanded watches, rings, or anything else of value. Since Thais routinely carried shotguns, their "requests" were complied with promptly. Refugees felt defenseless. None of us wanted to be accused of causing trouble. Our stay in Thailand was tenuous at best, and could be rescinded at any time. In a confrontation, Thai villagers were at an advantage with Thai authorities, so refugees simply acquiesced to the outrageous confiscations.

Petty theft was also a problem among the refugees. Objects that disappeared routinely were small, useful articles—a bowl, a teapot, a piece of clothing, a sheet of plastic, firewood, items not closely guarded.

Vitou could speak a little Thai, which allowed him to slip in and out of the camp occasionally to shop in the village where prices weren't inflated, and the selection was better. In anticipation of our impending emigration, we needed new clothing. The outfit I had worn across the border literally fell apart shortly after I reached the camp. Others in the family fared no better, and we did not want to meet our relatives or sponsors in the West looking like refugees.

By careful bargaining in the village, Leng and Vitou bought *sampot*s and a new outfit of Western clothing for each of us. We felt and looked civilized again, and my sisters and I even took time to fix our hair and nails.

Two weeks after we arrived in Thailand, days after turning in the forms, Keang and Mearadey, and their three daughters, left on a new air-conditioned bus bound for Bangkok, along with government officials and high-ranking military men of the former republic who had been given priority.

The rest of us were told our papers were being processed, and buses would come for us soon. We feared the separation but were assured it was only temporary. Without addresses of relatives in America, we each had to wait until sponsoring families could be matched to us, with no assurance we would all be sent to the same part of America. Though we would miss each other dreadfully, we had to remind ourselves we were lucky to have escaped at all, and couldn't expect to be sponsored by people in the same cities.

Now I wished I had put Mum's name on Keang and Mearadey's list. The camp near Bangkok, where they would stay for final processing, was reported to be much nicer than the makeshift temple compound. There Keang's family would receive medical checkups and immunizations. Once they were assigned a sponsor, airline tickets and pocket money would be issued, and they would be on their way.

I was excited about their quick sponsorship. I didn't even mind not being included, but I hated to see my mother living in miserable conditions merely because her name had been put on my list.

A week after Mearadey reached the camp near Bangkok, a letter from France reached her from Mum's youngest brother, our uncle who had invited us to live with him in western Cambodia at the time Phnom Penh was being bombarded. He had received Mearadey's letter from a distant relative, and his reply told of his life since escaping. He and his wife and children had settled in France, where he worked as a landscaper and his wife as a nurse. They had not acquired much money in the four years they had lived in their new country, but were willing to sponsor our entire family. Happy to learn we were still alive, he wanted to do whatever he could to help.

Mearadey was deeply touched by his kind offer, and wrote to tell us of it, but after serious reflection, she and Keang decided not to accept, and made the same decision for all of us. Our entire family wanted to settle in the United States, and our papers were already partially processed. Had the offer from France come sooner, she and Keang would have gladly accepted. Now they chose to keep to the course we had set. In his letter, our uncle also included current addresses of relatives in America. Mearadey wrote to them regarding the need the rest of us had for sponsorship.

Added to the joy of receiving our uncle's letter, Mearadey was surprised to discover a familiar name on a list of refugees in the Bangkok camp—Sarakun!

Chapter Seventeen

Refugees continued to pour into Thailand. Other nations talked about the need to help, but the process was slow, and the Thais needed immediate help. In desperation, Thailand announced illegal aliens would be returned to Cambodia.

In our border camp, Leng heard the dreaded message on a friend's radio. He had listened to the radio every day since our arrival, so he had known a crisis was brewing, but hoped it would not involve us. Because our emigration papers were partially processed, he felt quite secure that we would not be included in any order to go back.

We had been assured repeatedly that, even if we did not go to Bangkok soon, we would be sent to a more permanent facility. People simply had to be moved from the cesspool conditions. We couldn't have agreed more. The camp had become so crowded that not everyone could be contained in the compound. People camped outside the fence.

The day Leng heard the radio broadcast, another bus from Bangkok arrived in our camp. Naly's name was called. It was then she learned her husband was in Bangkok, and she was to join him. We were ecstatic.

Most names read out for transport, at the time Naly left, were for others in similar situations, where some members of the family had been processed but not others, or for people with verifiable relatives in America. Others in our group of forty went to Bangkok, including Aunt Satah and Uncle Mey Kamphot. Leng, Rasmei, and their children, Samol, Soorsdey, Mum, Tu, and I were left behind.

Three days passed. In midafternoon, a convoy of buses arrived at the gates. Our names were called to board. Mum insisted we pack the extra rice we had been issued, along with our plastic tarps, containers of water, and other accumulated items. If we were processed soon, we could discard the things in Bangkok. If we were sent to another camp, we would still need our possessions.

Leng made frantic inquiries about our destination while the rest of us packed. He asked bus drivers, officials, anyone. Two days before, a minister in the Thai government had been interviewed by a TV reporter. He stated Thailand did not recognize the illegal aliens in their country as genuine refugees. They were to be deported. Radio and newspapers echoed these views, which had been discussed with uneasiness in every refugee camp. Camp officials were besieged by people demanding to know if they had been listed as "refugee" or "illegal alien." Leng already knew our classification, so before we boarded a bus, he wanted to be sure where it was going.

He had previously been promised by embassy officials of various nationalities that everyone in our camp would be accommodated by one country or another, but now there were no embassy personnel available to talk to. More buses were on hand than had ever come before. The size of the convoy indicated that most people inside the temple complex would also be relocated with us. Leng could not determine if this was a good or bad sign.

One Thai official whom Leng cornered stated categorically that no one from this camp was being sent back to Cambodia. The buses were headed for Ubon, a less crowded refugee camp in northern Thailand. Some soldiers said the buses were going to Bangkok. The conflicting stories worried us. Reluctantly, we boarded. There was really no other option; armed guards saw to that.

We climbed aboard a comfortable air-conditioned bus with plush upholstered seats. It looked just like the bus that had taken Keang's family, and later Naly, to Bangkok. We felt better. Riding on a bus was an exciting new experience for Rota and Chenda Poong. However, Leng began to relax only when he saw the first road sign: BANGKOK 227 KM.

From the bus window, I saw, for the first time, the villages we had been camped near for the past month. In the markets, I noticed items we had not seen in four years or more. We had almost forgotten these things still existed. Rasmei and I busily pointed out everything to the enchanted children, whose little noses were pressed to the window, their eyes glued to the passing scenes.

A cacophony of voices filled the bus, as people eagerly directed attention toward once common sights.

"See the supermarket. You can't remember that. You were too young when we lived in Phnom Penh."

Vegetable markets, huge homes, a school, a lovely temple. We traveled toward Bangkok for over an hour in high spirits; only Leng sat silent. At a service station just beyond the village of Kabin Buri, the convoy stopped for gasoline. Villagers, hawking wares, carried snack-filled bamboo trays up and down the lines of buses. Food and coins changed hands through the open windows.

I leaned out the window and asked an educated-looking soldier where the buses were headed.

"Bangkok," he mechanically shot back.

I nodded and smiled my thanks. Though we had been heading west before the stop, now I, too, felt concern at this rehearsed reply.

There were too many buses. Other groups leaving for

camps near Bangkok had been much smaller. I wished his answer had been another refugee camp. I would have found that easier to believe. Years of Pol Pot's—and his cohorts'—deceitful behavior made me skeptical of pat replies. Seated next to my worried mother, I tried to appear optimistic.

I repeated what the soldier had said and hoped I sounded convincing. No need to upset Mum unnecessarily. A woman in the seat behind said she used to travel between Phnom Penh and Bangkok often on this road. We were indeed headed toward Bangkok, not the border, she asserted loud enough so most in the bus could hear.

All the buses were at last filled with gasoline, and the convoy started moving again—this time back through the village. An audible moan filled the bus. The woman behind me confidently assured everyone there were two routes to Bangkok from Kabin Buri. In fact, the southern route was even better. Hope revived. When we arrived at the crossroads, however, the buses turned north. We were definitely not going to Bangkok.

We pinned our hopes on being sent to another refugee camp, as the official at the gate had reported. Both Ubon and Buriram camps were northeast of Bangkok. Early evening, when the buses again stopped for fuel, Leng inquired where we were going. Two Thai soldiers told him, "Ubon." We clung to that reassurance as we stared out the window and watched twilight flow into night.

All night, the buses snaked through small villages and over mountain passes, uphill and down, back and forth, hour after hour. In the rain-whipped dark, it was impossible to be sure in which direction we were headed. Each time I woke from a fitful sleep, I could only ascertain, reassuringly, that the road was a major one and we were moving in a general northeasterly direction paralleling the Thai-Cambodian border. Occasionally, I glimpsed highway markers that indicated we were still on Highway 10. That was important. The radio had announced two days before, not long after the minister made his shocking pronouncement about Cambodians being sent back, that the Vietnamese had agreed to facilitate passage of those returning, and had food supplies and personnel located south of the Phnom Penh–Bangkok highway to receive the returnees. Since I knew we had not doubled back from our generally northeasterly route, I felt slightly reassured. I concluded we must be headed toward the Ubon refugee camp, as the soldiers had said. Again I dozed.

At 4:15 A.M. I jerked awake. The bus had veered sharply to the right onto a rutted, back road. Rays of the early-morning sun shot through the window on the wrong side of the bus, so others were also aware of our changed direction. In the early light, jungle-draped mountains loomed on every side. Ubon was in the rice-growing flatlands.

I knew beyond doubt we were being returned to our homeland. But why in this wild, forsaken region of northern Cambodia? Why not south of Poipet, where the Vietnamese were expecting us? There were no roads in this part of Cambodia, no possibility of getting food and water. What had happened to the plan to turn us over to the Vietnamese? How could we survive in this rough country?

Mum was not well. Rasmei was still weak from Helena's birth. Soorsdey was six months pregnant. I was just recovering from illness, and we had three small children to protect. The Khmer Rouge had their last remaining strongholds in this section of Cambodia. Why here?

Freedom had seemed so real when we crossed into Thailand. Now, exactly one month later, our dreams were dashed and death seemed certain.

In anguish, I repeatedly berated myself. Why hadn't I written Mum's name on Keang's list? It seemed such an arbitrary decision at the time, so unimportant. How stupid of me not to have realized Americans wanted educated men who could offer the nation something. Instead, I had stupidly, unthinkingly, put Mum on my own list. Fool! What had possessed me? Tu and I could stand whatever we must—stand it or die. It didn't matter. But Mum, my poor Mum.

Awareness of the forced return shocked my mother into numbed silence, as she stared unseeing at her knotted hands spasmodically clutching her wrinkled *sampot.* The bus rumbled on.

Each person, murmuring angrily or fighting back tears, tried to come to grips with catastrophe in his own way. Shocked disbelief showed on every face. I looked at Samol, then Soorsdey, heavy with child. We had just come from hell and were being sentenced to return. We couldn't believe our awful fate. Defeated, many wished only for a quick death.

In his innocence, little Rota frantically turned his tear-stained face to his father and asked, "But, Daddy, why did they lie to us? Why?"

Leng, in a choked whisper, voiced the obvious answer. "Son, the soldiers realized if we knew the truth, they would have had to kill us before we would have boarded the buses."

Cruel as it was, we could understand the lie, but it was doubly cruel to push us back across in the north when arrangements had been made for returning us to the south. It seemed little short of cold-blooded, premeditated murder. The remote jungle had been chosen deliberately. The Thais wanted an international incident and we were to be it.

Everyone in the convoy gaped in horror as we passed piles of possessions obviously jettisoned by other recent refugees forced out along the seldom-used road. Sheets of plastic, sacks of rice, clothing, pots, and water containers littered the roadside.

The buses lurched to a standstill. We were ordered out.

People refused to budge until forced from their seats at gunpoint. If only we could hold out a little longer without going back across the border, perhaps the order would be rescinded.

Everyone knew that shock waves from Thailand's decision to return us were reverberating throughout the world. Thailand's point had been made, and we did not want to be the victims of its strong message that help was needed *immediately*.

Camping on the Thai side of the border had been made impossible. Refugees, herded like cattle one busload at a time, were funneled between lines of soldiers to the summit of a steep ridge that marked the border, then pushed over. Wielding guns, Thai soldiers shouted, "Go down. Go down." They began shooting at those who refused to start down the face of the cliff.

Below the ridge, we could hear people screaming and moaning. Those who had been forced over the border during the past two days stubbornly refused to move off the mountainside trails, yet the press of refugees from above kept pushing them farther down. The entire face of the hill had been heavily mined by the Khmer Rouge four years ago, and everyone was terrified to break a new trail in the five-mile-wide no-man's-land. Occasionally, a mine exploded as the crowd pushed someone off the trail. Since everyone wanted to step only where they had seen others step, they slid cautiously downward only when forced from above by the pressure of others moving downhill. Descent proceeded at a snail's pace.

Stepping from the bus, I noticed Thai soldiers were stationed every twenty yards all along the ridge as far as I could see. That ruled out the possibility of going down the mountain face a short distance, then doubling back through the jungle to another point to sneak back into Thailand. Even if we could avoid the land mines, we would never get past the guards at the summit.

Leng thought about trying to buy our way out. We still had Mum's diamond ring, thanks to Vitou, and the diamond-studded bracelet, plus a little gold and some Thai bahts Leng had earned as an interpreter in the camp. We watched a rich Chinese man cautiously approach a nearby guard.

The Chinese gentleman and his party had pooled their Thai money in a red plastic bucket. Quietly, he offered it to the soldier, then asked to be pointed in a direction leading to freedom. The soldier accepted the bucket and motioned with his gun down a side path as he looked the other way. No sooner had the group started down this path, however, than the guard turned and raised the muzzle of his submachine gun. They fell like dominoes.

Most of the soldiers had no desire to kill, no hatred. They were just following orders. The Thai government had decided it had no alternative but forced repatriation, since no other countries were offering adequate aid for the overwhelming refugee problem. The order was inhumane and sentenced thousands of Cambodians to agonizing deaths, but we did not blame individual soldiers. We did not even blame the Thai government. That descent down the cliff was too hellish for such luxuries as fault-finding. It was as if something primal forced us off the edge of the world.

The concern some soldiers had for the plight of the refugees was evident. They dashed from bus to bus reminding people to be sure to take water and plenty of food. If people didn't have food, they were told to grab what had been left by others. Even at the ridge, some soldiers gently helped the old or the very young take the first tentative steps over the edge, so they wouldn't fall. Others sincerely wished them luck.

Faced with the descent, however, some families simply left their old, their very young, and their infirm on the ridge, knowing death awaited them if they entered the tangled vegetation of the jungle below. They could only hope for mercy from Thai soldiers for those abandoned loved ones. Even if they were shot, it would be kinder than slow death in the jungle. Old people who had no family to help them simply could not descend. They, too, lay down at the summit. Many were shot, others were left to die slowly. None were spared. None.

Much of the food Mum had so carefully accumulated had to be left on the ridge, along with the excess possessions of countless others. There was no way to carry it all and still cling to roots and overhanging vines. This time, however, we at least knew which objects would be of most value. We must have water. We took four full jugs. We must have food. We took a fifteen-day supply of rice. We needed plastic tarps, clothing, and items for barter.

All too soon our turn came, and we began the slippery drop over the edge of the cliff. Tree roots and vines slowed our sliding descent, as the three men and I helped the other six.

Finding footing on a narrow ledge to the side of the trail not far from the summit, Leng told Rota to fall down and moan as though he were hurt or ill. Perhaps Thai soldiers would allow us to remain there to nurse him. It didn't work. Soldiers threatened to shoot us if we did not move. Reluctantly but quickly we complied. About fifty yards below the summit the cliff ended and it was a little easier to walk.

We had seen Thai soldiers aim about shoulder height and fire along the trail, killing any who didn't duck or move forward on command. After a submachine-gun burst, little children, too short to be in the line of fire, were left as orphans. They whimpered by the side of slain parents, but few people dared stop long enough to help them.

Just ahead of Leng, near the trail at the base of the overhanging cliff, two young boys tried to battle their way back up the steep incline. One was shot between the eyes. Horror-stricken, Leng dropped his bag of rice as the second child's head was blown off. The boys were little older than Rota. Turning to retrieve his spilled rice, Leng could only scoop up part of it. The rest was strewn among the rocks. We no longer had a fifteen-day supply.

Bus after bus disgorged victims all that day. (Over forty-two thousand refugees would be returned to Cambodia at this

254

border.) Many were forced over the summit without any food or water, especially those who had not been in the camps long enough to save excess rice supplies.

A man told Leng it was impossible to go the way we were headed. There were no roads for miles and no one to lead us through the minefields, underbrush, and tangled vines. Yet there was no other choice.

We stopped for the night along the narrow confines of a trail blazed by those forced to move ahead. In the gathering darkness, the summit—our only chance of escape—was silhouetted above us. Then even that faded from view.

At the base of the cliff, Leng proposed one other option. Why not try to camp where we were to see if help might come or border security slacken? It was worth a try, but we would need more food.

Under cover of darkness, Vitou and Samol ventured to climb through the massed slumbering and dead bodies to the ridge top in order to claim rice left behind. As they cautiously inched toward the crest, they noted a strange rosy glow, like a second sunset. Peering through the bushes, they saw that the rice and all other possessions had been gathered into a pile and set on fire. Obviously, the Thais didn't want anyone to return to the summit or remain at the foot of the mountain tempted by the promise of food. Empty-handed, they slipped silently back down the cliff.

I thought the nightmare I had lived through for years and the trauma of our escape had exposed me to all the suffering and horrors this world had to offer. I was wrong. *Nothing* had prepared us for this first night on the trail. Descent from the cliff was like being lowered into the jaws of hell.

Fever-crazed, I cowered against the side of the muddy trail in torrential rain, not daring to shift position in the dark for fear of setting off a land mine. My nostrils were filled with the stench of bloated bodies of those who had already found mines.

This smell was coupled with the putrid odor of vomit and human waste from thousands of people, who dared not even step off a trail to relieve themselves. All this, and my own feverish state, left me faint. Propped against a tree, I fell into a fitful stupor, blotting out the pitiful cries of the distressed and damned who tried to cling to the mountainside and their sanity. Physically ill and sick at heart, I did not care if I lived until morning. It was the worst night of my life.

Chapter Eighteen

At dawn, after that first night on the mountain trail, Thai soldiers on the ridge resumed sending people over the cliff, shouting to those below to move, and shooting those who refused. Nudged forward, we joined the throngs inching down the dangerous trails, advancing twenty or thirty yards each day. Those near the front of the steep trail still only budged when forced by those descending upon them from above.

When someone found signs of a land mine, they stuck a branch in the ground and bent it over to point at the spot and tied a rag to the stick. Everyone looked out for his neighbor, partly out of simple concern and partly because someone in front or behind or to the side of you endangered your life as well as their own if they stepped on a mine. Fortunately, most of those who triggered mines were killed instantly. To be wounded in this mountainous terrain meant a slow, agonizing death. And it was impossible to bury the dead with mines all around. The bodies could only be left to rot where they lay, and trails rerouted around them.

A dense canopy of leaves trapped hot, fetid air near the forest floor. The putrid smell made me retch. Yet those tragic dead bodies provided a service to those seeking a way off the treacherous mountain. They marked paths where mines had been but were no longer. It was safe to step near the mangled remains.

All day, Rota and Chenda Poong whimpered, as did most children and many adults. Though I had both seen and smelled death and decay under Pol Pot's reign of terror, I had never been forced into the immediate presence of bloated cadavers day after day. For over a week, we lay beside, stepped over, ate near, and slept with the mutilated dead.

Four years before, when forced from Phnom Penh, we had all agreed that nothing could equal the horror of that mass exodus: the filth, stench, cruelty, and paralyzing fear we had endured at the time. But it couldn't begin to compare with the trials of this hellish place. Physically, we were not well, and we had less food, clothing, water. Worse than all the dangers and horror was the sure knowledge of the awful predicament we were in. Four years before, we had left Phnom Penh expecting to be inconvenienced for a few days before returning to the comforts of our home. This time, we had left the bus at the top of the cliff knowing survival on the mountain was almost impossible. There were no illusions to sustain us and our despair weighed us down.

Leng refused to leave the base of the mountain, so we found a spot to the side of the trail and waited. From a refugee with a radio, we learned the United Nations was rushing representatives to Bangkok to intervene on behalf of those being repatriated. Staying near the border was our best chance of returning to Thailand, but unless a UN decision was reached soon, we knew we would have to give up our vigil and join others who were trying to reach Cambodia's heartland before food and water ran out.

By collecting rainwater with our plastic sheets, we were able to make our food supply last longer. Thin rice gruel sustained us, as it had so often during the previous years; that and Vitou's uncanny ability to find dry wood in the wet forest and to keep damp wood burning. His knowledge of the jungle, of edible and poisonous plants, also stretched our food supply. The jungle held few fears for Vitou, but until we left the five-mile-wide swath of land mines, he could not really attempt to hunt.

Each day, we rehashed the possible escape routes and schemes. We were still convinced it was impossible to hike parallel with the border in this region, as it was unusually rugged country with no permanent rivers to supply fresh water. By the time we reached a brook, the season's torrential rains would have swollen the stream to a wide channel of unfordable water. Besides being heavily mined, there were no villages nearby where we could buy food. No roads. And we would be likely to encounter Khmer Rouge enclaves in these mountains. We had no guides, and, finally, if we ever crossed into Thailand in this region, we would still find no food, water, or nearby villages. Once we left the immediate area, our only chance of escape was to find a road leading back into Cambodia's heartland, and then once again follow Highway 6 toward Poipet and the border. We wanted to postpone that formidable trek as long as possible. Many others had made the same decision. We joined the massed humanity waiting huddled at the base of the mountain.

On a radio broadcast, Leng heard the explanation Thailand gave for sending us into Cambodia in this unpopulated area rather than the agreed-upon southern region. Thai officials knew most people had crossed into Thailand south of Poipet. Also, most refugee camps were located there. The government had reasoned that if they sent refugees back into southern Cambodia, they would quickly attempt another crossing to get back to the camps. That wouldn't solve the refugee problem. Instead, by sending us into Cambodia via the north, we would be forced into the interior of the country. Perhaps many would decide to stay in Cambodia, or at least it would take people much longer to reach the border again. By then other nations might have volunteered help so Thailand could better handle the influx.

Leng agreed the plan had merit—if human suffering was of no consequence. By the time the Vietnamese learned of the altered plans, however, and sent food and soldiers north, many refugees had already died. But there were a few who eventually found a way out of the wilderness on their own.

On the seventh day near the cliff, we learned the United Nations had been unable to stop deportation. With this news, most returnees concluded it no longer made sense to remain at the border. They would starve before the bureaucracy moved. By this time, also, some refugees had found their way to a Vietnamese army camp. They had not been shot, as they had feared, but had been fed and given food to take back to their families. Vietnamese soldiers helped detonate mines, making a wider, safer trail, and they pointed out the trail to the nearest road. They were quite kind and helpful, and their advice and food saved many lives.

After people made contact with the Vietnamese, hope again rose in our family. Until then, we had felt it was very likely we would die in the mountains, since we had no way of surviving long enough to find a way out on our own. Truthfully, we hadn't even been willing to try.

Many people were deathly ill. Diarrhea was rampant, yet knowledge that a way out had been found renewed their strength and everyone began to move as rapidly as possible toward the nearest road that would eventually lead to the French-built north-south highway linking Cambodia and Laos. Tens of thousands streamed down from the mountain jungles.

In a family council, it was determined that everyone still wanted to attempt escape. After all we had been through, we would still risk death rather than live under Communists. The craving for freedom was too strong.

We began the long march into central Cambodia to link up with Highway 6. Samol and Soorsdey's baby was due soon. They planned to go with us as far as Kompong Thom, then return to

Khum Speu to live with Samol's parents until the baby was old enough to travel, otherwise the rest of us would be slowed down.

Occasionally, along the route, we met bands of Vietnamese soldiers. They treated the refugees with gentleness, although those of obvious Chinese ancestry were poorly treated. (This reflected the Soviet-backed Vietnamese animosity toward China.) Thirty miles from the border, the Vietnamese helped everyone cross a large river, but made the Chinese-Cambodians wait until the rest of us had crossed. Even with over a thousand people ferried across in little boats each day, the process would take almost a month. Fortunately, our turn came early.

Many refugees died of malnutrition on the march back into the center of Cambodia, and a large percentage of these were Chinese. All of us were reduced to diets lacking in protein and salt, which caused legs to swell and bodies to retain excessive amounts of water. Leng and Samol suffered greatly from this affliction, but the Chinese we saw suffered even more because fewer supplies were made available to them. Since Chinese refugees were detained longer en route, they were reduced to a diet of bamboo shoots to supplement their limited rice supplies. This lopsided diet took its toll in lives and health.

Compared to those about us, our family felt quite healthy. Through sheer willpower, Mum managed to walk the fifteen miles per day we averaged once we reached a road. I recovered from my fever and suffered only from general malnutrition like the rest of my family. Soorsdey, although in the last stages of pregnancy, never complained that conditions were more than she could bear. Rasmei continued to breast-feed Helena and we marveled that her body could produce milk on her poor diet. Vitou, Rota, and Chenda Poong remained relatively healthy.

Each day we plodded steadily through the heat and heavy rain of the monsoon: late June, July, and part of August. We slept in puddles of stagnant water under leaky, plastic tarps, camped at the side of the road, since there were no villages.

261

Northern Cambodia's red mud colored our damp clothing and legs. We had no option but to sleep, eat, and live in it days on end.

There were no long delays, no rest. We seldom stopped long enough for Leng to fish or Vitou to hunt. Wild animals were abundant in the northern jungles, but refugees saw very few. Perhaps the thousands of returnees traveling this route scared animals away. Once a woman came screaming down the line of weary travelers claiming she had seen a tiger run across the road, but by the time Vitou reached the spot, the animal had long since disappeared.

Before we reached central Cambodia, the column of refugees was strung out the full length of the route. Despite our physical problems, we were traveling faster than most of the others. One reason for our rush was the desire to get Soorsdey back to her in-laws before the baby was born.

Villagers along this stretch of road were suspicious of strangers, but Leng had the rare ability of putting them at ease. As we had seen so many times before, people trusted Leng and traded with him when they would not deal with others. Peasants were eager to exchange their rice for our clothing, since they hadn't had new clothes for years. A shirt could be traded for a sack of rice and occasionally a chicken. Leng had a pencil he had used in the refugee camp to register people, and he was even able to trade the used pencil for rice. Because Leng and Vitou had outfitted each of us with new clothes while we were in the refugee camp, we were able to buy our way across Cambodia.

Peasants would not take gold or jewelry, so refugees with nothing else to offer found it impossible to get food. Families like ours became middlemen. Leng bought rice with our clothes and Mum traded it with fellow travelers for the gold and diamonds we knew we would need when we tried another border crossing.

Eventually, we reached the crossroads where Highway 12 from the north intersects Highway 6. It had taken almost a month to come from the northern border to the center of the country. This was a difficult juncture, for it was here Soorsdey and Samol would say good-bye to us. They would turn east toward Speu and we would turn west toward Siem Reap, Sisophon, Poipet, and another attempt at a crossing. From Kompong Thom, until we reached the border, we would retrace the route we had used on the first escape, although this time storehouses would be empty and there were no oxen or carts to carry Mum and the children.

Everyone knew how hard escape had been for Rasmei with a newborn, so it seemed likely it would be at least three or four months before Soorsdey and Samol could hope to again attempt to cross the border. In the meantime, Samol would have to find some way to acquire the capital to pay for a guide. We wondered whether it would ever be possible for them to leave the country.

During our last evening together in Kompong Thom, we tried to relive the fantasy that had cheered us on the first trip out—"When I get to America I will . . ."—but it just didn't work. We knew how unlikely it was that any of us would ever reach America or even Thailand.

On the morning of July 8, 1979, Samol and Soorsdey walked toward the rising sun with heavy hearts. The rest of us turned our backs on the warming rays, and slowly followed our long shadows down Highway 6, turning repeatedly to wave until a bend in the road obscured our view.

We arrived in Sisophon the first week of August, just a month and twenty-five days after we were forced down the cliff. We soon learned that new arrivals in Poipet and other villages close to the border were treated with suspicion and watched closely. Therefore, Leng settled us in Sisophon, thirty-five miles from the border, so our activities would draw less attention.

Our prime concern was to find some way to get reliable information regarding escape routes, and to ascertain the current political situation in Thailand. When we next crossed the border, we wanted some assurance we could reach an established camp. We wanted to be sent to a facility where we would not be expelled.

Aid from foreign countries seemed to come in waves, so we had to consider carefully the international situation in order to time our escape attempt. Sometimes there was outside help for Thailand, and refugees were processed quickly and sent to other countries. Then quotas filled and Thailand was left to deal with the continuing refugee problem as best it could. In order to pick the right time, we needed reliable information. We also needed gold to pay guides.

To meet our needs, Leng and Vitou turned to smuggling. Though it taxed Leng's strength, he and Tu joined a small band of smugglers and left the rest of us in Sisophon. For seed money to begin their new business venture, they took Mum's diamond-studded bracelet. With it, they bought contraband goods in Thailand and smuggled them back into a Cambodia hungry for radios, medicine, and luxury items that had been lacking for years.

Sometimes Thai border guards were lax, which allowed easy access to and from the country, and sometimes they could be bribed. Other times border patrols rounded up any suspected smugglers. Leng and Vitou well knew that other smugglers could be dangerous. To be caught by another band meant your trade goods were taken. Resist, and you might lose your life. Still, the greatest danger was to be caught by Khmer Rouge guerrillas. They shot first and stripped the body of its valuables afterward. Rasmei and I spent fear-filled nights waiting to learn whether our husbands had made a successful crossing. We hated to have them involved in such a dangerous occupation, but there was no other way to get gold or the firsthand information we needed.

Those of us remaining in Sisophon foraged for roots and tubers to stretch our rice. Some tasted like baked potato, others had a foul taste. We ate them anyway. Rice was still in short supply in the western provinces of Cambodia, and our own hoard was alarmingly low. Nonetheless, whenever Mum felt she could spare rice, she sold a cupful for a little more gold. Rasmei, the children, and I hunted for taro and tapioca roots, bamboo shoots, and other edible plants. We had already bartered most of our clothing away, so we were once again wearing rags. We didn't care.

To supplement our limited resources, I bought an expensive set of scales, carefully slid them into a woven shopping bag, and marched off to the local market where I located a busy corner, spread an old cloth on the ground in front of some open stalls, set up my scales and waited patiently for customers—all the time keeping a sharp eye out for local authorities.

Since there was no money in circulation, people bought and sold using gold. They did not trust shopkeepers to give honest weight, so after a price was finally agreed upon for the desired merchandise, the customer and the merchant went to an independent stall to have the gold weighed for a small fee.

By the time I began my enterprise, business licenses were required in Sisophon, but many people could not afford to pay the fees. As I was only planning to be in business a short time, I conducted an illegal, portable business. After finding a likely spot on the sidewalk, I set up my scales, and at the first sight of the police, scooped everything up and melted into the crowd.

I never earned much for my efforts, but it helped us survive while Leng and Tu were gone, and when we were ready to leave, I planned to sell the delicately balanced scales to some other enterprising person. My business also allowed me to listen to local market gossip regarding border crossings, the movements of soldiers, and other useful tidbits.

Vitou and Leng traveled in separate bands of smugglers, so they could gain more information, and one would remain to help the rest of us if tragedy befell the other. Each one-way crossing took a full day and a night of hard hiking. Then there would be a day or two of mingling with the local Thai shoppers, gathering news, and making purchases for the return trip.

On one trip, Vitou lugged a bicycle back to Cambodia. It was awkward carrying it through the rough terrain and tangled brush, but the price he received for the bike was well worth his efforts. Bikes were eagerly sought, since no one could afford more expensive transportation. With a bike, a person could establish himself in a delivery business or travel to the interior of Cambodia with letters from border towns and merchandise from Thailand to sell to an eager market.

Things from Thailand that sold especially well on Sisophon's black market were clothes, rice, sugar, medicine, watches, radios, and canned goods. A villager would willingly trade a large diamond ring for a bag of rice or three quinine pills. Before the month in Sisophon was over, Leng and Vitou had acquired a cache of valuables plus useful information about escape possibilities.

They learned that Aranyaprathet camp, the long-established refugee camp just across the border from Poipet, was the place we should try to reach.

Basically, Aranyaprathet housed those who did not wish to emigrate to a third country. Some refugees had lived in that camp for over five years and were waiting to return to Cambodia when it was safe. Others were waiting to see if more family members might escape before they disembarked for a Western nation.

Leng discovered it was possible for a family to be smuggled into the camp. That was important information, because new people were not often sent there. Once inside, we wanted to appear to be longtime residents, thus reducing the risk of being deported. When we were well established, we could venture to make contact with our relatives in the West and try again to emigrate.

When Vitou and Leng originally contemplated taking up the life of smugglers, they had hoped to learn the back trails between the two countries well enough to avoid the use of local guides. They soon concluded that was not feasible. The smugglers needed to alter their routes on every trip. Leng and Vitou could only follow along. It would take years to know the hills.

From some mountain villagers he traveled with, Vitou learned that Pol Pot's soldiers had somewhat eased the harsh treatment of peasants still under their control. No longer did they work them as hard or kill them as readily. Ever since the Vietnamese took over most of the country, the Khmer Rouge had feared villagers would revolt, so they had become more lenient. Most villagers understood the reasons for this benevolence and Vitou's companions reported that families in Khmer Rouge villages were eager for the Vietnamese to liberate them. They had no love for Vietnam, but they had even less regard for Pol Pot and his bloodthirsty followers.

Finally, Voice of America broadcasts reported that refugees were no longer being forced back to Cambodia. The time had come for us to try escape again.

Leng met a guide who had lived in the Aranyaprathet refugee camp for five years, but had left to become a smuggler in order to provide extra food and clothing for his family who still lived in the camp. He and four companions, also former refugees, could sneak us into the camp by bribing a guard. Leng made plans to hire the man and his four friends.

Rasmei, Mum, and I again packed, and eagerly waited for the men to return with updated information from their final trips across the border. We hoped they did well in their trading because it would take everything we had to pay the five guides, as well as bribe camp guards and officials.

Vitou returned with news that the chance of escape still looked promising. Rasmei and I talked him into staying in Sisophon until Leng got back. We didn't want anyone separated from the family this time.

We were unaware that Leng lay in a jungle thicket near death, too feverish to reach the Thai village. His companion volunteered to take his gold and jewels and make his purchases. Leng took a chance on the man and gave him the valuables, then waited for his friend's return, drifting into fitful sleep only to jerk awake wondering what day it was. He didn't know if his companion had been gone hours or days, and was too weak to care.

At the open-air market in the little border town of Aranyaprathet, a woman sidled up to Leng's companion. Though he knew most residents of the community, he did not know her. Not looking in his direction, she asked casually, "Do you know Leng Hong?"

He froze. Many residents of border towns inquired after refugees and smugglers, but so did government spies.

Noting his hesitancy, the woman continued in a low tone, while fingering merchandise in front of her. She had a letter from America, she said, and had gone to the border areas and nearby refugee camps every few days asking if anyone had word of Leng's family. She had checked with each incoming group of refugees. Some seemed to think his family was in Sisophon.

Leng's friend relaxed as the woman's story unfolded. He confessed he did know Leng, that Leng was ill in the jungle ten miles from the village and would not be coming to Aranyaprathet on this trip. Since he was meeting Leng soon, he volunteered to deliver the letter. She passed the envelope to him and moved on.

It had been an incredible coincidence that Leng's companion and Mearadey's friend had made contact. Once Leng learned of the letter, he couldn't wait to start back to Sisophon. His companion agreed Leng could follow him, as long as he kept pace. Since the man was carrying a heavy pack, Leng was able to trail along without losing sight of him. Almost unaware of his surroundings, Leng had to trust his friend to guide him to Rasmei. He concentrated on keeping his feet moving as he stumbled through the forest, determined to reach his wife with important news.

The forty-five-mile trip was made with few rests. Leng's companion kindly deposited him at our hut with the letter, which was from Mearadey and listed current addresses for relatives in the United States as well as in France and Canada. It was priceless.

The letter seemed to be the final piece of information we needed to complete our carefully worked-out escape. Armed with the vital addresses of potential sponsors, we hoped to be accepted by United States immigration authorities. We wept for joy, almost forgetting that in order for the dream to come true, we first had to cross into Thailand undetected.

Vitou and I wrote multiple copies of the addresses and paid several men to take the letters, hoping one would eventually reach Khum Speu. This scattershot approach had worked for Mearadey, and we felt it was the only method we could trust. Our couriers were smugglers going in that direction to trade. Samol also was to pay the smuggler once a letter was delivered, so I felt there was some chance of success. We had no idea how many letters Mearadey had written to us, or how many people might be looking for us to cross, but we were eternally grateful to her and wanted to perform the same service for Samol and Soorsdey.

In three days, Leng was well enough to travel. Earlier, we had formed a group with twenty-one other people who also were willing to pay the high price the guides required to smuggle us into the Aranyaprathet camp. Knowing this trip would take longer because we were starting thirty-five miles from the border, we took more food and water. However, it was still of utmost importance to travel as light as possible, so we left all nonessential goods behind.

Guides had warned us that the Thai patrols were more adept at locating valuables than they had been the first time we crossed. We would have to be clever in selecting hiding places if we hoped to keep any of the gold or jewels we had worked so hard to acquire. However, we, too, had picked up a few tricks in hiding things. Before we left the hut, Rasmei and I made rats' nests of our hair, as though it had not been combed for weeks. Then the six stones in Mum's diamond ring were pried from their mounting and wrapped in sticky pine gum. Rasmei carefully hid three diamonds among her snarls. I hid the rest in mine. Beeswax-wrapped jewels were again concealed in ears and teeth. We lined an old cooking pot with gold we had melted down. Then we blackened the pot in the fire until it looked well used, and tossed it into the bundle containing food and utensils.

Early on the morning of September 22, we met the five guides on a steamy jungle trail not far from Sisophon. More than four months had elapsed since we first ventured a border crossing and eight months since we had left Khum Speu and our Khmer Rouge masters.

We knew before we started that this would be a difficult escape attempt. Again, there were land mines and three armies to elude; but now the weather was worse and the hike more than twice as far. Walking would be much slower and more arduous. The heavy summer rains had eased somewhat by late September, but the ground was still saturated, and rivers were swollen to overflowing. Leng was weak. The last trek had been almost too much for Mum. Helena was now five months old, heavier and harder to keep quiet than she had been as a seven-week-old baby.

Guides told us the trip should take two strenuous days and nights of steady walking. There would be no sleep.

Though we didn't know it yet, Soorsdey's baby had been born in Khum Speu. Our letter with the all-important addresses, and our plans for escape, arrived while she convalesced. Determined not to be left behind, Samol redoubled his efforts and hit upon an unusual source of gold.

Early victims of mass murder under Pol Pot had been searched carefully for possible valuables hidden in their clothing. But as the pace for killing had increased, and the victims grew more wary, there had not been time to search so thoroughly. When the Vietnamese took control of Cambodia, they had paid villagers to lead them to the mass grave sites in order to chronicle Khmer Rouge atrocities, to use the evidence of mass murder to further their propaganda goals. Villagers and soldiers scavenged the decomposing bodies, helping themselves to gold-filled teeth, and the gold and jewels they occasionally found in the seams and linings of the victims' rotting clothes. But many burial sites had not yet been searched.

Samol's family had known of such a site in the dense jungle near the village of Bor Por, not far from Speu. Samol went to the eerie spot to see if he could find anything of value. The wretched smell of decay was gone. Only piles of bones and disintegrating clothing remained. The site had not been looted.

Rifling among the clothes, Samol found enough gold and jewels to make escape seem feasible. He found bundles of American dollars, but they were too badly decomposed to be of any value to him. He could still see red and green parachute cords among the piles of bones.

Once he had enough gold, he bribed a Vietnamese soldier to drive his family to the border in an army truck. Samol said he and his wife and baby daughter were returning to his home village near the Thai border; the soldier asked no questions, though the baby's name, Seri, which means "free," might have raised suspicions about their real destination.

Samol and Soorsdey with their baby, Seri, retraced our original route, but this time the four-month-long journey took only one day. They located a reliable guide a few days later and made an uneventful, though exhausting, crossing. They were sent to a camp near Aranyaprathet. Because Soorsdey spoke English, the Canadian embassy got in touch with them and processed their applications. Within three weeks, they were headed for Canada.

Our trek was a nightmare. By the third day, we were still in the wilds. The guides lost their way several times, making the trip even longer than the estimated fifty miles. Everyone had run out of food and water. Mum could no longer walk. Leng, Vitou, and the guides took turns carrying her. Helena and the other baby in the group began to cry and Rasmei and the other woman had no more breast milk, nor did they have drugs to keep them drowsy. Rags had to be stuffed in the infants' mouths to muffle the plaintive wails. Other children also had to be kept from crying.

We waded through leech- and snake-infested waters up to our necks, carrying Mum and the children on our shoulders and holding possessions over our heads, then slogged through ankle-deep mud and water. Leng was the only one who still owned sandals, but even those did not adequately protect his feet from sharp shoots and rocks. Insect bites and scratches festered. Cut and bruised by briers and thorn-covered underbrush, we continued to push forward. Each day was hell, and the nights were worse. In the dark, vision was limited to the back of the person ahead. Panic gripped me if that person slipped momentarily from view, yet no one dared call out for fear of attracting the attention of the Khmer Rouge or other patrols.

The longest rests came when some of the guides left us to scout ahead. These times were always frightening. Fearing abandonment, we had insisted that not all the guides leave the group at one time. We had also paid them only a third of the total before embarking. Midway, the guides demanded another third. Most of the gold we had accumulated had already been given for the initial payment, so Rasmei paid our family's share with the three small diamonds in her hair.

The guides were not pleased to be offered gems. But when they noticed how carefully Rasmei had hidden the stones, and how they had to be cut out of her matted hair, they concluded the diamonds must be valuable and begrudgingly accepted them.

We had always known we might fail to reach our final goal of a good, safe camp, but we had not expected to be foiled in our attempt to even gain the border. But after three days and two nights of exhausting, nerve-racking effort without reaching Thailand, we began to despair. Sometime during the third night on the trail, we reached a gently westward-sloping plateau and realized with gratitude that we were at last on Thai soil.

Still, no one felt secure. Three times that night we had had to hide from border guards. Each time had been a closer call than the previous one. The first time we heard an unusual noise and hid. An ox cart came by bearing an armed patrol. Later, a second, two-man patrol passed near our hiding place on a motorcycle. Another patrol, this time on foot, was almost upon us before we slipped silently into the dense undergrowth. It was vital we not be intercepted before we'd reached the safety of the refugee camp.

Before daylight, the guides concealed us in a thicket and instructed us to remain quietly hidden until nightfall. Then they left to make final arrangements to sneak us into the camp. We took turns sleeping and keeping a lookout for Thai patrols. With the morning sun, our spirits rose and our eyelids drooped, and our well-laid plans crashed down around us.

Exhausted by the long march and lack of sleep for over seventy-two hours, we grew inattentive. Those on lookout dozed. During the late afternoon, while we all slept, Helena awoke and started crying. She had not eaten in over twenty-four hours. In her hunger, she would not be stilled, and before Rasmei could clap her hand over the infant's mouth, her cry carried to nearby soldiers. We were surrounded before we knew what had happened.

It was 4:00 P.M. Only a few more hours and we would have been securely inside the Aranyaprathet camp. Just as others had done the first time we'd escaped, the soldiers demanded something or they would turn us back across the border. I still had the old wristwatch I had not worn since my wedding day. I volunteered this and the hidden jewels in my hair. The others gave most of what they had before the soldiers were satisfied.

Escorted by border guards, we were led away. Vitou carried my enfeebled mother piggyback. Rasmei held Helena, who continued to wail. Leng and I carried Rota and Chenda Poong.

Once more we limped toward the gate of a refugee camp in Thailand, tired and ragged, with our physical, emotional, and monetary resources spent. Circumstances were not what we had planned for so carefully, but we *had* made it—the camp *was* Aranyaprathet.

Chapter Nineteen

We had been in the camp only three hours when a friendly Englishman from the United Nations interviewed us. He copied the names and addresses Mearadey had sent. Before he left, he said he would have them verified. A short while later Thai soldiers came for us. In shocked disbelief, we were hustled directly to a nearby military prison.

For fifteen days, we endured interrogations to determine if we were agents for the Khmer Rouge or some other organization. Leng was especially suspect, since his rubber-tire sandals were the kind worn by Khmer Rouge guerrillas. He and Vitou were questioned for hours, accused alternately of being Vietnamese or Khmer Rouge infiltrators.

We could understand the Thais' need to be careful. Pro– and anti–Khmer Rouge, anti-Vietnamese, and right-wing Khmer Seri groups all flourished in the camps and actively recruited support from the thousands of refugees massed along the border. These various factions placed agents in the camps: the agents attempted to recruit soldiers for their causes, and to foment rebellion in Thailand.

If Vitou and Leng had not been accompanied by wives, children, and an aged mother-in-law, and if all of us had not been on the point of collapse when we reached Thailand, we would have found it impossible to convince our captors we were only seeking asylum. The authorities considered sending us back to Cambodia or incarcerating us indefinitely.

Our release was as unexpected as our imprisonment. Fifteen days after we were sent to prison, another representative from the United Nations came to see us. Mearadey's letter, with the names and addresses of relatives, had been checked and found to be valid. It verified our story, and we were officially classed as genuine refugees. Greatly relieved, we learned we would be transferred to the Buriram refugee camp. Leng's Ho Chi Minh sandals were confiscated—but that price we willingly paid for release.

A five-hour bus ride saw us in Buriram. In contrast to our last bus trip through Thailand, we felt only a little apprehension this time, though much of the route followed the same Highway 10 we had traveled before.

We were to be housed in the camp only until our papers were processed for immigration. We did not know how long that might take, but at last we began to feel safe. It was simply a matter of waiting for sponsorship and the completion of the paperwork. Mearadey's blessed addresses had made all the difference.

Buriram was a new, well-run facility. We had ready access to representatives from the various embassies on a regular basis. The camp was clean; there were real toilets. A French doctor visited once or twice a week. Everyone was allowed outside the main compound during the day and could go to a nearby river to bathe where the water was clear and refreshing. We again enjoyed the luxury of feeling clean.

Refugees were housed in a huge barrack, overcrowded but a big improvement over muddy fields of rice stubble. Each family was allotted a ten-by-ten-foot section of the building for its use, and sleeping mats and mosquito nets were provided. Compared to our recent conditions, our quarters almost seemed luxurious.

Huge caldrons of rice were prepared each day in a central kitchen. The food was bland and filling. To improve our health, Mum insisted we buy fruits and vegetables and occasionally meat from the local market, so we used our almost exhausted resources and prepared our own meals. Drinking water in the camp was not free from contamination and was the cause of some illnesses among refugees, so we purchased water from village vendors. As a consequence, we were healthier and suffered less than poorer refugees, especially those who had arrived in an already-starved condition. Despite conscientious care in the camps, hundreds were so weakened by chronic disease that they died shortly after arrival.

Among the poorest refugees in the camp were the mountain people, many of whom entered Thailand barely alive. These were predominantly Cambodian villagers of the northwest who had continued to live in Pol Pot–controlled areas after Vietnam took over the central government. Many were families of unwilling Khmer Rouge soldiers. These families had had to escape from their own army in order to survive.

Our basic needs were met, so Leng and Vitou utilized the last of the gold from our cooking pot to again bargain in the town market for clothing for each of us. Some clothing was also distributed in the camp by humanitarian groups. Once more we felt decently attired.

Refugees could sign up for a pass to leave the camp boundaries during the day in order to make purchases from the Thai merchants in Buriram, or to play tennis, badminton, volleyball, or soccer. However, everyone had to be accounted for each evening when the gates were locked. This freedom to leave the compound helped relieve but not eliminate tensions within the crowded camp. Inactivity was a serious problem. Most people slept during the hottest part of each day, visited with others in the camp, and complained.

Our uncle in France sent some money. Leng bought a watch in the village market to replace the expensive Omega

277

requested by my father at the time of his capture. We also purchased a portable radio for news of the outside world.

Mearadey, in California, set about trying to secure sponsors for us. A stream of letters flowed between Thailand, France, and America.

Leng was elected to the camp council and worked with the United Nations officials and camp authorities. Vitou joined a volleyball team and spent much of his time competing against other teams. He was also the wood gatherer for our family, and organized expeditions with his niece and nephew to collect a supply for the cooking fire. He and I were at last able to spend time by ourselves and went to the town of Buriram occasionally to see a movie or just look in the shops.

I earned a little money filling out forms for those who wanted to emigrate to the United States. I also taught Chenda Poong, Rota, and their friends some English words. They learned to count and became familiar with the sounds of another language; however, they were too impatient for long sessions. They had never been exposed to school and knew nothing of formal learning. The discipline they knew was of a different type: to endure hunger, to steel themselves to the terrors of war and the slaughter of relatives, to suffer disease without medication, to elude death daily.

Entertainment in the camp was minimal, so Leng and the other leaders arranged for Thai dancers to perform occasionally. There are subtle differences between Thai and Cambodian dancing, but both forms originated in India and tell the religious myths of the Hindu and Buddhist deities through intricate hand, body, foot, and head motions. Watching these graceful finger movements and controlled body postures renewed an almost forgotten pride in our heritage. Despite the systematic annihilation of education and culture by the Khmer Rouge, a few refugees knew the ancient dances and stories and organized classes to teach others. Girls of five and six began the rigorous discipline, mimicking the facial expressions of the adult dancers and moving to the exacting steps of the traditional dances.

Others in camp crafted the instruments needed to provide Cambodian classical music. Orchestras performed for weddings and special occasions. A young man who had been a guitarist in Phnom Penh located a battered guitar and played popular Cambodian and Western songs and I sang with the group. People wove baskets and *sampots*, carved religious statuettes, painted scenes of tranquil rural life or graphically recorded on canvas the horrors of war and grief.

Doctors trained in Western medicine worked with *krou* Khmer to treat the sick. Mum was the only one of us who remained in poor health during the five months we stayed in the camp. She contracted a chest ailment that resulted in a persistent cough. Helping Rasmei with the cooking and pampering little Helena took most of her limited energy. She did not tell the camp doctor about her prolapsed uterus, since it was a major health problem that might keep her from emigrating. This time we would allow nothing to stop us from joining Mearadey and Keang in California. Mearadey had found sponsors for us—five American families to whom we would be eternally grateful.

Almost daily, officials came to the camp for those who were bound for Bangkok for final processing. Shouts of joy accompanied the reading of each name on the list, especially if it was for America. Anticipation was building in camp, and we joined in the excitement. Then Rota fell.

He stumbled playing soccer and hit his leg on a rock. It throbbed and even after a day or two had not improved. In fact, it was worse. If he required treatment, our papers would again be delayed, and we didn't think we could endure any more disappointments. Leng took his nine-year-old son aside and explained the problem. Rota agreed: he would not let anyone know his leg hurt and gave no sign of a limp whenever officials were near.

Though we suspected his leg was broken, we said nothing to camp officials or doctors.

Our names were read when the next buses arrived a few days later. Rota boarded the bus without help and without limping. Mum suppressed her persistent cough and hid the fact it was difficult to walk. Both she and Rota felt they had endured far worse, and they could certainly bear this discomfort for a chance to go to America.

In the staging camp near Bangkok, we had chest X rays, blood tests, and cursory physical exams. All passed. We breathed a sigh of relief. Then a doctor noticed Rota's leg. It was broken and had to be set, but fortunately there was no infection or further damage as a result of waiting. We decided Mum, Vitou, and I would fly to California as scheduled. Leng's family would follow a few days later.

Many refugees, when they boarded buses for the airport, refused to part with their bundles of sleeping mats, cooking pots, rice, and implements they thought were essential to start a new life in a new land. Officials could not convince them these things would not be needed in America. Too often in the past they had been told everything would be provided.

At the airport, terrified tribesmen even refused to have their small hoards taken from them to be put in the luggage compartments. Some women clutched bundles in their laps for the entire flight—at the same time keeping their young children strapped to their backs. They had been fooled once too often to be cajoled into relaxing now. When food was served on board the flight, villagers simply scooped it all into their bags to save for later, when they might be really hungry in the new land.

Until this flight, Vitou, my mother, and I had never been the prime decision-makers in our family, and we had grown to rely on the consensus of the group. Now we were expected to manage on our own, get through customs, make a connecting flight, and hope Mearadey would meet us. I especially felt the pressure, because Vitou and Mum didn't speak English and mine was poor.

Landing in San Francisco, we called Mearadey before we boarded an evening flight to Sacramento. We'd had little sleep in the past twenty-four hours. Everything seemed new and different. Not knowing what was expected of us, we were eager, yet frightened, to meet our sponsoring families.

As we circled above the Sacramento airport that evening, the lights of the city loomed below. Once we stepped from the plane, life would be indescribably different, we knew, but we could not begin to fathom in what ways it would unfold.

I had been robbed by the Khmer Rouge of five very important years in my life. The four years I served them, and the year I spent trying to escape, were years I should have been in school, preparing for adulthood. These were years I could never get back, but I was determined to overcome that handicap. To grow. To be someone after having been considered a zero, a mere grain of rice, for so long.

I would have to learn to count time in minutes, not seasons, master freeways, computers, and an incredible array of machines for every task. I would have to learn to cook and maintain a home.

A home.

The plane made its final approach. Knowing we would soon be reunited with Mearadey, Keang, Tevi, Moni, and little Chenda made it easier for us to face the uncertainty, pry ourselves out of the seats, walk the length of the plane, and enter the brightly lit lobby at the end of the tunnel.

I had an immediate impression some celebrity had been on our plane because we saw TV cameras ahead focused on the disembarking passengers. Only when I flew into Mearadey's waiting arms, and my sister whispered in my ear, did I realize *we* were the ones being photographed. I had ceased to be a cipher.

Epilogue

Seven exciting years have passed since our arrival was featured on Sacramento's evening news in March 1980. It was the end of our long odyssey, and the exciting beginning of another. Once again, we faced *Tchap Pdum Pee Saun*—starting from scratch. But this time, in addition to our bare hands, and freedom, we had the support of warmhearted American friends.

Sponsors provided Leng's family and ours with our first homes in America—two apartments near Mearadey and Keang in Davis, California. Five months later, all thirteen of us moved into a big house, where we all lived together for a year and from where Mearadey and Rasmei started a housecleaning business. Mum watched Helena and little Chenda while the rest of us went to school.

A year later, Keang found employment at the computer center at the University of California at Davis. Hoping to find a way to advance more rapidly, he trained on weekends to become a doughnut-shop manager. When a manager's position in San Jose was offered to him, he moved his family there. Leng's family and Mum also moved to San Jose a few months later. They lived with Keang and Mearadey so Mum could watch all four children, while the adults pooled resources, worked, and went to school.

Vitou and I spent our first year in America mastering English and other basic subjects at a full-time continuing-education high school, with the additional aid of tutors. During the summer, Vitou bicycled twenty miles round-trip each day to attend classes in a nearby community.

With this minimal preparation, we were accepted at Sacramento City College, and two years later completed associate degrees, graduating with honors. Vitou graduated as an aeronautical mechanic, and I in data processing. Our language handicap meant it took us many long hours outside class to read and prepare assignments but then long hours of tedious effort was nothing new to us.

Tu and I remained in the big house until our second year in college, when we moved to an apartment in Sacramento, and became fully self-supporting. Working evenings and weekends, I took over my sisters' housecleaning clients. Vitou worked at an auto body shop and a service station, and did lawn and yard maintenance. During this time, I also took on Mearadey's role as a volunteer interpreter for my countrymen. I took them to appointments with doctors, and helped them fill out welfare forms. (The government granted welfare aid to Asian refugees for the first eighteen months in America, after which healthy adults were expected to be self-supporting.)

I found an excellent job as a computer programmer in Silicon Valley, and moonlighted on a second job while continuing my education. At first, Vitou could not find satisfactory employment in his field, so he worked for Keang. Then he ran a doughnut shop of his own for a while. He joined the Naval Reserve to get additional training in aeronautical mechanics, and found a job at a small local airport. He is now a mechanic for a major airline at the San Francisco International Airport.

Within a year of moving to San Jose, Mearadey and Keang had saved enough to buy a doughnut shop for Mearadey and her girls to run, while Keang continued to manage the other shop and go to school. After building up the clientele in the second shop, they sold it a year later for a profit and gave up management of the first shop as well. Mearadey went back to school to gain typing and computer skills. Keang worked for a computer company and was sent to school by them to take electrical engineering courses. Then he and Mearadey decided to change careers. They trained as social workers for the county in order to help Cambodians and other minorities adjust to America. Having arrived eight months before the rest of us, their family was the first to gain U.S. citizenship.

Vitou and I became citizens a few months before our daughter, Laura Tevary, was born in October 1986.

In San Jose, Rasmei trained as a key punch operator and soon found satisfying employment. Leng works for a precision instruments manufacturing company. All of us continue to take night classes.

Each of the children has skipped a grade in school, so they are only a year behind American students. Vivacious Tevi has set the pace for the younger ones by getting excellent grades and mastering French while working part-time. This ambitious, tri-lingual young woman has her eye on a college education and a career before marriage. Tevi, Moni, Chenda Peach, and their cousins have adopted Western dress, pizza, and popular music as their own, but have retained the Cambodian custom of deferring to their parents when making important decisions.

We all dream that someday Samol and Soorsdey will be able to move from Vancouver to California to be near us.

In the four years Tu and I have lived and worked in the San Jose area, our family has almost regained the status within the local Cambodian community that we enjoyed in Phnom Penh. Each family owns a beautiful new home, each household has two new cars, each of us works in our chosen field and feels comfortable with English as a second language. And Mum, at long last, reigns in serenity as the beloved matriarch of us all.

We cherish the few mementos we brought from Cambodia. My mother's antique silver bowl has a place of honor on my coffee table. We look at the old photos of our family often, and my little Buddha necklace is always around my neck. We held a reunion in 1986 of the forty people who left Cambodia with us. Most of them came. They have all made remarkable adjustments to Western life.

I have lived in three very different worlds. For fifteen years, I was a pampered child of a well-to-do family in Phnom Penh, then, for four years, a slave in a rural Communist commune. And I am now a professional woman with a demanding career, a wife and mother; an American citizen.

Repeatedly, the Khmer Rouge told us that we were insignificant, that to destroy us was no loss. Revenge in the Western sense can be a destructive force in the life of a wronged person, but for Cambodians revenge has a different meaning. By our actions, by what we can accomplish, we intend to show that we do have significance. When we have proven the Khmer Rouge wrong in their assessment of our culture and of us as individuals, our revenge will be complete.

Cambodian Historical Time Line

1ST CENTURY A.D.

Dawn of known Cambodian history/ India influences tribal culture

8TH CENTURY

Ancient Khmer Kingdom with its god-kings

9TH–14TH CENTURY

Kingdom reaches greatest size— Angkor Wat built

15TH CENTURY

Thailand Conquers part of Khmer Kingdom

16–18TH CENTURY

Ancient Kingdom declines and history is forgotten

1864

Cambodia becomes a French Protectorate

LATE 1800'S

Angkor Wat rediscovered— history made known to modern-day Cambodians

20TH CENTURY

France makes 19 year-old Sihanouk a puppet king/ World War II/ Japanese occupy Cambodia 1941–1945

1945–1953	**1954**	**1955**	**1970**
Sihanouk applies pressure on France via world opinion & gains independence for Cambodia	Cambodian independence/ Vietnamese defeat the French at Diem Bien Phu/ French leave Indochina/ Vietnam divide into North and South	Sihanouk renounces Kingship to become Prince & President	Sihanouk replaced in bloodless coup/ Khmer Republic established under General Lon Nol

SPRING 1975	**JUNE 1975**	**JULY 1975**	**OCTOBER 1975**
Khmer Republic defeated by Khmer Rouge/citizens driven from cities/ Communists also rule in Laos & Vietnam	Choun Butt killed/ Exodus ends/ city residents in villages	Wet Monsoon "Killing Time" for royalty, top government men, professional and business men/ food rations cut —widespread hunger	Angka's private communique: former military & government leaders are expendable after fall harvests

JANUARY 1976
Communique:
1 million
men . . . are
enough.
Prisoners of
war
(those expelled
from
cities) . . .
dispose of
as (you) please.

JULY 1976
Wet Monsoon
"Killing
Time" for
lesser
military and
government
men,
and the
educated
and skilled

JULY 1977
Wet Monsoon
"Killing
Time" for
families
of men already
killed,
including many
Butt
relatives/Keang
imprisoned

JULY 1978
Wet Monsoon
"Killing
Time"—anyone
from previous
groups who
had been
missed, plus
any who might
threaten
regime, e.g.,
Vietnamese-
Cambodians

FALL 1978

Khmer Rouge
war with
Vietnam
intensifies/
Repressive
measures
increase/ Many
killed or
moved/
Leng taken for
questioning

JANUARY 1979

3rd—Teeda
marries/
7th—Vietnam
"liberates"
Cambodia/
21st—Teeda
begins
escape to
Thailand

**REMAINDER
1979**
May 10, Teeda
arrives
in Thailand/
June 10, Teeda
sent back to
Cambodia/
Oct., Teeda
returns
to Thailand

MARCH 1980

Teeda arrives
in California

1983
Teeda earns
associate degree
as a computer
programmer/begins
work in Silicon
Valley

1985
Teeda buys a
home

1986
Teeda gains
American
citizenship